D0975402

The One Year Book
OF
Bible Readings

THE ONE YEAR®

book of

Bible Readings

TYNDALE HOUSE PUBLISHERS, INC.
WHEATON, ILLINOIS

Visit Tyndale's exciting Web site at www.tyndale.com

The readings in *The One Year Book of Bible Readings* are taken from *In Touch,* a compilation created by Edythe Draper.

Notes are taken from the *Life Application Bible. Life Application* is a registered trademark of Tyndale House Publishers, Inc.

ISBN 0-8423-5364-X

Printed in the United States of America

03 02 01 00
6 5 4 3 2 1

Publisher's Note

The One Year Book of Bible Readings has been prepared to help you in the discipline of daily devotional Bible reading. Each day's reading is a short compilation of several topically related Scriptures. The passages included are referenced at the bottom of each page so that favorite verses can be easily located in your Bible.

Each day's reading is introduced by a special thought that speaks to pressing needs and concerns that everyone has experienced. This thought is followed by Scripture passages that speak to these issues, bringing God's perspective and power into the problems, fears, and joys of everyday life. And each reading includes a powerful application note taken from the *Life Application Bible.*

This book will help you get in touch with God, who is able to solve even the deepest of problems. Each reading is filled with the hope, comfort, and wisdom that God offers to all who are willing to look to him for guidance and help. May this year and every year be enriched as you enjoy these daily portions from God's holy Word.

And now, just as you accepted Christ Jesus as your Lord, you must continue to live in obedience to him. Let your roots grow down into him and draw up nourishment from him, so you will grow in faith, strong and vigorous in the truth you were taught. Let your lives overflow with thanksgiving for all he has done.

Colossians 2:6-7

January

All Things New

Another year of promise and of blessings
A year of uncertainties and of unknowns
A year for seeking God's heart

Whether you are looking forward to the excitement and possibilities of a new job, relationship, discovery, or any other new event, God desires to share each step of the way with you. Take his hand, and begin a new year full of God's abundant life!

January 1

Do not be afraid or discouraged, for the LORD is the one who goes before you. He will be with you; he will neither fail you nor forsake you.

I know, LORD, that a person's life is not his own. No one is able to plan his own course. ▪ If you don't go with us personally, don't let us move a step from this place.

The steps of the godly are directed by the LORD. He delights in every detail of their lives. Though they stumble, they will not fall, for the LORD holds them by the hand.

Yet I still belong to you; you are holding my right hand. You will keep on guiding me with your counsel, leading me to a glorious destiny. ▪ And I am convinced that nothing can ever separate us from his love. Death can't, and life can't. The angels can't, and the demons can't. Our fears for today, our worries about tomorrow, and even the powers of hell can't keep God's love away. Whether we are high above the sky or in the deepest ocean, nothing in all creation will ever be able to separate us from the love of God that is revealed in Christ Jesus our Lord.

The person in whom God delights is one who follows God, trusts him, and tries to do his will. God watches over and makes firm every step that person takes. If you would like to have God direct your way, then seek his advice before you step out. *LAB note for Psalm 37:23-24*

(DEUTERONOMY 31:8) (JEREMIAH 10:23) (EXODUS 33:15) (PSALM 37:23-24) (PSALM 73:23-24) (ROMANS 8:38-39)

January 2

Sing a new song to the LORD! Sing his praises from the ends of the earth!

Sing praises to God, our strength. Sing to the God of Israel. Sing! Beat the tambourine. Play the sweet lyre and harp. ▩ He has given me a new song to sing, a hymn of praise to our God. Many will see what he has done and be astounded. They will put their trust in the LORD.

I command you—be strong and courageous! Do not be afraid or discouraged. For the LORD your God is with you wherever you go. ▩ The joy of the LORD is your strength! ▩ Paul . . . thanked God and took courage.

The night is almost gone; the day of salvation will soon be here. So don't live in darkness. Get rid of your evil deeds. Shed them like dirty clothes. Clothe yourselves with the armor of right living, as those who live in the light. We should be decent and true in everything we do, so that everyone can approve of our behavior. Don't participate in wild parties and getting drunk, or in adultery and immoral living, or in fighting and jealousy. But let the Lord Jesus Christ take control of you, and don't think of ways to indulge your evil desires.

Look at all the Lord will do for us and through us! Majestic works prompt majestic responses. Do you really appreciate the good things that God does for you and through you? If so, let your praise to him reflect how you really feel. *LAB note for Isaiah 42:10*

(ISAIAH 42:10) (PSALM 81:1-2) (PSALM 40:3) (JOSHUA 1:9) (NEHEMIAH 8:10) (ACTS 28:15) (ROMANS 13:12-14)

January 3

I will not fail you or abandon you.

All of the good promises that the LORD had given Israel came true.

God is not a man, that he should lie. He is not a human, that he should change his mind. Has he ever spoken and failed to act? Has he ever promised and not carried it through?

Understand, therefore, that the LORD your God is indeed God. He is the faithful God who keeps his covenant for a thousand generations and constantly loves those who love him and obey his commands. ❖ He always remembers his covenant. ❖ So don't worry about tomorrow, for tomorrow will bring its own worries. Today's trouble is enough for today.

Can a mother forget her nursing child? Can she feel no love for a child she has borne? But even if that were possible, I would not forget you! See, I have written your name on my hand.

The LORD your God has arrived to live among you. He is a mighty savior. He will rejoice over you with great gladness. With his love, he will calm all your fears. He will exult over you by singing a happy song.

The more we learn of the promises God has fulfilled and continues to fulfill, the easier it is to hope for those yet to come. Sometimes we become impatient, wanting God to act in a certain way now. Instead, we should faithfully do what we know he wants us to do and trust him for the future. *LAB note for Joshua 21:43-45*

(JOSHUA 1:5) (JOSHUA 21:45) (NUMBERS 23:19) (DEUTERONOMY 7:9) (PSALM 111:5) (MATTHEW 6:34) (ISAIAH 49:15-16) (ZEPHANIAH 3:17)

January 4

You will keep in perfect peace all who trust in you, whose thoughts are fixed on you!

Give your burdens to the LORD, and he will take care of you. He will not permit the godly to slip and fall. ▩ I will trust in him and not be afraid. The LORD God is my strength and my song; he has become my salvation.

Why are you afraid? You have so little faith! ▩ Don't worry about anything; instead, pray about everything. Tell God what you need, and thank him for all he has done. If you do this, you will experience God's peace, which is far more wonderful than the human mind can understand. His peace will guard your hearts and minds as you live in Christ Jesus. ▩ In quietness and confidence is your strength.

Righteousness will bring peace. Quietness and confidence will fill the land forever. ▩ I am leaving you with a gift—peace of mind and heart. And the peace I give isn't like the peace the world gives. So don't be troubled or afraid. ▩ Grace and peace from the one who is, who always was, and who is still to come.

We can never avoid strife in the world around us, but when we fix our thoughts on God, we can know perfect peace even in turmoil. As we focus our mind on God and his Word, we become steady and stable. Supported by God's unchanging love and mighty power, we are not shaken by the surrounding chaos. *LAB note for Isaiah 26:3*

(ISAIAH 26:3) (PSALM 55:22) (ISAIAH 12:2) (MATTHEW 8:26) (PHILIPPIANS 4:6-7) (ISAIAH 30:15) (ISAIAH 32:17) (JOHN 14:27) (REVELATION 1:4)

January 5

Jesus asked the man, "What do you want me to do for you?" "Lord," he pleaded, "I want to see!"

Open my eyes to see the wonderful truths in your law.

Then he opened their minds to understand these many Scriptures. ▪ When the Father sends the Counselor as my representative—and by the Counselor I mean the Holy Spirit—he will teach you everything and will remind you of everything I myself have told you. ▪ Whatever is good and perfect comes to us from God above, who created all heaven's lights. Unlike them, he never changes or casts shifting shadows.

God, the glorious Father of our Lord Jesus Christ . . . give you spiritual wisdom and understanding, so that you might grow in your knowledge of God. I pray that your hearts will be flooded with light so that you can understand the wonderful future he has promised to those he called. I want you to realize what a rich and glorious inheritance he has given to his people. I pray that you will begin to understand the incredible greatness of his power for us who believe him. This is the same mighty power that raised Christ from the dead and seated him in the place of honor at God's right hand in the heavenly realms.

Most of us chafe under rules, for we think they restrict us from doing what we want. But God's laws were given to free us to be all he wants us to be. They help us follow his path and avoid paths that lead to destruction. *LAB note for Psalm 119:12-24*

(LUKE 18:41) (PSALM 119:18) (LUKE 24:45) (JOHN 14:26) (JAMES 1:17) (EPHESIANS 1:17-20)

January 6

Take control of what I say, O LORD, and keep my lips sealed.

LORD, if you kept a record of our sins, who, O Lord, could ever survive?

You are not defiled by what you eat; you are defiled by what you say and do.

Gossip separates the best of friends. ▩ Some people make cutting remarks, but the words of the wise bring healing. Truth stands the test of time; lies are soon exposed. ▩ No one can tame the tongue. It is an uncontrollable evil, full of deadly poison. Blessing and cursing come pouring out of the same mouth. Surely, my brothers and sisters, this is not right!

Now is the time to get rid of anger, rage, malicious behavior, slander, and dirty language. Don't lie to each other, for you have stripped off your old evil nature and all its wicked deeds. ▩ God wants you to be holy.

Gentle words bring life and health.

Even though we may not achieve perfect control of our tongues, the Holy Spirit will help us learn self-control, giving us increasing power to monitor and control what we say. Then when we are criticized, the Spirit will heal the hurt and help us not to lash out. *LAB note for James 3:8*

(PSALM 141:3) (PSALM 130:3) (MATTHEW 15:11) (PROVERBS 16:28) (PROVERBS 12:18-19) (JAMES 3:8, 10) (COLOSSIANS 3:8-9) (1 THESSALONIANS 4:3) (PROVERBS 15:4)

January 7

You have raised a banner for those who honor you—a rallying point in the face of attack.

The LORD Is My Banner. ▩ They will respect and glorify the name of the LORD throughout the world. For he will come like a flood tide driven by the breath of the LORD.

May we shout for joy when we hear of your victory, flying banners to honor our God. May the LORD answer all your prayers. ▩ The LORD has vindicated us. Come, let us announce in Jerusalem everything the LORD our God has done. ▩ Overwhelming victory is ours through Christ, who loved us. ▩ How we thank God, who gives us victory over sin and death through Jesus Christ our Lord! ▩ Jesus . . . a perfect leader.

Be strong with the Lord's mighty power. ▩ Prove yourself to be a real warrior by fighting the LORD's battles. ▩ Take courage and work, for I am with you, says the LORD Almighty. . . . Do not be afraid. ▩ Look around you! Vast fields are ripening all around us and are ready now for the harvest.

In the Christian life we battle against rulers and authorities. To withstand their attacks, we must depend on God's strength and use every piece of his armor. As you do battle against the "mighty powers of darkness," ask for the Holy Spirit's help in the fight.

LAB note for Ephesians 6:10-17

(PSALM 60:4) (EXODUS 17:15) (ISAIAH 59:19) (PSALM 20:5) (JEREMIAH 51:10) (ROMANS 8:37) (1 CORINTHIANS 15:57) (HEBREWS 2:10) (EPHESIANS 6:10) (1 SAMUEL 18:17) (HAGGAI 2:4-5) (JOHN 4:35)

January 8

There is really only one thing worth being concerned about.

Many people say, "Who will show us better times?" Let the smile of your face shine on us, LORD. You have given me greater joy than those who have abundant harvests of grain and wine.

As the deer pants for streams of water, so I long for you, O God. I thirst for God, the living God. ▩ O God, you are my God; I earnestly search for you. My soul thirsts for you; my whole body longs for you in this parched and weary land where there is no water.

"I am the bread of life. No one who comes to me will ever be hungry again. Those who believe in me will never thirst." "Sir . . . give us that bread every day of our lives." ▩ Mary . . . sat at the Lord's feet, listening to what he taught. ▩ The one thing I ask of the LORD—the thing I seek most—is to live in the house of the LORD all the days of my life, delighting in the LORD's perfections and meditating in his Temple. ▩ Surely your goodness and unfailing love will pursue me all the days of my life, and I will live in the house of the LORD forever.

As the life of a deer depends upon water, so our lives depend upon God. Those who seek him and long to understand him find eternal life. When you feel separated from God, you shouldn't rest until you have restored your relationship with God. Your very life depends on it.

LAB note for Psalm 42:1-2

(LUKE 10:42) (PSALM 4:6-7) (PSALM 42:1-2) (PSALM 63:1) (JOHN 6:35, 34) (LUKE 10:39) (PSALM 27:4) (PSALM 23:6)

January 9

Oh, that you would burst from the heavens and come down!

Come quickly, my love! Move like a swift gazelle or a young deer on the mountains of spices. ▪ Even we Christians, although we have the Holy Spirit within us as a foretaste of future glory, also groan to be released from pain and suffering. We, too, wait anxiously for that day when God will give us our full rights as his children, including the new bodies he has promised us. ▪ Bend down the heavens, LORD, and come down. Touch the mountains so they billow smoke.

Jesus has been taken away from you into heaven. And someday . . . he will return. ▪ He will come again but not to deal with our sins again. This time he will bring salvation to all those who are eagerly waiting for him. ▪ In that day the people will proclaim, "This is our God. We trusted in him, and he saved us. This is the LORD, in whom we trusted. Let us rejoice in the salvation he brings!"

He who is the faithful witness to all these things says, "Yes, I am coming soon!" Amen! Come, Lord Jesus! ▪ We look forward to that wonderful event when the glory of our great God and Savior, Jesus Christ, will be revealed. ▪ We are citizens of heaven, where the Lord Jesus Christ lives.

Because Christ died and rescued us from sin, we are free from sin's control. God gives us the power and understanding to live according to his will and do good. Then we will look forward to Christ's wonderful return with eager expectation and hope. *LAB note for Titus 2:11-14*

(ISAIAH 64:1) (SONG OF SONGS 8:14) (ROMANS 8:23) (PSALM 144:5) (ACTS 1:11) (HEBREWS 9:28) (ISAIAH 25:9) (REVELATION 22:20) (TITUS 2:13) (PHILIPPIANS 3:20)

January 10

Don't sin by letting anger gain control over you.

"If another believer sins against you, go privately and point out the fault. If the other person listens and confesses it, you have won that person back." "Lord, how often should I forgive someone who sins against me? Seven times?" "No!" Jesus replied, "seventy times seven!"

When you are praying, first forgive anyone you are holding a grudge against, so that your Father in heaven will forgive your sins, too.

Since God chose you to be the holy people whom he loves, you must clothe yourselves with tenderhearted mercy, kindness, humility, gentleness, and patience. You must make allowance for each other's faults and forgive the person who offends you. Remember, the Lord forgave you, so you must forgive others. ▪ Be kind to each other, tenderhearted, forgiving one another, just as God through Christ has forgiven you.

The key to forgiving others is remembering how much God has forgiven you. Is it difficult for you to forgive someone who has wronged you a little when God has forgiven you so much? Realizing God's infinite love and forgiveness can help you love and forgive others.

LAB note for Colossians 3:13

(Ephesians 4:26) (Matthew 18:15, 21–22) (Mark 11:25)
(Colossians 3:12–13) (Ephesians 4:32)

January 11

I lie in the dust, completely discouraged; revive me by your word.

Since you have been raised to new life with Christ, set your sights on the realities of heaven, where Christ sits at God's right hand in the place of honor and power. Let heaven fill your thoughts. Do not think only about things down here on earth. For you died when Christ died, and your real life is hidden with Christ in God. ▩ We are citizens of heaven, where the Lord Jesus Christ lives. And we are eagerly waiting for him to return as our Savior. He will take these weak mortal bodies of ours and change them into glorious bodies like his own, using the same mighty power that he will use to conquer everything, everywhere.

The old sinful nature loves to do evil, which is just opposite from what the Holy Spirit wants. ▩ Dear brothers and sisters, you have no obligation whatsoever to do what your sinful nature urges you to do. For if you keep on following it, you will perish. But if through the power of the Holy Spirit you turn from it and its evil deeds, you will live. ▩ You are foreigners and aliens here. So I warn you to keep away from evil desires because they fight against your very souls.

Setting your sights on heaven means striving to put heaven's priorities into daily practice. Letting heaven fill our thoughts means concentrating on the eternal rather than the temporal.

LAB note for Colossians 3:1-2

(PSALM 119:25) (COLOSSIANS 3:1-3) (PHILIPPIANS 3:20-21) (GALATIANS 5:17) (ROMANS 8:12-13) (1 PETER 2:11)

January 12

Be honest in your estimate of yourselves, measuring your value by how much faith God has given you.

[He is] weak in faith. ▩ His faith grew stronger, and in this he brought glory to God.

"You don't have much faith," Jesus said. "Why did you doubt me?" ▩ Your faith is great. Your request is granted.

"Do you believe I can make you see?" "Yes, Lord," they told him, "we do." "Because of your faith, it will happen."

We need more faith. ▩ Continue to build your lives on the foundation of your holy faith. ▩ Let your roots grow down into him and draw up nourishment from him, so you will grow in faith, strong and vigorous in the truth you were taught. ▩ It is God who gives us, along with you, the ability to stand firm for Christ. ▩ After you have suffered a little while, he will restore, support, and strengthen you, and he will place you on a firm foundation.

We must be considerate of the doubts and fears of [others]. . . . We should please others. ▩ Don't condemn each other anymore. Decide instead to live in such a way that you will not put an obstacle in another Christian's path.

Although we start out with good intentions, sometimes our faith falters. But we can be afraid and still look to Christ. When you are apprehensive about the troubles around you and doubt Christ's presence or ability to help, remember that he is always with you and is the only one who can really help. *LAB note for Matthew 14:30-31*

(Romans 12:3) (Romans 14:1) (Romans 4:20) (Matthew 14:31) (Matthew 15:28) (Matthew 9:28-29) (Luke 17:5) (Jude 20) (Colossians 2:7) (2 Corinthians 1:21) (1 Peter 5:10) (Romans 15:1) (Romans 14:13)

January 13

You have rescued me from death and have forgiven all my sins.

God showed how much he loved us by sending his only Son into the world so that we might have eternal life through him. This is real love. It is not that we loved God, but that he loved us and sent his Son as a sacrifice to take away our sins.

Where is another God like you, who pardons the sins of the survivors among his people? You cannot stay angry with your people forever, because you delight in showing mercy. Once again you will have compassion on us. You will trample our sins under your feet and throw them into the depths of the ocean! ▪ O LORD my God, I cried out to you for help, and you restored my health. You brought me up from the grave, O LORD. You kept me from falling into the pit of death. ▪ When I had lost all hope, I turned my thoughts once more to the LORD. And my earnest prayer went out to you in your holy Temple. ▪ I waited patiently for the LORD to help me, and he turned to me and heard my cry. He lifted me out of the pit of despair, out of the mud and the mire. He set my feet on solid ground and steadied me as I walked along.

God delights to show mercy! He does not forgive grudgingly but is glad when we repent, and he offers forgiveness to all who come back to him. Today you can confess your sins and receive his loving forgiveness.

LAB note for Micah 7:18

(ISAIAH 38:17) (1 JOHN 4:9-10) (MICAH 7:18-19) (PSALM 30:2-3) (JONAH 2:7) (PSALM 40:1-2)

January 14

All that I know now is partial and incomplete.

Now we see things imperfectly as in a poor mirror, but then we will see everything with perfect clarity. . . . Then I will know everything completely, just as God knows me now.

We have even greater confidence in the message proclaimed by the prophets. Pay close attention to what they wrote, for their words are like a light shining in a dark place—until the day Christ appears and his brilliant light shines in your hearts. ▪ Your word is a lamp for my feet and a light for my path.

You, my dear friends, must remember what the apostles of our Lord Jesus Christ told you, that in the last times there would be scoffers. ▪ The Holy Spirit tells us clearly that in the last times some will turn away from what we believe; they will follow lying spirits and teachings that come from demons.

Dear children, the last hour is here. ▪ The night is almost gone; the day of salvation will soon be here. . . . Clothe yourselves with the armor of right living, as those who live in the light.

We have the hope that one day we will be complete when we see God face-to-face. This truth should strengthen our faith. We don't have all the answers now, but one day we will. Someday we will meet Christ in person and be able to see with God's perspective.

LAB note for 1 Corinthians 13:12

(1 Corinthians 13:12) (1 Corinthians 13:12) (2 Peter 1:19) (Psalm 119:105) (Jude 1:17-18) (1 Timothy 4:1) (1 John 2:18) (Romans 13:12)

January 15

Serve each other in humility.

Whoever wants to be a leader among you must be your servant, and whoever wants to be first must become your slave. For even I, the Son of Man, came here not to be served but to serve others, and to give up my life as a ransom for many.

If you think you are too important to help someone in need, you are only fooling yourself. You are really a nobody. ▪ As God's messenger, I give each of you this warning: Be honest in your estimate of yourselves, measuring your value by how much faith God has given you. ▪ When you obey me, you should say, "We are not worthy of praise. We are servants who have simply done our duty."

When we are weighed down with troubles, it is for your benefit and salvation! For when God comforts us, it is so that we, in turn, can be an encouragement to you. Then you can patiently endure the same things we suffer. We are confident that as you share in suffering, you will also share God's comfort. ▪ This precious treasure—this light and power that now shine within us—is held in perishable containers, that is, in our weak bodies. So everyone can see that our glorious power is from God and is not our own.

A real leader has a servant's heart. Servant leaders appreciate others' worth and realize that they're not above any job. If you see something that needs to be done, don't wait to be asked. Take the initiative and do it like a faithful servant. *LAB note for Matthew 20:27*

(1 PETER 5:5) (MATTHEW 20:26-28) (GALATIANS 6:3) (ROMANS 12:3) (LUKE 17:10) (2 CORINTHIANS 1:6-7) (2 CORINTHIANS 4:7)

January 16

His special possession.

You belong to Christ, and Christ belongs to God. ▪ I am my lover's, the one he desires. ▪ I am his. ▪ The Son of God . . . loved me and gave himself for me.

You do not belong to yourself, for God bought you with a high price. So you must honor God with your body. ▪ Remember that the LORD rescued you . . . to become his own people and special possession; that is what you are today.

You are God's field, God's building. ▪ But Christ, the faithful Son, was in charge of the entire household. And we are God's household, if we keep up our courage and remain confident in our hope in Christ. ▪ God is building you, as living stones, into his spiritual temple.

"They will be my people," says the LORD Almighty. "On the day when I act, they will be my own special treasure." ▪ And all of them, since they are mine, belong to you; and you have given them back to me, so they are my glory!

What did Paul mean when he said that our body belongs to God? Many people say they have the right to do whatever they want with their own bodies. But when we become Christians, the Holy Spirit comes to live in us. Therefore we no longer own our bodies.

LAB note for 1 Corinthians 6:19-20

(DEUTERONOMY 32:9) (1 CORINTHIANS 3:23) (SONG OF SONGS 7:10) (SONG OF SONGS 2:16) (GALATIANS 2:20) (1 CORINTHIANS 6:19-20) (DEUTERONOMY 4:20) (1 CORINTHIANS 3:9) (HEBREWS 3:6) (1 PETER 2:5) (MALACHI 3:17) (JOHN 17:10)

January 17

He prunes the branches that do bear fruit so they will produce even more.

He will be like a blazing fire that refines metal or like a strong soap that whitens clothes. He will sit and judge like a refiner of silver, watching closely as the dross is burned away.

We can rejoice, too, when we run into problems and trials, for we know that they are good for us—they help us learn to endure. And endurance develops strength of character in us, and character strengthens our confident expectation of salvation. And this expectation will not disappoint us. For we know how dearly God loves us, because he has given us the Holy Spirit to fill our hearts with his love. ▪ As you endure this divine discipline, remember that God is treating you as his own children. Whoever heard of a child who was never disciplined? If God doesn't discipline you as he does all of his children, it means that you are illegitimate and are not really his children after all. No discipline is enjoyable while it is happening—it is painful! But afterward there will be a quiet harvest of right living for those who are trained in this way. So take a new grip with your tired hands and stand firm on your shaky legs.

Christ is the vine, and God is the gardener who cares for the branches to make them fruitful. The branches are all those who claim to be followers of Christ. The fruitful branches are true believers who by their living union with Christ produce much fruit. *LAB note for John 15:1ff.*

(JOHN 15:2) (MALACHI 3:2-3) (ROMANS 5:3-5) (HEBREWS 12:7-8, 11-12)

*J*anuary 18

He is our God forever and ever, and he will be our guide until we die.

O LORD, I will honor and praise your name, for you are my God. You do such wonderful things! You planned them long ago, and now you have accomplished them. ▩ LORD, you alone are my inheritance, my cup of blessing. You guard all that is mine.

He renews my strength. He guides me along right paths, bringing honor to his name. Even when I walk through the dark valley of death, I will not be afraid, for you are close beside me. ▩ You are holding my right hand. You will keep on guiding me with your counsel, leading me to a glorious destiny. Whom have I in heaven but you? I desire you more than anything on earth. My health may fail, and my spirit may grow weak, but God remains the strength of my heart; he is mine forever. ▩ In him our hearts rejoice, for we are trusting in his holy name. ▩ The LORD will work out his plans for my life—for your faithful love, O LORD, endures forever. Don't abandon me, for you made me.

As we struggle with decisions, we need both a map that gives us directions and a constant companion who has an intimate knowledge of the way and will make sure we interpret the map correctly. The Bible is such a map, and the Holy Spirit is our constant companion and guide. As you make your way through life, use both. *LAB note for Psalm 48:14*

(PSALM 48:14) (ISAIAH 25:1) (PSALM 16:5) (PSALM 23:3-4) (PSALM 73:23-26) (PSALM 33:21) (PSALM 138:8)

January 19

When doubts filled my mind, your comfort gave me renewed hope and cheer.

My heart is overwhelmed. Lead me to the towering rock of safety.

I am in trouble, Lord. Help me! ▪ Give your burdens to the LORD, and he will take care of you. He will not permit the godly to slip and fall.

I am like a little child who doesn't know his way around. ▪ If you want to know what God wants you to do—ask him, and he will gladly tell you.

Who is adequate for such a task? ▪ I am rotten through and through so far as my old sinful nature is concerned. ▪ My gracious favor is all you need. My power works best in your weakness.

"Take heart, son! Your sins are forgiven." "Daughter, be encouraged! Your faith has made you well."

You satisfy me more than the richest of foods. I will praise you with songs of joy. I lie awake thinking of you, meditating on you through the night. I think how much you have helped me; I sing for joy in the shadow of your protecting wings. I follow close behind you; your strong right hand holds me securely.

Who is adequate for the task of representing Christ? Our adequacy is always from God, who has already commissioned and sent us. As we realize that God has equipped us, we can overcome our feelings of inadequacy. Serving Christ, therefore, requires that we focus on what he can do through us, not on what we can't do by ourselves.

LAB note for 2 Corinthians 2:16-17

(PSALM 94:19) (PSALM 61:2) (ISAIAH 38:14) (PSALM 55:22) (1 KINGS 3:7) (JAMES 1:5) (2 CORINTHIANS 2:16) (ROMANS 7:18) (2 CORINTHIANS 12:9) (MATTHEW 9:2, 22) (PSALM 63:5-8)

January 20

The fact that I am still being persecuted proves that I am still preaching salvation through the cross of Christ alone.

If any of you wants to be my follower, you must put aside your selfish ambition, shoulder your cross, and follow me.

Don't you realize that friendship with this world makes you an enemy of God? I say it again, that if your aim is to enjoy this world, you can't be a friend of God. ▪ They must enter into the Kingdom of God through many tribulations.

Anyone who believes in him will not be disappointed. ▪ He is very precious to you who believe.

God forbid that I should boast about anything except the cross of our Lord Jesus Christ. Because of that cross, my interest in this world died long ago, and the world's interest in me is also long dead. ▪ I have been crucified with Christ. ▪ Those who belong to Christ Jesus have nailed the passions and desires of their sinful nature to his cross and crucified them there.

If we endure hardship, we will reign with him. If we deny him, he will deny us.

God is faithful to his children, and although we may suffer great hardships here, God promises that someday we will live eternally with him. Are you facing hardships? Don't turn away from God—he promises you a wonderful future with him. *LAB note for 2 Timothy 2:11–13*

(Galatians 5:11) (Matthew 16:24) (James 4:4) (Acts 14:22) (Romans 9:33) (1 Peter 2:7) (Galatians 6:14) (Galatians 2:19) (Galatians 5:24) (2 Timothy 2:12)

January 21

The Lord is coming soon.

The Lord himself will come down from heaven with a commanding shout, with the call of the archangel, and with the trumpet call of God. First, all the Christians who have died will rise from their graves. Then, together with them, we who are still alive and remain on the earth will be caught up in the clouds to meet the Lord in the air and remain with him forever. So comfort and encourage each other with these words. ▩ He who is the faithful witness to all these things says, "Yes, I am coming soon!" Amen! Come, Lord Jesus!

Dear friends, while you are waiting for these things to happen, make every effort to live a pure and blameless life. And be at peace with God. ▩Keep away from every kind of evil. Now may the God of peace make you holy in every way, and may your whole spirit and soul and body be kept blameless until that day when our Lord Jesus Christ comes again. God, who calls you, is faithful; he will do this.

Be patient. And take courage, for the coming of the Lord is near.

Because Jesus Christ came back to life, so will all believers. All Christians, including those living when Christ returns, will live with Christ forever. All believers throughout history will stand reunited in God's very presence, safe and secure. *LAB note for 1 Thessalonians 4:15–18*

(PHILIPPIANS 4:5) (1 THESSALONIANS 4:16–18) (REVELATION 22:20)
(2 PETER 3:14) (1 THESSALONIANS 5:22–24) (JAMES 5:8)

January 22

A choice vine.

My beloved has a vineyard on a rich and fertile hill. He plowed the land, cleared its stones, and planted it with choice vines. . . . Then he waited for a harvest of sweet grapes, but the grapes that grew were wild and sour. ▩ How could this happen? When I planted you, I chose a vine of the purest stock—the very best. How did you grow into this corrupt wild vine?

When you follow the desires of your sinful nature, your lives will produce these evil results: sexuality immorality, impure thoughts, eagerness for lustful pleasure, . . . envy, drunkenness, wild parties, and other kinds of sin. . . . But when the Holy Spirit controls our lives, he will produce this kind of fruit in us: love, joy, peace, patience, kindness, goodness, faithfulness, gentleness, and self-control.

I am the true vine, and my Father is the gardener. He cuts off every branch that doesn't produce fruit, and he prunes the branches that do bear fruit so they will produce even more. Remain in me, and I will remain in you. My true disciples produce much fruit. This brings great glory to my Father.

Jesus makes a distinction between cutting off and cutting back branches. Fruitful branches are cut back to promote growth (meaning God must sometimes discipline us to strengthen our character and faith). But branches that don't bear fruit are cut off at the trunk (meaning people who don't bear fruit for God or who try to block the efforts of God's followers will be cut off from his life-giving power). *LAB note for John 15:2-3*

(GENESIS 49:11) (ISAIAH 5:1-2) (JEREMIAH 2:21) (GALATIANS 5:19, 21-23) (JOHN 15:1-2, 4, 8)

January 23

We are made right in God's sight when we trust in Jesus Christ to take away our sins.

For God made Christ, who never sinned, to be the offering for our sin, so that we could be made right with God through Christ. ▪ Christ . . . took upon himself the curse for our wrongdoing. ▪ God alone made it possible for you to be in Christ Jesus. For our benefit God made Christ to be wisdom itself. He is the one who made us acceptable to God. He made us pure and holy, and he gave himself to purchase our freedom. ▪ He saved us, not because of the good things we did, but because of his mercy. He washed away our sins and gave us a new life through the Holy Spirit. He generously poured out the Spirit upon us because of what Jesus Christ our Savior did.

Everything else is worthless when compared with the priceless gain of knowing Christ Jesus my Lord. I have discarded everything else, counting it all as garbage, so that I may have Christ and become one with him. I no longer count on my own goodness or my ability to obey God's law, but I trust Christ to save me. For God's way of making us right with himself depends on faith.

There is a way to be declared not guilty—by trusting Jesus Christ to take away our sins. Trusting means putting our confidence in Christ to forgive our sins, to make us right with God, and to empower us to live the way he taught us. *LAB note for Romans 3:21-29*

(ROMANS 3:22) (2 CORINTHIANS 5:21) (GALATIANS 3:13) (1 CORINTHIANS 1:30) (TITUS 3:5-6) (PHILIPPIANS 3:8-9)

January 24

Adopted into his family—calling him "Father, dear Father."

Jesus . . . looked up to heaven and said, "Father . . . Holy Father . . . righteous Father." ▩ Because you Gentiles have become his children, God has sent the Spirit of his Son into your hearts, and now you can call God your dear Father. ▩ All of us, both Jews and Gentiles, may come to the Father through the same Holy Spirit because of what Christ has done for us. So now you Gentiles are no longer strangers and foreigners. You are citizens along with all of God's holy people. You are members of God's family.

I will go home to my father and say, "Father, I have sinned against both heaven and you, and I am no longer worthy of being called your son. Please take me on as a hired man." So he returned home to his father. And while he was still a long distance away, his father saw him coming. Filled with love and compassion, he ran to his son, embraced him, and kissed him.

Surely you are still our Father! . . . You are our Redeemer from ages past.

As adopted children of God, we share with Jesus all rights to God's resources. As God's heirs, we can claim what he has provided for us—our full identity as his children. *LAB note for Galatians 4:5-7*

(ROMANS 8:15) (JOHN 17:1, 11, 25) (GALATIANS 4:6) (EPHESIANS 2:18-19) (LUKE 15:18-20) (ISAIAH 63:16)

January 25

Let us go out to him outside the camp and bear the disgrace he bore. For this world is not our home; we are looking forward to our city in heaven, which is yet to come.

Dear friends, don't be surprised at the fiery trials you are going through, as if something strange were happening to you. Instead, be very glad—because these trials will make you partners with Christ in his suffering, and afterward you will have the wonderful joy of sharing his glory when it is displayed to all the world. ▪ We are confident that as you share in suffering, you will also share God's comfort.

Be happy if you are insulted for being a Christian, for then the glorious Spirit of God will come upon you.

The apostles left the high council rejoicing that God had counted them worthy to suffer dishonor for the name of Jesus. ▪ Moses . . . chose to share the oppression of God's people instead of enjoying the fleeting pleasures of sin. He thought it was better to suffer for the sake of the Messiah than to own the treasures of Egypt, for he was looking ahead to the great reward that God would give him.

It is easy to be deceived by the temporary benefits of wealth, popularity, status, and achievement, and to be blind to the long-range benefits of God's Kingdom. Faith helps us look beyond the world's value system to see the eternal values of God's Kingdom.

LAB note for Hebrews 11:24-28

(HEBREWS 13:13-14) (1 PETER 4:12-13) (2 CORINTHIANS 1:7) (1 PETER 4:14) (ACTS 5:41) (HEBREWS 11:24-26)

January 26

May your strength match the length of your days!

When you are arrested and stand trial, don't worry about what to say in your defense. Just say what God tells you to. Then it is not you who will be speaking, but the Holy Spirit. ▪ Don't worry about tomorrow, for tomorrow will bring its own worries. Today's trouble is enough for today.

The God of Israel gives power and strength to his people. Praise be to God! ▪ He gives power to those who are tired and worn out; he offers strength to the weak.

"My gracious favor is all you need. My power works best in your weakness." So now I am glad to boast about my weaknesses, so that the power of Christ may work through me. Since I know it is all for Christ's good, I am quite content with my weaknesses and with insults, hardships, persecutions, and calamities. For when I am weak, then I am strong. ▪ For I can do everything with the help of Christ who gives me the strength I need. ▪ March on, my soul, with courage!

The fact that God's power is displayed in our weaknesses should give us courage and hope. As we recognize our limitations, we will depend more on God for our effectiveness rather than on our own energy, effort, or talent.

LAB note for 2 Corinthians 12:9

(DEUTERONOMY 33:25) (MARK 13:11) (MATTHEW 6:34) (PSALM 68:35) (ISAIAH 40:29) (2 CORINTHIANS 12:9-10) (PHILIPPIANS 4:13) (JUDGES 5:21)

January 27

Don't be discouraged when he corrects you.

No discipline is enjoyable while it is happening—it is painful! But afterward there will be a quiet harvest of right living for those who are trained in this way. ▪ The Holy Spirit . . . will produce fruit in us.

The LORD is like a father to his children, tender and compassionate to those who fear him.

Though our bodies are dying, our spirits are being renewed every day. For our present troubles are quite small and won't last very long. Yet they produce for us an immeasurably great glory that will last forever! So we don't look at the troubles we can see right now; rather, we look forward to what we have not yet seen. For the troubles we see will soon be over, but the joys to come will last forever.

Even though Jesus was God's Son, he learned obedience from the things he suffered. ▪ He faced all of the same temptations we do, yet he did not sin.

We may respond to discipline in several ways: (1) We can accept it with resignation; (2) we can accept it with self-pity, thinking we really don't deserve it; (3) we can be angry and resentful toward God; or (4) we can accept it gratefully, as the appropriate response we owe a loving Father.

LAB note for Hebrews 12:11

(PROVERBS 3:11) (HEBREWS 12:11) (GALATIANS 5:22) (PSALM 103:13) (2 CORINTHIANS 4:16-18) (HEBREWS 5:8) (HEBREWS 4:15)

January 28

The God who sees me.

O LORD, you have examined my heart and know everything about me. You know when I sit down or stand up. You know my every thought when far away. You chart the path ahead of me and tell me where to stop and rest. Every moment you know where I am. You know what I am going to say even before I say it, LORD. Such knowledge is too wonderful for me, too great for me to know! I can never escape from your spirit! I can never get away from your presence!

The LORD is watching everywhere, keeping his eye on both the evil and the good. ■ For the LORD sees clearly what a man does, examining every path he takes. ■ You like to look good in public, but God knows your evil hearts. What this world honors is an abomination in the sight of God. ■ The eyes of the LORD search the whole earth in order to strengthen those whose hearts are fully committed to him.

Jesus . . . knew what people were really like. No one needed to tell him about human nature. ■ Lord, you know everything. ■ You know I love you.

God already knows everything about us, and still he accepts and loves us. He is with us through every situation, in every trial—protecting, loving, guiding. He knows and loves us completely. *LAB note for Psalm 139:1–5*

(GENESIS 16:13) (PSALM 139:1–4, 6–7) (PROVERBS 15:3) (PROVERBS 5:21) (LUKE 16:15) (2 CHRONICLES 16:9) (JOHN 2:24–25) (JOHN 21:17) (JOHN 21:16)

January 29

When the Holy Spirit controls our lives, he will produce . . . self-control.

All athletes practice strict self-control. They do it to win a prize that will fade away, but we do it for an eternal prize. So I run straight to the goal with purpose in every step. I am not like a boxer who misses his punches. I discipline my body like an athlete, training it to do what it should. Otherwise, I fear that after preaching to others I myself might be disqualified.

Don't be drunk with wine, because that will ruin your life. Instead, let the Holy Spirit fill and control you.

If any of you wants to be my follower, you must put aside your selfish ambition, shoulder your cross, and follow me.

Be on your guard, not asleep like the others. Stay alert and be sober. Night is the time for sleep and the time when people get drunk. But let us who live in the light think clearly. ▪ We are instructed to turn from godless living and sinful pleasures. We should live in this evil world with self-control, right conduct, and devotion to God.

At times we must even give up something good in order to do what God wants. Without a goal, discipline is nothing but self-punishment. With the goal of pleasing God, our denial seems like nothing compared to the eternal imperishable reward that will be ours.

LAB note for 1 Corinthians 9:25

(GALATIANS 5:22-23) (1 CORINTHIANS 9:25-27) (EPHESIANS 5:18) (MATTHEW 16:24) (1 THESSALONIANS 5:6-8) (TITUS 2:12)

January 30

Let us run with endurance the race that God has set before us. We do this by keeping our eyes on Jesus, on whom our faith depends from start to finish.

If any of you wants to be my follower, you must put aside your selfish ambition, shoulder your cross daily, and follow me. ▩ No one can become my disciple without giving up everything for me. ▩ Don't live in darkness. Get rid of your evil deeds.

All athletes practice strict self-control. They do it to win a prize that will fade away, but we do it for an eternal prize. I discipline my body like an athlete, training it to do what it should. ▩ I am still not all I should be, but I am focusing all my energies on this one thing: Forgetting the past and looking forward to what lies ahead, I strain to reach the end of the race and receive the prize for which God, through Christ Jesus, is calling us up to heaven. ▩ Oh, that we might know the LORD! Let us press on to know him! Then he will respond to us as surely as the arrival of dawn or the coming of rains in early spring.

The Christian life involves hard work. It requires us to give up whatever endangers our relationship with God, to run patiently, and to struggle against sin with the power of the Holy Spirit. To live effectively, we must keep our eyes on Jesus. *LAB note for Hebrews 12:1-4*

(HEBREWS 12:1-2) (LUKE 9:23) (LUKE 14:33) (ROMANS 13:12) (1 CORINTHIANS 9:25, 27) (PHILIPPIANS 3:13-14) (HOSEA 6:3)

January 31

It is good for the young to submit to the yoke of his discipline.

Teach your children to choose the right path, and when they are older, they will remain upon it.

Since we respect our earthly fathers who disciplined us, should we not all the more cheerfully submit to the discipline of our heavenly Father and live forever? For our earthly fathers disciplined us for a few years, doing the best they knew how. But God's discipline is always right and good for us because it means we will share in his holiness.

LORD, in distress we searched for you. We were bowed beneath the burden of your discipline. ▪ I used to wander off until you disciplined me; but now I closely follow your word. The suffering you sent was good for me, for it taught me to pay attention to your principles.

"I know the plans I have for you," says the LORD. "They are plans for good and not for disaster, to give you a future and a hope." ▪ Humble yourselves under the mighty power of God, and in his good time he will honor you.

When parents teach a child how to make decisions, they don't have to watch every step he or she takes. They know their children will remain on the right path because they have made the choice themselves.

LAB note for Proverbs 22:6

(LAMENTATIONS 3:27) (PROVERBS 22:6) (HEBREWS 12:9-10) (ISAIAH 26:16) (PSALM 119:67, 71) (JEREMIAH 29:11) (1 PETER 5:6)

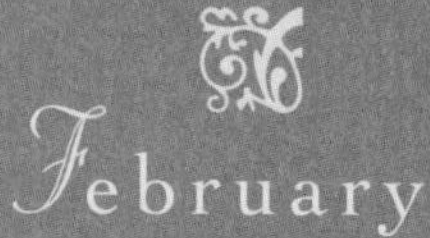

February

Above All . . . Love

Love speaks honestly and pardons graciously.
Love rejoices in victories and comforts in sorrows.
Love overcomes circumstances.

God is the giver of true love. He created it, and he rejoices in seeing us learn it from him. May you experience more of God's perfect love this year so that your peace and joy will inspire others.

February 1

How kind and gracious the Lord was! He filled me completely with faith and the love of Christ Jesus.

You know how full of love and kindness our Lord Jesus Christ was. Though he was very rich, yet for your sakes he became poor, so that by his poverty he could make you rich. ▩ As people sinned more and more, God's wonderful kindness became more abundant.

God saved you by his special favor when you believed. And you can't take credit for this; it is a gift from God. Salvation is not a reward for the good things we have done, so none of us can boast about it. ▩ We have believed in Christ Jesus, that we might be accepted by God because of our faith in Christ—and not because we have obeyed the law. For no one will ever be saved by obeying the law. ▩ He saved us, not because of the good things we did, but because of his mercy. He washed away our sins and gave us a new life through the Holy Spirit. He generously poured out the Spirit upon us because of what Jesus Christ our Savior did.

Jesus did not give up his eternal power when he became human, but he did set aside his glory and his rights. He became "poor" when he became human because he set aside so much. Yet by doing so, he made us "rich" because we received salvation and eternal life.

LAB note for 2 Corinthians 8:9

(1 Timothy 1:14) (2 Corinthians 8:9) (Romans 5:20) (Ephesians 2:8-9) (Galatians 2:16) (Titus 3:5-6)

February 2

If someone sins against another person, God can mediate for the guilty party. But if someone sins against the LORD, who can intercede?

If you do sin, there is someone to plead for you before the Father. He is Jesus Christ, the one who pleases God completely. He is the sacrifice for our sins. He takes away not only our sins but the sins of all the world. ▪ For God sent Jesus to take the punishment for our sins and to satisfy God's anger against us. We are made right with God when we believe that Jesus shed his blood, sacrificing his life for us. God was being entirely fair and just when he did not punish those who sinned in former times. And he is entirely fair and just in this present time when he declares sinners to be right in his sight because they believe in Jesus.

What can we say about such wonderful things as these? If God is for us, who can ever be against us? Who dares accuse us whom God has chosen for his own? Will God? No! He is the one who has given us right standing with himself. Who then will condemn us? Will Christ Jesus? No, for he is the one who died for us and was raised to life for us and is sitting at the place of highest honor next to God, pleading for us.

When you feel guilty and condemned, don't give up hope—the best defense attorney in the universe is pleading your case. Jesus Christ, your defender, has already suffered your penalty in your place. You can't be tried for a case that is no longer on the docket. *LAB note for 1 John 2:1-2*

(1 SAMUEL 2:25) (1 JOHN 2:1-2) (ROMANS 3:25-26) (ROMANS 8:31, 33-34)

February 3

The stars differ from each other in their beauty and brightness.

They had been arguing about which one of them was the greatest. He sat down and called the twelve disciples over to him. Then he said, "Anyone who wants to be the first must take last place and be the servant of everyone else." ▪ Serve each other in humility, for "God sets himself against the proud, but he shows favor to the humble." So humble yourselves under the mighty power of God, and in his good time he will honor you.

Your attitude should be the same that Christ Jesus had. Though he was God . . . he took the humble position of a slave and appeared in human form. Because of this, God raised him up to the heights of heaven and gave him a name that is above every other name, so that at the name of Jesus every knee will bow, in heaven and on earth and under the earth, and every tongue will confess that Jesus Christ is Lord, to the glory of God the Father.

Those who are wise will shine as bright as the sky, and those who turn many to righteousness will shine like stars forever.

If we say we follow Christ, we must also say we want to live as he lived. We should develop his attitude of humility as we serve, even when we are not likely to get recognition for our efforts. Are you selfishly clinging to your rights, or are you willing to serve? *LAB note for Philippians 2:5-11*

(1 Corinthians 15:41) (Mark 9:34-35) (1 Peter 5:5-6) (Philippians 2:5-7, 9-10) (Daniel 12:3)

February 4

Take courage and work, for I am with you, says the LORD Almighty.

I am the vine; you are the branches. Those who remain in me, and I in them, will produce much fruit. For apart from me you can do nothing. ▩ I can do everything with the help of Christ who gives me the strength I need. ▩ Be strong with the Lord's mighty power. ▩ The joy of the LORD is your strength!

This is what the LORD Almighty says: "Take heart and finish the task! You have heard what the prophets have been saying." ▩ Strengthen those who have tired hands, and encourage those who have weak knees. Say to those who are afraid, "Be strong, and do not fear, for your God is coming to destroy your enemies. He is coming to save you." ▩ The LORD . . . said, "Go with the strength you have."

If God is for us, who can ever be against us? ▩ And so, since God in his mercy has given us this wonderful ministry [of telling his Good News to others], we never give up.

So don't get tired of doing what is good. Don't get discouraged and give up, for we will reap a harvest of blessing at the appropriate time. ▩ How we thank God, who gives us victory over sin and death through Jesus Christ our Lord!

It is discouraging to continue to do right and receive no word of thanks or see any tangible results. But we must keep on doing good and trust God for the results. In due time we will reap a harvest of blessing.

LAB note for Galatians 6:9-10

(HAGGAI 2:4) (JOHN 15:5) (PHILIPPIANS 4:13) (EPHESIANS 6:10) (NEHEMIAH 8:10) (ZECHARIAH 8:9) (ISAIAH 35:3-4) (JUDGES 6:14) (ROMANS 8:31) (2 CORINTHIANS 4:1) (GALATIANS 6:9) (1 CORINTHIANS 15:57)

February 5

Even in darkness I cannot hide from you.

God carefully watches the way people live; he sees everything they do. No darkness is thick enough to hide the wicked from his eyes. ▩ Can anyone hide from me? Am I not everywhere in all the heavens and the earth?

Do not be afraid of the terrors of the night, nor fear the dangers of the day, nor dread the plague that stalks in darkness, nor the disaster that strikes at midday. If you make the LORD your refuge, if you make the Most High your shelter, no evil will conquer you; no plague will come near your dwelling. ▩ He will not let you stumble and fall; the one who watches over you will not sleep.

The LORD himself watches over you! The LORD stands beside you as your protective shade. The sun will not hurt you by day, nor the moon at night. The LORD keeps you from all evil and preserves your life.

Even though I walk through the dark valley of death, I will not be afraid, for you are close beside me. Your rod and your staff protect and comfort me.

We should never trust a lesser power than God himself. Not only is he all-powerful, he also watches over us. Nothing diverts or deters him. We are safe. We never outgrow our need for God's untiring watch over our life. *LAB note for Psalm 121:1ff.*

(PSALM 139:12) (JOB 34:21-22) (JEREMIAH 23:24) (PSALM 91:5-6, 9-10) (PSALM 121:3) (PSALM 121:5-7) (PSALM 23:4)

February 6

Never return.

If they had meant the country they came from, they would have found a way to go back. But they were looking for a better place, a heavenly homeland. Moses . . . chose to share the oppression of God's people instead of enjoying the fleeting pleasures of sin. He thought it was better to suffer for the sake of the Messiah than to own the treasures of Egypt. ▪ A righteous person will live by faith. But I will have no pleasure in anyone who turns away. ▪ Anyone who puts a hand to the plow and then looks back is not fit for the Kingdom of God.

God forbid that I should boast about anything except the cross of our Lord Jesus Christ. Because of that cross, my interest in this world died long ago, and the world's interest in me is also long dead. ▪ Therefore come out from them and separate yourselves from them, says the Lord. Don't touch their filthy things, and I will welcome you.

I am sure that God, who began the good work within you, will continue his work until it is finally finished on that day when Christ Jesus comes back again.

What does Jesus want from us? Total dedication, not halfhearted commitment. We can't pick and choose among Jesus' ideas and follow him selectively; we have to accept the cross along with the crown, judgment as well as mercy. *LAB note for Luke 9:62*

(Deuteronomy 17:16) (Hebrews 11:15-16, 24-26) (Hebrews 10:38) (Luke 9:62) (Galatians 6:14) (2 Corinthians 6:17) (Phlippians 1:6)

February 7

My purpose is to give life in all its fullness.

The wages of sin is death, but the free gift of God is eternal life through Christ Jesus our Lord. ▪ The sin of this one man, Adam, caused death to rule over us, but all who receive God's wonderful, gracious gift of righteousness will live in triumph over sin and death through this one man, Jesus Christ. ▪ Just as death came into the world through a man, Adam, now the resurrection from the dead has begun through another man, Christ. Everyone dies because all of us are related to Adam, the first man. But all who are related to Christ, the other man, will be given new life. ▪ Christ Jesus, our Savior . . . broke the power of death and showed us the way to everlasting life through the Good News.

And this is what God has testified: He has given us eternal life, and this life is in his Son. So whoever has God's Son has life; whoever does not have his Son does not have life. ▪ God did not send his Son into the world to condemn it, but to save it.

The life Jesus gives right now is abundantly rich and full. It is eternal, yet it begins immediately. Life in Christ is lived on a higher plane because of his overflowing forgiveness, love, and guidance. Have you taken Christ's offer of life? *LAB note for John 10:10*

(JOHN 10:10) (ROMANS 6:23) (ROMANS 5:17) (1 CORINTHIANS 15:21-22) (2 TIMOTHY 1:10) (1 JOHN 5:11-12) (JOHN 3:17)

February 8

If you fail to drive out the people who live in the land, those who remain will be like splinters in your eyes and thorns in your sides.

Fight the good fight for what we believe. ▩ We use God's mighty weapons, not mere worldly weapons, to knock down the Devil's strongholds. With these weapons we break down every proud argument that keeps people from knowing God. With these weapons we conquer their rebellious ideas, and we teach them to obey Christ.

Dear brothers and sisters, you have no obligation whatsoever to do what your sinful nature urges you to do. For if you keep on following it, you will perish. But if through the power of the Holy Spirit you turn from it and its evil deeds, you will live.

The old sinful nature loves to do evil, which is just opposite from what the Holy Spirit wants. And the Spirit gives us desires that are opposite from what the sinful nature desires. These two forces are constantly fighting each other, and your choices are never free from this conflict. ▩ But there is another law at work within me that is at war with my mind. ▩ Despite all these things, overwhelming victory is ours through Christ, who loved us.

Some think Christianity is a passive religion that advocates waiting for God to act. On the contrary, we must have an active faith, obeying God with courage and doing what we know is right. Is it time for action on your part? Don't wait—get going! *LAB note for 1 Timothy 6:11-12*

(NUMBERS 33:55) (1 TIMOTHY 6:12) (2 CORINTHIANS 10:4-5) (ROMANS 8:12-13) (GALATIANS 5:17) (ROMANS 7:23) (ROMANS 8:37)

February 9

When you have eaten your fill, praise the LORD your God for the good land he has given you.

Beware that in your plenty you do not forget the LORD your God. ▩ One of them, when he saw that he was healed, came back to Jesus, shouting, "Praise God, I'm healed!" He fell face down on the ground at Jesus' feet, thanking him for what he had done. This man was a Samaritan. Jesus asked, "Didn't I heal ten men? Where are the other nine? Does only this foreigner return to give glory to God?"

Since everything God created is good, we should not reject any of it. We may receive it gladly, with thankful hearts. For it is made holy by the word of God and prayer. ▩ The blessing of the LORD makes a person rich, and he adds no sorrow with it.

Praise the LORD, I tell myself; with my whole heart, I will praise his holy name. Praise the LORD, I tell myself, and never forget the good things he does for me. He forgives all my sins and heals all my diseases. He ransoms me from death and surrounds me with love and tender mercies. He fills my life with good things. My youth is renewed like the eagle's!

It is easy to get so busy collecting and managing wealth that we push God right out of our lives. But it is God who gives us everything we have, and it is God who asks us to manage it for him.

LAB note for Deuteronomy 8:11-20

(DEUTERONOMY 8:10) (DEUTERONOMY 8:11) (LUKE 17:15-18) (1 TIMOTHY 4:4-5) (PROVERBS 10:22) (PSALM 103:1-5)

February 10

He had compassion on them.

Jesus Christ is the same yesterday, today, and forever. ▩ We have a High Priest who has gone to heaven, Jesus the Son of God. Let us cling to him and never stop trusting him. This High Priest of ours understands our weaknesses, for he faced all of the same temptations we do, yet he did not sin. ▩ Because he is human, he is able to deal gently with the people, though they are ignorant and wayward. For he is subject to the same weaknesses they have. ▩ Then he returned and found the disciples asleep. "Simon!" he said to Peter. "Are you asleep? Couldn't you stay awake and watch with me even one hour? Keep alert and pray. Overwise temptation will overpower you. For though the spirit is willing enough, the body is weak."

The LORD is like a father to his children, tender and compassionate to those who fear him. For he understands how weak we are; he knows we are only dust.

You, O Lord, are a merciful and gracious God, slow to get angry, full of unfailing love and truth. Look down and have mercy on me. Give strength to your servant; yes, save me, for I am your servant.

Jesus is like us because he experienced a full range of temptations throughout his life as a human being. We can be comforted, knowing that Jesus faced temptation—he can sympathize with us. We can be encouraged, knowing that Jesus faced temptation without giving in to sin.

LAB note for Hebrews 4:15

(MATTHEW 14:14) (HEBREWS 13:8) (HEBREWS 4:14-15) (HEBREWS 5:2) (MARK 14:37-38) (PSALM 103:13-14) (PSALM 86:15-16)

February 11

Your eye is a lamp for your body. A pure eye lets sunshine into your soul.

People who aren't Christians can't understand these truths from God's Spirit. It all sounds foolish to them because only those who have the Spirit understand what the Spirit means. ◈ Open my eyes to see the wonderful truths in your law.

I am the light of the world. If you follow me, you won't be stumbling through the darkness, because you will have the light that leads to life. ◈ All of us have had that veil removed so that we can be mirrors that brightly reflect the glory of the Lord. And as the Spirit of the Lord works within us, we become more and more like him and reflect his glory even more. ◈ For God, who said, "Let there be light in the darkness," has made us understand that this light is the brightness of the glory of God that is seen in the face of Jesus Christ.

God, the glorious Father of our Lord Jesus Christ, . . . give you spiritual wisdom and understanding, so that you might grow in your knowledge of God . . . [and] understand the wonderful future he has promised to those he called.

Jesus Christ is the Creator of life, and his life brings light to humankind. In his light we see ourselves as we really are (sinners in need of a Savior). When we follow Jesus, he lights the path ahead of us so we can see how to live. He removes the darkness of sin from our lives.

LAB note for John 1:4–5

(Luke 11:34) (1 Corinthians 2:14) (Psalm 119:18) (John 8:12) (2 Corinthians 3:18) (2 Corinthians 4:6) (Ephesians 1:17–18)

February 12

Who can say, "I have cleansed my heart; I am pure and free from sin"?

The LORD looks down from heaven on the entire human race; he looks to see if there is even one with real understanding, one who seeks for God. But no, all have turned away from God; all have become corrupt. ▩ Those who are still under the control of their sinful nature can never please God.

I know I am rotten through and through so far as my old sinful nature is concerned. No matter which way I turn, I can't make myself do right. I want to, but I can't. ▩ We are all infected and impure with sin. When we proudly display our righteous deeds, we find they are but filthy rags.

If the law could have given us new life, we could have been made right with God by obeying. But the Scriptures have declared that we are all prisoners of sin, so the only way to receive God's promise is to believe in Jesus Christ. ▩ For God was in Christ, reconciling the world to himself, no longer counting people's sins against them.

If we say we have no sin, we are only fooling ourselves and refusing to accept the truth. But if we confess our sins to him, he is faithful and just to forgive us and to cleanse us from every wrong.

No one is without sin. We all need ongoing cleansing, moment by moment. Thank God he provides forgiveness by his mercy when we ask for it. Make confession and repentance a regular part of your talks with God. Rely on him moment by moment for the cleansing you need.

LAB note for Proverbs 20:9

(PROVERBS 20:9) (PSALM 14:2-3) (ROMANS 8:8) (ROMANS 7:18) (ISAIAH 64:6) (GALATIANS 3:22) (2 CORINTHIANS 5:19) (1 JOHN 1:8-9)

February 13

I am your inheritance and your share.

Whom have I in heaven but you? I desire you more than anything on earth. My health may fail, and my spirit may grow weak, but God remains the strength of my heart; he is mine forever. ❖ LORD, you alone are my inheritance, my cup of blessing. You guard all that is mine. The land you have given me is a pleasant land. What a wonderful inheritance!

I say to myself, "The LORD is my inheritance; therefore, I will hope in him!"

Your decrees are my treasure; they are truly my heart's delight.

O God, you are my God; I earnestly search for you. My soul thirsts for you; my whole body longs for you in this parched and weary land where there is no water. You satisfy me more than the richest of foods. I will praise you with songs of joy. I lie awake thinking of you, meditating on you through the night. I think how much you have helped me; I sing for joy in the shadow of your protecting wings.

My lover is mine, and I am his.

If you are lonely or thirsty for something lasting in your life, remember David's prayer: "O God . . . my soul thirsts for you . . . in this parched and weary land." God alone can satisfy our deepest longings!

LAB note for Psalm 63:1-5

(NUMBERS 18:20) (PSALM 73:25-26) (PSALM 16:5-6) (LAMENTATIONS 3:24) (PSALM 119:111) (PSALM 63:1, 5-7) (SONG OF SONGS 2:16)

February 14

Those who feared the LORD spoke with each other, and the LORD listened to what they said. In his presence, a scroll of remembrance was written to record the names of those who feared him and loved to think about him.

Suddenly, Jesus himself came along and joined them and began walking beside them. ▩ For where two or three gather together because they are mine, I am there among them.

Let the words of Christ, in all their richness, live in your hearts and make you wise. Use his words to teach and counsel each other. Sing psalms and hymns and spiritual songs to God with thankful hearts. ▩ You must warn each other every day, as long as it is called "today," so that none of you will be deceived by sin and hardened against God. ▩ Talk about [God's Word] when you are at home and when you are away on a journey, when you are lying down and when you are getting up again.

I tell you this, that you must give an account on judgment day of every idle word you speak. The words you say now reflect your fate then; either you will be justified by them or you will be condemned.

I will tell about your righteous deeds all day long.

What kinds of words come from your mouth? That is an indication of what is in your heart. You can't solve your heart problem, however, just by cleaning up your speech. You must allow the Holy Spirit to fill you with new attitudes and motives. *LAB note for Matthew 12:34-36*

(MALACHI 3:16) (LUKE 24:15) (MATTHEW 18:20) (COLOSSIANS 3:16) (HEBREWS 3:13) (DEUTERONOMY 6:7) (MATTHEW 12:36-37) (PSALM 71:24)

February 15

The mighty oceans have roared, O LORD.

Mightier than the violent raging of the seas, mightier than the breakers on the shore—the LORD above is mightier than these! ▩ O LORD God Almighty! Where is there anyone as mighty as you, LORD? Faithfulness is your very character. You are the one who rules the oceans. When their waves rise in fearful storms, you subdue them.

Do you have no respect for me? Why do you not tremble in my presence? I, the LORD, am the one who defines the ocean's sandy shoreline, an everlasting boundary that the waters cannot cross. The waves may toss and roar, but they can never pass the bounds I set.

When you go through deep waters and great trouble, I will be with you. When you go through rivers of difficulty, you will not drown!

Peter went over the side of the boat and walked on the water toward Jesus. But when he looked around at the high waves, he was terrified and began to sink. "Save me, Lord!" he shouted. Instantly Jesus reached out his hand and grabbed him. "You don't have much faith," Jesus said. "Why did you doubt me?"

When I am afraid, I put my trust in you.

What is your attitude when you come into God's presence? We should come with respect and trembling because God sets the boundaries of the roaring seas and sends the rain, assuring us of plentiful harvests.

LAB note for Jeremiah 5:22-24

(PSALM 93:3) (PSALM 93:4) (PSALM 89:8-9) (JEREMIAH 5:22) (ISAIAH 43:2) (MATTHEW 14:29-31) (PSALM 56:3)

February 16

How fragrant your cologne, and how pleasing your name!

Christ . . . loved you and gave himself as a sacrifice to take away your sins. And God was pleased, because that sacrifice was like sweet perfume to him. ▪ He is very precious to you who believe. ▪ God raised him up to the heights of heaven and gave him a name that is above every other name, so that at the name of Jesus every knee will bow, in heaven and on earth and under the earth. ▪ For in Christ the fullness of God lives in a human body.

If you love me, obey my commandments. ▪ We know how dearly God loves us, because he has given us the Holy Spirit to fill our hearts with his love. ▪ Our lives are a fragrance presented by Christ to God. But this fragrance is perceived differently by those being saved and by those perishing.

O LORD, our Lord, the majesty of your name fills the earth! Your glory is higher than the heavens. ▪ Immanuel . . . God is with us. ▪ These will be his royal titles: Wonderful Counselor, Mighty God, Everlasting Father, Prince of Peace. ▪ The LORD is a strong fortress; the godly run to him and are safe.

Just as children imitate their parents, we should follow God's example. His great love for us led him to sacrifice himself so that we might live. Our love for others should be of the same kind—a love that goes beyond affection to self-sacrificing service. *LAB note for Ephesians 5:1-2*

(SONG OF SONGS 1:3) (EPHESIANS 5:2) (1 PETER 2:7) (PHILIPPIANS 2:9-10) (COLOSSIANS 2:9) (JOHN 14:15) (ROMANS 5:5) (2 CORINTHIANS 2:15) (PSALM 8:1) (MATTHEW 1:23) (ISAIAH 9:6) (PROVERBS 18:10)

February 17

LORD, do not desert me now! You alone are my hope.

Many people say, "Who will show us better times?" Let the smile of your face shine on us, LORD. ▩ I will sing about your power. I will shout with joy each morning because of your unfailing love. For you have been my refuge, a place of safety in the day of distress.

When I was prosperous I said, "Nothing can stop me now!" Your favor, O LORD, made me as secure as a mountain. Then you turned away from me, and I was shattered. I cried out to you, O LORD. I begged the Lord for mercy, saying, "What will you gain if I die, if I sink down into the grave? Can my dust praise you from the grave? Can it tell the world of your faithfulness? Hear me, LORD, and have mercy on me. Help me, O LORD."

"For a brief moment I abandoned you, but with great compassion I will take you back. In a moment of anger I turned my face away for a little while. But with everlasting love I will have compassion on you," says the LORD, your Redeemer. ▩ Your grief will suddenly turn to wonderful joy. ▩ Weeping may go on all night, but joy comes with the morning.

The God we serve is holy, and he cannot tolerate sin. But if we confess our sin and repent, then God will forgive us. Have you ever been separated from a loved one and then experienced joy when that person returned? That is like the joy God experiences when you repent and return to him.

LAB note for Isaiah 54:6-8

(JEREMIAH 17:17) (PSALM 4:6) (PSALM 59:16) (PSALM 30:6-10) (ISAIAH 54:7-8) (JOHN 16:20) (PSALM 30:5)

February 18

God's law was given so that all people could see how sinful they were.

Who can create purity in one born impure? ▩ For I was born a sinner—yes, from the moment my mother conceived me.

Once you were dead, doomed forever because of your many sins. We were born with an evil nature, and we were under God's anger just like everyone else. ▩ I don't understand myself at all, for I really want to do what is right, but I don't do it. Instead, I do the very thing I hate. I know I am rotten through and through so far as my old sinful nature is concerned. No matter which way I turn, I can't make myself do right.

When Adam sinned, sin entered the entire human race. Adam's sin brought death, so death spread to everyone, for everyone sinned. What a contrast between Adam and Christ, who was yet to come! This other man, Jesus Christ, brought forgiveness to many through God's bountiful gift. Because one person disobeyed God, many people became sinners. But because one other person obeyed God, many people will be made right in God's sight.

For the power of the life-giving Spirit has freed you through Christ Jesus from the power of sin that leads to death.

How we thank God, who gives us victory over sin and death through Jesus Christ our Lord!

As a sinner separated from God, you see his law from below, as a ladder to be climbed to get to God. What relief it is to see Jesus' open arms offering to lift you above the ladder of the law and take you directly to God! *LAB note for Romans 5:20*

(ROMANS 5:20) (JOB 14:4) (PSALM 51:5) (EPHESIANS 2:1, 3) (ROMANS 7:15, 18) (ROMANS 5:12, 14-15, 19) (ROMANS 8:2) (1 CORINTHIANS 15:57)

February 19

The LORD grants wisdom! From his mouth come knowledge and understanding.

Trust in the LORD with all your heart; do not depend on your own understanding. ▪ If you need wisdom—if you want to know what God wants you to do—ask him, and he will gladly tell you. He will not resent your asking. ▪ God is far wiser than the wisest of human plans, and God's weakness is far stronger than the greatest of human strength. God chose things despised by the world, things counted as nothing at all, and used them to bring to nothing what the world considers important, so that no one can ever boast in the presence of God.

As your words are taught, they give light; even the simple can understand them. ▪ I have hidden your word in my heart, that I might not sin against you.

All who were there spoke well of him and were amazed by the gracious words that fell from his lips. ▪ We have never heard anyone talk like this! ▪ God alone made it possible for you to be in Christ Jesus.

Wisdom comes in two ways: It is a God-given gift and also the result of an energetic search. Wisdom's starting point is God and his revealed Word, the source of "knowledge and understanding."

LAB note for Proverbs 2:3-6

(PROVERBS 2:6) (PROVERBS 3:5) (JAMES 1:5) (1 CORINTHIANS 1:25, 28-29) (PSALM 119:130) (PSALM 119:11) (LUKE 4:22) (JOHN 7:46) (1 CORINTHIANS 1:30)

February 20

Don't harden your hearts against him as Israel did when they rebelled, when they tested God's patience in the wilderness.

In the wilderness, their desires ran wild, testing God's patience in that dry land.

Jesus, full of the Holy Spirit, left the Jordan River. He was led by the Spirit to go out into the wilderness, where the Devil tempted him for forty days. He ate nothing all that time and was very hungry. Then the Devil said to him, "If you are the Son of God, change this stone into a loaf of bread." But Jesus told him, "No! The Scriptures say, 'People need more than bread for their life.'"

No one who wants to do wrong should ever say, "God is tempting me." God is never tempted to do wrong, and he never tempts anyone else either. Temptation comes from the lure of our own evil desires. These evil desires lead to evil actions, and evil actions lead to death.

Since he himself has gone through suffering and temptation, he is able to help us when we are being tempted. ◆ Simon, Simon, Satan has asked to have all of you, to sift you like wheat. But I have pleaded in prayer for you, Simon, that your faith should not fail.

In many places the Bible warns us not to "harden" our hearts. This means stubbornly setting ourselves against God so that we are no longer able to turn to him for forgiveness. Be careful to obey God's Word, and do not allow your heart to become hardened. *LAB note for Exodus 3:7-15*

(HEBREWS 3:8) (PSALM 106:14) (LUKE 4:1-4) (JAMES 1:13-15) (HEBREWS 2:18) (LUKE 22:31-32)

February 21

Light shines on the godly, and joy on those who do right.

Those who plant in tears will harvest with shouts of joy. They weep as they go to plant their seed, but they sing as they return with the harvest. ※ Plant the good seeds of righteousness, and you will harvest a crop of my love.

All honor to the God and Father of our Lord Jesus Christ, for it is by his boundless mercy that God has given us the privilege of being born again. Now we live with a wonderful expectation because Jesus Christ rose again from the dead. So be truly glad! There is wonderful joy ahead, even though it is necessary for you to endure many trials for a while. These trials are only to test your faith, to show that it is strong and pure. It is being tested as fire tests and purifies gold—and your faith is far more precious to God than mere gold. So if your faith remains strong after being tried by fiery trials, it will bring you much praise and glory and honor on the day when Jesus Christ is revealed to the whole world.

Don't get discouraged and give up, for we will reap a harvest of blessing at the appropriate time.

God's ability to restore life is beyond our understanding. Our tears can be seeds that will grow into a harvest of joy because God is able to bring good out of tragedy. When burdened by sorrow, know that your times of grief will end and you will again find God's harvest of joy.

LAB note for Psalm 126:5-6

(PSALM 97:11) (PSALM 126:5-6) (HOSEA 10:12) (1 PETER 1:3, 6-7) (GALATIANS 6:9)

February 22

Who are those who fear the LORD? He will show them the path they should choose.

The LORD guided them by a pillar of cloud during the day and a pillar of fire at night.

Your word is a lamp for my feet and a light for my path. ▩ You will hear a voice say, "This is the way; turn around and walk here." ▩ The LORD says, "I will guide you along the best pathway for your life. I will advise you and watch over you. Do not be like a senseless horse or mule that needs a bit and bridle to keep it under control." Many sorrows come to the wicked, but unfailing love surrounds those who trust the LORD. So rejoice in the LORD and be glad, all you who obey him! ▩ The LORD leads with unfailing love and faithfulness all those who keep his covenant and obey his decrees.

I know, LORD, that a person's life is not his own. No one is able to plan his own course. ▩ Show me the path where I should walk, O LORD; point out the right road for me to follow.

To fear the Lord is to recognize God's attributes: He is holy, almighty, righteous, pure, all-knowing, all-powerful, and all-wise. When we recognize who God is and who we are, we will fall at his feet in humble respect. Only then will he show us how to choose his way.

LAB note for Psalm 25:12

(PSALM 25:12) (EXODUS 13:21) (PSALM 119:105) (ISAIAH 30:21) (PSALM 32:8-11) (PSALM 25:10) (JEREMIAH 10:23) (PSALM 25:4)

February 23

You can lie down without fear and enjoy pleasant dreams.

Soon a fierce storm arose. High waves began to break into the boat until it was nearly full of water. Jesus was sleeping at the back of the boat with his head on a cushion.

Don't worry about anything; instead, pray about everything. Tell God what you need, and thank him for all he has done. If you do this, you will experience God's peace, which is far more wonderful than the human mind can understand. His peace will guard your hearts and minds as you live in Christ Jesus.

I will lie down in peace and sleep, for you alone, O LORD, will keep me safe. ▪ God gives rest to his loved ones.

As they stoned him, Stephen prayed, "Lord Jesus, receive my spirit." And he fell to his knees, shouting, "Lord, don't charge them with this sin!" And with that, he died. ▪ We are fully confident, and we would rather be away from these bodies, for then we will be at home with the Lord.

Imagine never worrying about anything! It seems like an impossibility; we all have worries on the job, in our homes, at school. But if you want to worry less, pray more! Whenever you start to worry, stop and pray.

LAB note for Philippians 4:6-7

(PROVERBS 3:24) (MARK 4:37-38) (PHILIPPIANS 4:6-7) (PSALM 4:8) (PSALM 127:2) (ACTS 7:59-60) (2 CORINTHIANS 5:8)

February 24

Who can comprehend the power of your anger?

At noon, darkness fell across the whole land until three o'clock. At about three o'clock, Jesus called out with a loud voice, "Eli, Eli, lema sabachthani?" which means, "My God, my God, why have you forsaken me?" ▪ The LORD laid on him the guilt and sins of us all.

So now there is no condemnation for those who belong to Christ Jesus. ▪ Since we have been made right in God's sight by faith, we have peace with God because of what Jesus Christ our Lord has done for us. ▪ Christ has rescued us from the curse pronounced by the law. When he was hung on the cross, he took upon himself the curse for our wrongdoing.

God showed how much he loved us by sending his only Son into the world so that we might have eternal life through him. This is real love. It is not that we loved God, but that he loved us and sent his Son as a sacrifice to take away our sins. ▪ He declares sinners to be right in his sight because they believe in Jesus.

"Not guilty; let him go free." What would those words mean to you if you were on death row? The whole human race is on death row, justly condemned for repeatedly breaking God's holy law. But thank God! He has declared us not guilty and has offered us freedom from sin and power to do his will.

LAB note for Romans 8:1

(PSALM 90:11) (MATTHEW 27:45-46) (ISAIAH 53:6) (ROMANS 8:1) (ROMANS 5:1) (GALATIANS 3:13) (1 JOHN 4:9-10) (ROMANS 3:26)

February 25

The Sovereign LORD says, I am ready to hear . . . and . . . grant them their requests.

The reason you don't have what you want is that you don't ask God for it.

Keep on asking, and you will be given what you ask for. Keep on looking, and you will find. Keep on knocking, and the door will be opened. For everyone who asks, receives. Everyone who seeks, finds. And the door is opened to everyone who knocks. ▪ We can be confident that he will listen to us whenever we ask him for anything in line with his will. And if we know he is listening when we make our requests, we can be sure that he will give us what we ask for. ▪ If you need wisdom—if you want to know what God wants you to do—ask him, and he will gladly tell you. He will not resent your asking.

The eyes of the LORD watch over those who do right; his ears are open to their cries for help. The LORD hears his people when they call to him for help. He rescues them from all their troubles.

Ask in my name. I'm not saying I will ask the Father on your behalf, for the Father himself loves you dearly because you love me.

When you talk to God, what do you talk about? Do you ask only to satisfy your desires? Do you seek God's approval for what you already plan to do? Your prayers will become powerful when you allow God to change your desires so that they perfectly correspond to his will for you.

LAB note for James 4:2-3

(EZEKIEL 36:37) (JAMES 4:2) (MATTHEW 7:7-8) (1 JOHN 5:14-15) (JAMES 1:5) (PSALM 34:15, 17) (JOHN 16:26-27)

February 26

Should we accept only good things from the hand of God and never anything bad?

I know, O LORD, that your decisions are fair; you disciplined me because I needed it. ▩ LORD, you are our Father. We are the clay, and you are the potter. We are all formed by your hand. ▩ It is the LORD's will. . . . Let him do what he thinks best.

He will sit and judge like a refiner of silver, watching closely as the dross is burned away. ▩ For the Lord disciplines those he loves, and he punishes those he accepts as his children. ▩ The student shares the teacher's fate. The servant shares the master's fate. ▩ Even though Jesus was God's Son, he learned obedience from the things he suffered.

Be very glad—because these trials will make you partners with Christ in his suffering, and afterward you will have the wonderful joy of sharing his glory when it is displayed to all the world. ▩ He said to me, "These are the ones coming out of the great tribulation. They washed their robes in the blood of the Lamb and made them white."

Many people think that believing in God protects them from trouble, so when calamity comes, they question God's goodness and justice. But you should not give up on God because he allows you to have bad experiences. God is capable of rescuing us from suffering, but he may also allow suffering to come for reasons we cannot understand.

LAB note for Job 2:10

(JOB 2:10) (PSALM 119:75) (ISAIAH 64:8) (1 SAMUEL 3:18) (MALACHI 3:3) (HEBREWS 12:6) (MATTHEW 10:25) (HEBREWS 5:8) (1 PETER 4:13) (REVELATION 7:14)

February 27

Resist the Devil, and he will flee from you.

"Get out of here, Satan," Jesus told him. "For the Scriptures say, 'You must worship the Lord your God; serve only him.'" Then the Devil went away, and angels came and cared for Jesus.

Be strong with the Lord's mighty power. Put on all of God's armor so that you will be able to stand firm against all strategies and tricks of the Devil. ▩ Take no part in the worthless deeds of evil and darkness; instead, rebuke and expose them. ▩ Satan will not outsmart us. For we are very familiar with his evil schemes. ▩ Be careful! Watch out for attacks from the Devil, your great enemy. He prowls around like a roaring lion, looking for some victim to devour. Take a firm stand against him, and be strong in your faith. Remember that your Christian brothers and sisters all over the world are going through the same kind of suffering you are. ▩ Every child of God defeats this evil world by trusting Christ to give the victory.

I am convinced that nothing can ever separate us from his love. Death can't, and life can't. The angels can't, and the demons can't. . . . Even the powers of hell can't keep God's love away.

Although God and the Devil are at war, we don't have to wait until the end to see who will win. God has already defeated Satan, and when Christ returns, the Devil and all he stands for will be eliminated forever. With the Holy Spirit's power we can resist the Devil, and he will flee from us.

LAB note for James 4:7

(JAMES 4:7) (MATTHEW 4:10-11) (EPHESIANS 6:10-11) (EPHESIANS 5:11) (2 CORINTHIANS 2:11) (1 PETER 5:8-9) (1 JOHN 5:4) (ROMANS 8:38)

February 28

The glow of an emerald circled his throne like a rainbow.

I am giving you a sign as evidence of my eternal covenant with you and all living creatures. I have placed my rainbow in the clouds. It is the sign of my permanent promise to you and to all the earth. When I see the rainbow in the clouds, I will remember the eternal covenant between God and every living creature on earth. ▪ An everlasting covenant . . . eternal, final, sealed. ▪ God has given us both his promise and his oath. These two things are unchangeable because it is impossible for God to lie. Therefore, we who have fled to him for refuge can take new courage, for we can hold on to his promise with confidence. This confidence is like a strong and trustworthy anchor for our souls. It leads us through the curtain of heaven into God's inner sanctuary. Jesus has already gone in there for us. He has become our eternal High Priest in the line of Melchizedek. ▪ In this man Jesus there is forgiveness for your sins. Everyone who believes in him is freed from all guilt and declared right with God.

Jesus Christ is the same yesterday, today, and forever.

Because God is truth, you can be secure in his promises; you don't need to wonder if he will change his plans. Our hope is secure and immovable, anchored in God. This truth should give you encouragement, assurance, and confidence. *LAB note for Hebrews 6:18-19*

(Revelation 4:3) (Genesis 9:12-13, 16) (2 Samuel 23:5) (Hebrews 6:18-20) (Acts 13:38-39) (Hebrews 13:8)

February 29

God . . . always does just what he says, and he is the one who invited you into this wonderful friendship with his Son, Jesus Christ our Lord.

Without wavering, let us hold tightly to the hope we say we have, for God can be trusted to keep his promise. ▩ We are the temple of the living God. As God said: "I will live in them and walk among them. I will be their God, and they will be my people." ▩ You may have fellowship with us. And our fellowship is with the Father and with his Son, Jesus Christ. ▩ Be very glad—because these trials will make you partners with Christ in his suffering, and afterward you will have the wonderful joy of sharing his glory when it is displayed to all the world.

I pray that Christ will be more and more at home in your hearts as you trust in him. May your roots go down deep into the soil of God's marvelous love. And may you have the power to understand, as all God's people should, how wide, how long, how high, and how deep his love really is. May you experience the love of Christ, though it is so great you will never fully understand it. Then you will be filled with the fullness of life and power that comes from God.

We have significant privileges associated with our new life in Christ: (1) we have personal access to God through Christ; (2) we may grow in faith, overcome doubts and questions, and deepen our relationship with him; (3) we may enjoy encouragement from one another; (4) we may worship together. *LAB note for Hebrews 10:22-25*

(1 CORINTHIANS 1:9) (HEBREWS 10:23) (2 CORINTHIANS 6:16) (1 JOHN 1:3) (1 PETER 4:13) (EPHESIANS 3:17-19)

March

New Life in Spring

Abundant life and new beginnings
Warm sunny days and cool rainy evenings
Spring brings a sense of refreshment and peace.

Take a moment each morning to pause outside your door and breathe deeply of the scent of fresh air and new life. Listen for the chirping of birds, and revel in the gift of the season.

March 1

The LORD made the heavens, the earth, the sea, and everything in them.

The heavens tell of the glory of God. The skies display his marvelous craftsmanship. ▩ The LORD merely spoke, and the heavens were created. He breathed the word, and all the stars were born. He gave the sea its boundaries and locked the oceans in vast reservoirs. When he spoke, the world began! It appeared at his command. ▩ All the nations of the world are nothing in comparison with him. They are but a drop in the bucket, dust on the scales. He picks up the islands as though they had no weight at all.

Who else has held the oceans in his hand? Who has measured off the heavens with his fingers? Who else knows the weight of the earth or has weighed out the mountains and the hills?

By faith we understand that the entire universe was formed at God's command, that what we now see did not come from anything that can be seen.

When I look at the night sky and see the work of your fingers—the moon and the stars you have set in place—what are mortals that you should think of us, mere humans that you should care for us?

As God reveals himself through nature, we learn about his power and our finiteness. As God reveals himself through Scripture, we learn about his holiness and our sinfulness. As God reveals himself through daily experiences, we learn about his gracious forgiveness that frees us from guilt.

LAB note for Psalm 19:1ff.

(EXODUS 20:11) (PSALM 19:1) (PSALM 33:6-7, 9) (ISAIAH 40:15) (ISAIAH 40:12) (HEBREWS 11:3) (PSALM 8:3-4)

M a r c h 2

Don't brag about tomorrow, since you don't know what the day will bring.

At just the right time, I heard you. On the day of salvation, I helped you. ▩ My light will shine out for you just a little while longer. Walk in it while you can, so you will not stumble when the darkness falls. If you walk in the darkness, you cannot see where you are going. Believe in the light while there is still time; then you will become children of the light.

Whatever you do, do well. For when you go to the grave, there will be no work or planning or knowledge or wisdom.

And I'll sit back and say to myself, "My friend, you have enough stored away for years to come. Now take it easy! Eat, drink, and be merry!" But God said to him, "You fool! You will die this very night. Then who will get it all?" Yes, a person is a fool to store up earthly wealth but not have a rich relationship with God.

Your life is like the morning fog—it's here a little while, then it's gone. ▩ This world is fading away, along with everything it craves. But if you do the will of God, you will live forever.

Life is short, no matter how many years we live. Don't be deceived into thinking that you have lots of remaining time to live for Christ, to enjoy your loved ones, or to do what you know you should. Live for God today! Then no matter when your life ends, you will have fulfilled God's plan for you.

LAB note for James 4:14

(PROVERBS 27:1) (2 CORINTHIANS 6:2) (JOHN 12:35-36) (ECCLESIASTES 9:10) (LUKE 12:19-21) (JAMES 4:14) (1 JOHN 2:17)

March 3

You are always the same; your years never end.

Before the mountains were created, before you made the earth and the world, you are God, without beginning or end.

I am the LORD, and I do not change. That is why you descendants of Jacob are not already completely destroyed. ▪ Jesus Christ is the same yesterday, today, and forever.

Whatever is good and perfect comes to us from God above, who created all heaven's lights. Unlike them, he never changes or casts shifting shadows. ▪ God's gifts and his call can never be withdrawn.

God is not a man, that he should lie. He is not a human, that he should change his mind. ▪ The unfailing love of the LORD never ends! By his mercies we have been kept from complete destruction.

Jesus remains a priest forever; his priesthood will never end. Therefore he is able, once and forever, to save everyone who comes to God through him. He lives forever to plead with God on their behalf. ▪ Don't be afraid! I am the First and the Last.

Though human leaders have much to offer, we must keep our eyes on Christ, our ultimate leader. Unlike any human leaders, he will never change. Christ has been and will be the same forever. In a changing world we can trust our unchanging Lord. *LAB note for Hebrews 13:8*

(PSALM 102:27) (PSALM 90:2) (MALACHI 3:6) (HEBREWS 13:8) (JAMES 1:17) (ROMANS 11:29) (NUMBERS 23:19) (LAMENTATIONS 3:22) (HEBREWS 7:24-25) (REVELATION 1:17)

March 4

The LORD Is My Banner.

If God is for us, who can ever be against us? ▩ The LORD is for me, so I will not be afraid. What can mere mortals do to me?

You have raised a banner for those who honor you—a rallying point in the face of attack.

The LORD is my light and my salvation—so why should I be afraid? The LORD protects me from danger—so why should I tremble? Though a mighty army surrounds me, my heart will know no fear. Even if they attack me, I remain confident.

God is with us. He is our leader. ▩ The LORD Almighty is here among us; the God of Israel is our fortress.

They will wage war against the Lamb, but the Lamb will defeat them.

Why do the nations rage? Why do the people waste their time with futile plans? The one who rules in heaven laughs. The Lord scoffs at them. ▩ Call your councils of war, develop your strategies, prepare your plans of attack—and then die! For God is with us!

We can conquer fear by using the bright liberating light of the Lord, who brings salvation. If we want to dispel the darkness of fear, let us remember with the psalmist that "the LORD is my light and my salvation."

LAB note for Psalm 27:1

(EXODUS 17:15) (ROMANS 8:31) (PSALM 118:6) (PSALM 60:4) (PSALM 27:1, 3) (2 CHRONICLES 13:12) (PSALM 46:7) (REVELATION 17:14) (PSALM 2:1, 4) (ISAIAH 8:10)

*M*arch 5

Trust in the LORD with all your heart; do not depend on your own understanding.

Seek his will in all you do, and he will direct your paths. ▩ O my people, trust in him at all times. Pour out your heart to him, for God is our refuge.

The LORD says, "I will guide you along the best pathway for your life. I will advise you and watch over you. Do not be like a senseless horse or mule that needs a bit and bridle to keep it under control." Many sorrows come to the wicked, but unfailing love surrounds those who trust the LORD. ▩ You will hear a voice say, "This is the way; turn around and walk here." ▩ The LORD will guide you continually, watering your life when you are dry and keeping you healthy, too. You will be like a well-watered garden, like an ever-flowing spring.

I know, LORD, that a person's life is not his own. No one is able to plan his own course. ▩ If you don't go with us personally, don't let us move a step from this place.

When we have an important decision to make, we sometimes feel that we can't trust anyone—not even God. But God knows what is best for us. He is a better judge of what we want than we are! We must trust him completely in every choice we make. *LAB note for Proverbs 3:5-6*

(PROVERBS 3:5) (PROVERBS 3:6) (PSALM 32:8-10) (ISAIAH 30:21) (ISAIAH 58:11) (JEREMIAH 10:23) (EXODUS 33:15)

March 6

The prize for which God, through Christ Jesus, is calling us up to heaven.

You will have treasure in heaven. . . . Come, follow me. ▩ Your reward will be great.

The master was full of praise. "Well done, my good and faithful servant. You have been faithful in handling this small amount, so now I will give you many more responsibilities. Let's celebrate together!" ▩ They will reign forever and ever.

Your reward will be a never-ending share in his glory and honor. ▩ [You] will receive the crown of life. ▩ An eternal prize.

Father, I want these whom you've given me to be with me, so they can see my glory. You gave me the glory because you loved me even before the world began! ▩ We who are still alive . . . will be caught up in the clouds . . . and remain with him forever.

What we suffer now is nothing compared to the glory he will give us later.

"No eye has seen, no ear has heard, and no mind has imagined what God has prepared for those who love him." But we know these things because God has revealed them to us by his Spirit.

God's crown of life is not glory and honor here on earth but the reward of eternal life—living with God forever. The way to be in God's winners' circle is by loving him and staying faithful even under pressure.

LAB note for James 1:12

(PHILIPPIANS 3:14) (MATTHEW 19:21) (GENESIS 15:1) (MATTHEW 25:21) (REVELATION 22:5) (1 PETER 5:4) (JAMES 1:12) (1 CORINTHIANS 9:25) (JOHN 17:24) (1 THESSALONIANS 4:17) (ROMANS 8:18) (1 CORINTHIANS 2:9-10)

March 7

He will bend his shoulder to the task.

For examples of patience in suffering, dear brothers and sisters, look at the prophets who spoke in the name of the Lord. ▩ All these events happened to them as examples for us. They were written down to warn us, who live at the time when this age is drawing to a close.

Should we accept only good things from the hand of God and never anything bad? ▩ Job is an example of a man who endured patiently. From his experience we see how the Lord's plan finally ended in good, for he is full of tenderness and mercy. ▩ It is the LORD's will. . . . Let him do what he thinks best.

Give your burdens to the LORD, and he will take care of you. He will not permit the godly to slip and fall. ▩ It was our weaknesses he carried; it was our sorrows that weighed him down.

Come to me, all of you who are weary and carry heavy burdens, and I will give you rest. Take my yoke upon you. Let me teach you, because I am humble and gentle, and you will find rest for your souls. For my yoke fits perfectly, and the burden I give you is light.

Jesus frees people from burdens. The rest that Jesus promises is love, healing, and peace with God, not the end of all labor. A relationship with God changes meaningless, wearisome toil into spiritual productivity and purpose.

LAB note for Matthew 11:28-30

(GENESIS 49:15) (JAMES 5:10) (1 CORINTHIANS 10:11) (JOB 2:10) (JAMES 5:11) (1 SAMUEL 3:18) (PSALM 55:22) (ISAIAH 53:4) (MATTHEW 11:28-30)

March 8

I am in trouble, Lord. Help me!

I lift my eyes to you, O God, enthroned in heaven. We look to the LORD our God for his mercy, just as servants keep their eyes on their master, as a slave girl watches her mistress for the slightest signal. ▩ O God, listen to my cry! Hear my prayer! From the ends of the earth, I will cry to you for help, for my heart is overwhelmed. Lead me to the towering rock of safety, for you are my safe refuge, a fortress where my enemies cannot reach me. Let me live forever in your sanctuary, safe beneath the shelter of your wings! ▩ To the poor, O LORD, you are a refuge from the storm. To the needy in distress, you are a shelter from the rain and the heat.

Christ, who suffered for you, is your example. Follow in his steps. He never sinned, and he never deceived anyone. He did not retaliate when he was insulted. When he suffered, he did not threaten to get even. He left his case in the hands of God, who always judges fairly. ▩ This High Priest of ours understands our weaknesses, for he faced all of the same temptations we do, yet he did not sin. So let us come boldly to the throne of our gracious God. There we will receive his mercy, and we will find grace to help us when we need it.

The psalmist lifted his eyes to God, waiting and watching for God to send his mercy. The more he waited, the more he cried out to God, because he knew that the evil and proud offered no help—they had only contempt for God. *LAB note for Psalm 123:1ff.*

(ISAIAH 38:14) (PSALM 123:1-2) (PSALM 61:1-4) (ISAIAH 25:4) (1 PETER 2:21-23) (HEBREWS 4:15-16)

M a r c h 9

Fight the good fight.

Outside there was conflict from every direction, and inside there was fear. ▩ Don't be afraid! . . . For there are more on our side than on theirs! ▩ Be strong with the Lord's mighty power.

You come to me with sword, spear, and javelin, but I come to you in the name of the LORD Almighty—the God of the armies of Israel, whom you have defied. ▩ God is my strong fortress. . . . He prepares me for battle; he strengthens me to draw a bow of bronze. ▩ Our only power and success come from God.

The angel of the LORD guards all who fear him, and he rescues them. ▩ "O LORD, open his eyes and let him see!" The LORD opened his servant's eyes, and when he looked up, he saw that the hillside around Elisha was filled with horses and chariots of fire.

How much more do I need to say? It would take too long to recount the stories. . . . By faith these people overthrew kingdoms. . . . Their weakness was turned to strength. They became strong in battle and put whole armies to flight.

When you face difficulties that seem insurmountable, remember that spiritual resources are there even if you can't see them. Look through the eyes of faith, and let God show you his resources. *LAB note for 2 Kings 6:16*

(1 TIMOTHY 6:12) (2 CORINTHIANS 7:5) (2 KINGS 6:16) (EPHESIANS 6:10) (1 SAMUEL 17:45) (2 SAMUEL 22:33, 35) (2 CORINTHIANS 3:5) (PSALM 34:7) (2 KINGS 6:17) (HEBREWS 11:32-34)

*M*arch 10

He guards the paths of justice and protects those who are faithful to him.

The LORD your God . . . goes before you looking for the best places to camp, guiding you by a pillar of fire at night and a pillar of cloud by day. ▧ Like an eagle that rouses her chicks and hovers over her young, so he spread his wings to take them in and carried them aloft on his pinions. The LORD alone guided them. ▧ The steps of the godly are directed by the LORD. He delights in every detail of their lives. Though they stumble, they will not fall, for the LORD holds them by the hand. ▧ The righteous face many troubles, but the LORD rescues them from each and every one. ▧ For the LORD watches over the path of the godly, but the path of the wicked leads to destruction. ▧ And we know that God causes everything to work together for the good of those who love God and are called according to his purpose for them. ▧ We have the LORD our God to help us and to fight our battles for us!

The LORD your God has arrived to live among you. He is a mighty savior. He will rejoice over you with great gladness.

The Israelites had no excuse for abandoning God. He had been the encircling protector, like a mother eagle who protects her young. The Lord alone had led them. And he alone leads us. Let us remember to trust in him. *LAB note for Deuteronomy 32:10-11*

(PROVERBS 2:8) (DEUTERONOMY 1:32-33) (DEUTERONOMY 32:11-12)
(PSALM 37:23-24) (PSALM 34:19) (PSALM 1:6) (ROMANS 8:28)
(2 CHRONICLES 32:8) (ZEPHANIAH 3:17)

March 11

You . . . have forgiven all my sins.

Where is another God like you, who pardons the sins of the survivors among his people? You cannot stay angry with your people forever, because you delight in showing mercy. Once again you will have compassion on us. You will trample our sins under your feet and throw them into the depths of the ocean!

"For a brief moment I abandoned you, but with great compassion I will take you back. In a moment of anger I turned my face away for a little while. But with everlasting love I will have compassion on you," says the LORD, your Redeemer. ▪ I will forgive their wickedness and will never again remember their sins.

Oh, what joy for those whose rebellion is forgiven, whose sin is put out of sight! Yes, what joy for those whose record the LORD has cleared of sin, whose lives are lived in complete honesty! ▪ The blood of Jesus, his Son, cleanses us from every sin. If we say we have no sin, we are only fooling ourselves and refusing to accept the truth. But if we confess our sins to him, he is faithful and just to forgive us and to cleanse us from every wrong.

Prayer brings deliverance, forgiveness, and good from even a bitter experience. The next time you have difficult struggles, pray for God's help to gain something beneficial from them.

LAB note for Isaiah 38:16-18

(ISAIAH 38:17) (MICAH 7:18-19) (ISAIAH 54:7-8) (JEREMIAH 31:34) (PSALM 32:1-2) (1 JOHN 1:7-9)

March 12

I know the one in whom I trust, and I am sure that he is able to guard what I have entrusted to him until the day of his return.

He is able to accomplish infinitely more than we would ever dare to ask or hope.

God will generously provide all you need. Then you will always have everything you need and plenty left over to share with others.

He is able to help us when we are being tempted.

He is able, once and forever, to save everyone who comes to God through him. He lives forever to plead with God on their behalf.

God . . . is able to keep you from stumbling, and . . . will bring you into his glorious presence innocent of sin and with great joy.

He is able to guard what I have entrusted to him until the day of his return.

He will take these weak mortal bodies of ours and change them into glorious bodies like his own, using the same mighty power that he will use to conquer everything, everywhere.

"Do you believe?" . . . "Yes, Lord," they told him, "we do." . . . "Because of your faith, it will happen!"

Even in prison, the apostle Paul knew that God was still in control. No matter what setbacks or problems we face, we can trust fully in God.

LAB note for 2 Timothy 1:12

(2 Timothy 1:12) (Ephesians 3:20) (2 Corinthians 9:8) (Hebrews 2:18) (Hebrews 7:25) (Jude 1:24) (2 Timothy 1:12) (Philippians 3:21) (Matthew 9:28-29)

March 13

The LORD Will Provide.

I trust in you, my God! Do not let me be disgraced, or let my enemies rejoice in my defeat.

The LORD is not too weak to save you, and he is not becoming deaf. He can hear you when you call. ▩ A Deliverer will come from Jerusalem.

Happy are those who have the God of Israel as their helper, whose hope is in the LORD their God. ▩ The LORD watches over those who fear him, those who rely on his unfailing love. He rescues them from death and keeps them alive in times of famine.

This same God who takes care of me will supply all your needs from his glorious riches, which have been given to us in Christ Jesus. ▩ For God has said, "I will never fail you. I will never forsake you." That is why we can say with confidence, "The Lord is my helper, so I will not be afraid. What can mere mortals do to me?" ▩ The LORD is my strength, my shield from every danger. I trust in him with all my heart. He helps me, and my heart is filled with joy. I burst out in songs of thanksgiving. The LORD protects his people.

We do not have an ironclad guarantee that all believers will be delivered from death and starvation. God can (and often does) miraculously deliver his followers from pain and death; although sometimes, for purposes known only to him, he chooses not to.

LAB note for Psalm 33:18-19

(GENESIS 22:14) (PSALM 25:2) (ISAIAH 59:1) (ROMANS 11:26) (PSALM 146:5) (PSALM 33:18-19) (PHILIPPIANS 4:19) (HEBREWS 13:5-6) (PSALM 28:7-8)

*M*arch 14

The things that please him.

It is impossible to please God without faith. ▩ Those who are still under the control of their sinful nature can never please God. ▩ The LORD delights in his people; he crowns the humble with salvation.

God is pleased with you when, for the sake of your conscience, you patiently endure unfair treatment. Of course, you get no credit for being patient if you are beaten for doing wrong. But if you suffer for doing right and are patient beneath the blows, God is pleased with you. ▩ You should be known for the beauty that comes from within, the unfading beauty of a gentle and quiet spirit, which is so precious to God.

Giving thanks is a sacrifice that truly honors me. If you keep to my path, I will reveal to you the salvation of God. ▩ Then I will praise God's name with singing, and I will honor him with thanksgiving. For this will please the LORD more than sacrificing an ox or presenting a bull with its horns and hooves.

Dear brothers and sisters, I plead with you to give your bodies to God. Let them be a living and holy sacrifice—the kind he will accept. When you think of what he has done for you, is this too much to ask?

God wants us to offer ourselves as living sacrifices—daily laying aside our own desires to follow him, putting all our energy and resources at his disposal, and trusting him to guide us. We do this out of gratitude that our sins have been forgiven. *LAB note for Romans 12:1*

(1 JOHN 3:22) (HEBREWS 11:6) (ROMANS 8:8) (PSALM 149:4) (1 PETER 2:19-20) (1 PETER 3:4) (PSALM 50:23) (PSALM 69:30-31) (ROMANS 12:1)

*M*arch 15

I am deeply discouraged.

You will keep in perfect peace all who trust in you, whose thoughts are fixed on you! Trust in the LORD always, for the LORD GOD is the eternal Rock.

Give your burdens to the LORD, and he will take care of you. He will not permit the godly to slip and fall. ▩ He has not ignored the suffering of the needy. He has not turned and walked away. He has listened to their cries for help. ▩ Are any among you suffering? They should keep praying about it.

Don't be troubled or afraid. ▩ Don't worry about everyday life—whether you have enough food, drink, and clothes. Doesn't life consist of more than food and clothing? Look at the birds. They don't need to plant or harvest or put food in barns because your heavenly Father feeds them. And you are far more valuable to him than they are. Can all your worries add a single moment to your life? Of course not. And why worry about your clothes? Look at the lilies and how they grow. They don't work or make their clothing, yet Solomon in all his glory was not dressed as beautifully as they are. And if God cares so wonderfully for flowers that are here today and gone tomorrow, won't he more surely care for you? ▩ Don't be faithless any longer. Believe! ▩ I am with you always.

Sin, fear, uncertainty, doubt, and numerous other forces are at war within us. The peace of God moves into our hearts and lives to restrain these hostile forces and offer comfort in place of conflict. Jesus says he will give us that peace if we are willing to accept it from him.

LAB note for John 14:27-29

(PSALM 42:6) (ISAIAH 26:3-4) (PSALM 55:22) (PSALM 22:24) (JAMES 5:13) (JOHN 14:27) (MATTHEW 6:25-30) (JOHN 20:27) (MATTHEW 28:20)

March 16

Don't hide your light under a basket! Instead, put it on a stand and let it shine for all. In the same way, let your good deeds shine out for all to see, so that everyone will praise your heavenly Father.

Live in a manner worthy of the Good News about Christ, as citizens of heaven. ▪ Keep away from every kind of evil. ▪ Be happy if you are insulted for being a Christian, for then the glorious Spirit of God will come upon you. If you suffer, however, it must not be for murder, stealing, making trouble, or prying into other people's affairs. ▪ In everything you do, stay away from complaining and arguing, so that no one can speak a word of blame against you. You are to live clean, innocent lives as children of God in a dark world full of crooked and perverse people. Let your lives shine brightly before them. ▪ Make the teaching about God our Savior attractive in every way.

Never let loyalty and kindness get away from you! Wear them like a necklace; write them deep within your heart. Then you will find favor with both God and people, and you will gain a good reputation. Trust in the LORD with all your heart; do not depend on your own understanding. ▪ Fix your thoughts on what is true and honorable and right. Think about things that are pure and lovely and admirable. Think about things that are excellent and worthy of praise.

Can you hide a city that is sitting on top of a mountain? Its light at night can be seen for miles. If we live for Christ, we will glow like lights, showing others what Christ is like. Be a beacon of truth—don't shut your light off from the rest of the world. *LAB note for Matthew 5:14-16*

(MATTHEW 5:15-16) (PHILIPPIANS 1:27) (1 THESSALONIANS 5:22) (1 PETER 4:14-15) (PHILIPPIANS 2:14-15) (TITUS 2:10) (PROVERBS 3:3-5) (PHILIPPIANS 4:8)

March 17

The LORD Is Our Righteousness.

We are all infected and impure with sin. When we proudly display our righteous deeds, we find they are but filthy rags.

I will praise your mighty deeds, O Sovereign LORD. I will tell everyone that you alone are just and good. ▪ I am overwhelmed with joy in the LORD my God! For he has dressed me with the clothing of salvation and draped me in a robe of righteousness. I am like a bridegroom in his wedding suit or a bride with her jewels.

Bring the finest robe in the house and put it on. ▪ Wear the finest white linen. (Fine linen represents the good deeds done by the people of God.)

Everything else is worthless when compared with the priceless gain of knowing Christ Jesus my Lord. I have discarded everything else, counting it all as garbage, so that I may have Christ and become one with him. I no longer count on my own goodness or my ability to obey God's law, but I trust Christ to save me. For God's way of making us right with himself depends on faith.

Sin makes us unclean so that we cannot approach God any more than a beggar in filthy rags could dine at a king's table. Our best efforts are still infected with sin. Our only hope, therefore, is faith in Jesus Christ, who can cleanse us and bring us into God's presence. *LAB note for Isaiah 64:6*

(JEREMIAH 23:6) (ISAIAH 64:6) (PSALM 71:16) (ISAIAH 61:10) (LUKE 15:22) (REVELATION 19:8) (PHILIPPIANS 3:8-9)

*M*arch 18

Through the suffering of Jesus, God made him a perfect leader.

"My soul is crushed with grief to the point of death. Stay here and watch with me." He went on a little farther and fell face down on the ground, praying, "My Father! If it is possible, let this cup of suffering be taken away from me. Yet I want your will, not mine." ▪ He prayed more fervently, and he was in such agony of spirit that his sweat fell to the ground like great drops of blood.

Death had its hands around my throat; the terrors of the grave overtook me. I saw only trouble and sorrow. ▪ Their insults have broken my heart, and I am in despair. If only one person would show some pity; if only one would turn and comfort me. ▪ No one gives me a passing thought! No one will help me; no one cares a bit what happens to me.

He was despised and rejected—a man of sorrows, acquainted with bitterest grief. We turned our backs on him and looked the other way when he went by. He was despised, and we did not care. But he was wounded and crushed for our sins. He was beaten that we might have peace. He was whipped, and we were healed! He was oppressed and treated harshly, yet he never said a word.

I will give him the honors of one who is mighty and great, because he exposed himself to death.

The man of sorrows was despised and rejected by those around him, and he is still despised and rejected by many today. Some reject Christ by standing against him. Others despise Christ and his great gift of forgiveness. Do you despise him, reject him, or accept him?

LAB note for Isaiah 53:3

(HEBREWS 2:10) (MATTHEW 26:38-39) (LUKE 22:44) (PSALM 116:3) (PSALM 69:20) (PSALM 142:4) (ISAIAH 53:3, 5, 7) (ISAIAH 53:12)

*M*arch 19

The LORD's searchlight penetrates the human spirit, exposing every hidden motive.

"All right, stone her. But let those who have never sinned throw the first stones!" When the accusers heard this, they slipped away one by one, beginning with the oldest.

"Who told you that you were naked?" the LORD God asked. "Have you eaten the fruit I commanded you not to eat?"

It is sin to know what you ought to do and then not do it. ▪ We will be confident when we stand before the Lord, even if our hearts condemn us. For God is greater than our hearts, and he knows everything. Dear friends, if our conscience is clear, we can come to God with bold confidence.

There is nothing wrong with these things in themselves. But it is wrong to eat anything if it makes another person stumble. Blessed are those who do not condemn themselves by doing something they know is all right.

Search me, O God, and know my heart; test me and know my thoughts. Point out anything in me that offends you, and lead me along the path of everlasting life.

We tend to think that doing wrong is sin. But sin is also not doing right. If God has directed you to do a kind act, to render a service, or to restore a relationship, do it. You will experience a renewed vitality in your Christian faith. *LAB note for James 4:17*

(PROVERBS 20:27) (JOHN 8:7, 9) (GENESIS 3:11) (JAMES 4:17) (1 JOHN 3:19-21) (ROMANS 14:20, 22) (PSALM 139:23-24)

March 20

I will pray in the spirit, and I will pray in words I understand. I will sing in the spirit, and I will sing in words I understand.

Let the Holy Spirit fill and control you. Then you will sing psalms and hymns and spiritual songs among yourselves, making music to the Lord in your hearts. ▩ Let the words of Christ, in all their richness, live in your hearts and make you wise. Use his words to teach and counsel each other. Sing psalms and hymns and spiritual songs to God with thankful hearts.

I will praise the LORD, and everyone on earth will bless his holy name forever and forever.

How good it is to sing praises to our God! How delightful and how right! Sing out your thanks to the LORD; sing praises to our God, accompanied by harps.

I heard a sound from heaven like the roaring of a great waterfall or the rolling of mighty thunder. It was like the sound of many harpists playing together. ▩ Then I saw in heaven another significant event. . . . They were all holding harps that God had given them. And they were singing the song of Moses, the servant of God, and the song of the Lamb: "Great and marvelous are your actions, Lord God Almighty. Just and true are your ways, O King of the nations."

In praying and singing, both the mind and the spirit are to be fully engaged. When we sing, we should also think about the meaning of the words. When we pour out our feelings to God in prayer, we should not turn off our capacity to think. *LAB note for 1 Corinthians 14:15*

(1 CORINTHIANS 14:15) (EPHESIANS 5:18-19) (COLOSSIANS 3:16) (PSALM 145:21) (PSALM 147:1, 7) (REVELATION 14:2) (REVELATION 15:1-3)

March 21

God in all his fullness was pleased to live in Christ.

The Father loves his Son, and he has given him authority over everything. ▩ God raised him up to the heights of heaven and gave him a name that is above every other name, so that at the name of Jesus every knee will bow, in heaven and on earth and under the earth, and every tongue will confess that Jesus Christ is Lord, to the glory of God the Father. ▩ Now he is far above any ruler or authority or power or leader or anything else in this world or in the world to come. ▩ Christ is the one through whom God created everything in heaven and earth. He made the things we can see and the things we can't see—kings, kingdoms, rulers, and authorities. Everything has been created through him and for him.

Christ died and rose again for this very purpose, so that he might be Lord of those who are alive and of those who have died. ▩ You are complete through your union with Christ. He is the Lord over every ruler and authority in the universe. ▩ We have all benefited from the rich blessings he brought to us—one gracious blessing after another.

Christ was fully human; he was also fully divine. Christ has always been God and always will be God. When we have Christ, we have all of God in human form. Don't diminish any aspect of Christ—either his humanity or his divinity.

LAB note for Colossians 1:19

(Colossians 1:19) (John 3:35) (Phlippians 2:9-11) (Ephesians 1:21) (Colossians 1:16) (Romans 14:9) (Colossians 2:10) (John 1:16)

March 22

He faced all of the same temptations we do, yet he did not sin.

The fruit looked so fresh and delicious, and it would make her so wise! So she ate some of the fruit. She also gave some to her husband, who was with her. Then he ate it, too. ▩ Stop loving this evil world and all that it offers you, for when you love the world, you show that you do not have the love of the Father in you.

Then the Devil came and said to him, "If you are the Son of God, change these stones into loaves of bread." But Jesus told him, "No! The Scriptures say, 'People need more than bread for their life; they must feed on every word of God.'" Next the Devil took him to the peak of a very high mountain and showed him the nations of the world and all their glory. "I will give it all to you," he said, "if you will only kneel down and worship me." "Get out of here, Satan," Jesus told him. ▩ The world offers only the lust for physical pleasure, the lust for everything we see, and pride in our posessions. These are not from the Father. They are from this evil world.

Since he himself has gone through suffering and temptation, he is able to help us when we are being tempted.

God blesses the people who patiently endure testing.

Prepare yourself for the attractive temptations that may come your way. We cannot always prevent temptation, but there is always a way of escape. Use God's Word and God's people to help you stand against it.

LAB note for Genesis 3:6

(HEBREWS 4:15) (GENESIS 3:6) (1 JOHN 2:15) (MATTHEW 4:3-4, 8-10) (1 JOHN 2:16) (HEBREWS 2:18) (JAMES 1:12)

March 23

My eyes grew tired of looking to heaven for help.

Have compassion on me, LORD, for I am weak. Heal me, LORD, for my body is in agony. I am sick at heart. How long, O LORD, until you restore me? Return, O LORD, and rescue me. Save me because of your unfailing love. ▩ My heart is in anguish. The terror of death overpowers me. Fear and trembling overwhelm me. I can't stop shaking. Oh, how I wish I had wings like a dove; then I would fly away and rest!

Patient endurance is what you need now, so you will continue to do God's will. ▩ Don't get tired of doing what is good. Don't get discouraged and give up, for we will reap a harvest of blessing at the appropriate time.

As they were straining their eyes to see him, two white-robed men suddenly stood there among them. They said, "Men of Galilee, why are you standing here staring at the sky? Jesus has been taken away from you into heaven. And someday, just as you saw him go, he will return!" ▩ We are citizens of heaven, where the Lord Jesus Christ lives. And we are eagerly waiting for him to return as our Savior. ▩ We look forward to that wonderful event when the glory of our great God and Savior, Jesus Christ, will be revealed.

Don't abandon your faith in times of persecution, but show by your endurance that your faith is real. Faith means resting in what Christ has done for us in the past, but it also means trusting him for what he will do for us in the present and in the future. *LAB note for Hebrews 10:35-38*

(ISAIAH 38:14) (PSALM 6:2-4) (PSALM 55:4-6) (HEBREWS 10:36) (GALATIANS 6:9) (ACTS 1:10-11) (PHILIPPIANS 3:20) (TITUS 2:13)

March 24

When God raised up his servant, he sent him . . . to bless you by turning each of you back from your sinful ways.

All honor to the God and Father of our Lord Jesus Christ, for it is by his boundless mercy that God has given us the privilege of being born again. Now we live with a wonderful expectation because Jesus Christ rose again from the dead.

Our great God and Savior, Jesus Christ . . . gave his life to free us from every kind of sin, to cleanse us, and to make us his very own people, totally committed to doing what is right. ▪ Be holy in everything you do, just as God—who chose you to be his children—is holy. For he himself has said, "You must be holy because I am holy."

God, the Father of our Lord Jesus Christ . . . has blessed us with every spiritual blessing in the heavenly realms because we belong to Christ. ▪ For in Christ the fullness of God lives in a human body, and you are complete through your union with Christ. ▪ We have all benefited from the rich blessings he brought to us—one gracious blessing after another.

Since God did not spare even his own Son but gave him up for us all, won't God, who gave us Christ, also give us everything else?

Christ's freeing us from sin opens the way for him to purify us. He freed us from sin (redeemed us) by purchasing our release from the captivity of sin with a ransom. We are not only free from the sentence of death for our sin, but we are also purified from sin's influence as we grow in Christ.

LAB note for Titus 2:14

(ACTS 3:26) (1 PETER 1:3) (TITUS 2:13-14) (1 PETER 1:15-16) (EPHESIANS 1:3) (COLOSSIANS 2:9-10) (JOHN 1:16) (ROMANS 8:32)

March 25

Encourage me by your word.

Remember your promise to me, for it is my only hope. ▩ I am in trouble, Lord. Help me!

Heaven and earth will disappear, but my words will remain forever. ▩ Deep in your hearts you know that every promise of the LORD your God has come true.

Don't be afraid, for I am with you. Do not be dismayed, for I am your God. I will strengthen you. I will help you. I will uphold you with my victorious right hand. ▩ Take courage and work, for I am with you, says the LORD Almighty. ▩ Not by force nor by strength, but by my Spirit, says the LORD Almighty. ▩ Study this Book of the Law continually. Meditate on it day and night so you may be sure to obey all that is written in it. Only then will you succeed. I command you—be strong and courageous! Do not be afraid or discouraged. For the LORD your God is with you wherever you go.

Be strong with the Lord's mighty power.

To succeed you must (1) be strong and courageous, (2) obey God's law, and (3) constantly read and study God's Word. You may not succeed by the world's standards, but you will be a success in God's eyes—and his opinion lasts forever. *LAB note for Joshua 1:6-8*

(PSALM 119:28) (PSALM 119:49) (ISAIAH 38:14) (LUKE 21:33) (JOSHUA 23:14) (ISAIAH 41:10) (HAGGAI 2:4) (ZECHARIAH 4:6) (JOSHUA 1:8-9) (EPHESIANS 6:10)

March 26

Wake up! Strengthen what little remains, for even what is left is at the point of death.

The end of the world is coming soon. Therefore, be earnest and disciplined in your prayers. ▪ Be careful! Watch out for attacks from the Devil, your great enemy. He prowls around like a roaring lion, looking for some victim to devour. ▪ Watch out! Be very careful never to forget what you have seen the LORD do for you. Do not let these things escape from your mind as long as you live! ▪ A righteous person will live by faith. But I will have no pleasure in anyone who turns away. . . . We have faith that assures our salvation.

Keep a sharp lookout! For you do not know when the homeowner will return—at evening, midnight, early dawn, or late daybreak. Don't let him find you sleeping when he arrives without warning. What I say to you I say to everyone: Watch for his return!

Don't be afraid, for I am with you. Do not be dismayed, for I am your God. I will strengthen you. I will help you. I will uphold you with my victorious right hand. I am holding you by your right hand—I, the LORD your God. And I say to you, "Do not be afraid. I am here to help you."

We should live expectantly because Christ is coming soon. Getting ready to meet Christ involves continually growing in love for God and for others. It is important to pray regularly and to reach out to needy people. Invest your time and talents where they will make an eternal difference.

LAB note for 1 Peter 4:7-9

(REVELATION 3:2) (1 PETER 4:7) (1 PETER 5:8) (DEUTERONOMOY 4:9) (HEBREWS 10:38-39) (MARK 13:35-37) (ISAIAH 41:10, 13)

*M*arch 27

Is his unfailing love gone forever?

He remembered our utter weakness. His faithful love endures forever. ▩ The LORD is slow to anger and rich in unfailing love, forgiving every kind of sin and rebellion. ▩ Where is another God like you, who pardons the sins of the survivors among his people? You cannot stay angry with your people forever, because you delight in showing mercy. Once again you will have compassion on us. You will trample our sins under your feet and throw them into the depths of the ocean! ▩ He saved us, not because of the good things we did, but because of his mercy. He washed away our sins and gave us a new life through the Holy Spirit.

All praise to the God and Father of our Lord Jesus Christ. He is the source of every mercy and the God who comforts us. He comforts us in all our troubles.

Our merciful and faithful High Priest before God . . . could offer a sacrifice that would take away the sins of the people. Since he himself has gone through suffering and temptation, he is able to help us when we are being tempted.

Here are several unchanging characteristics of God we can rely on: (1) God is immensely patient; (2) God's love is one promise we can always count on; (3) God forgives again and again; (4) God is merciful, listening to and answering our requests. *LAB note for Micah 14:17-20*

(PSALM 77:8) (PSALM 136:23) (NUMBERS 14:18) (MICAH 7:18-19) (TITUS 3:5) (2 CORINTHIANS 1:3-4) (HEBREWS 2:17-18)

March 28

Lot took a long look at the fertile plains of the Jordan Valley in the direction of Zoar. The whole area was well watered everywhere, like the garden of the LORD or the beautiful land of Egypt. (This was before the LORD had destroyed Sodom and Gomorrah.) Lot chose that land for himself—the Jordan Valley to the east of them.

Lot . . . was a good man.

Don't be misled. Remember that you can't ignore God and get away with it. You will always reap what you sow! ▩ Remember what happened to Lot's wife!

Don't team up with those who are unbelievers. How can goodness be a partner with wickedness? How can light live with darkness? Therefore, come out from them and separate yourselves from them, says the Lord. Don't touch their filthy things, and I will welcome you. ▩ Don't participate in the things these people do. For though your hearts were once full of darkness, now you are full of light from the Lord, and your behavior should show it! Try to find out what is pleasing to the Lord. Take no part in the worthless deeds of evil and darkness; instead, rebuke and expose them. ▩ Knowing God leads to self-control. Self-control leads to patient endurance, and patient endurance leads to godliness. The more you grow like this, the more you will become productive and useful in your knowledge of our Lord Jesus Christ.

Just as God rescued Lot from Sodom, so he is able to rescue us from the temptations and trials we face in a wicked world. Lot was not sinless, but he put his trust in God and was spared when Sodom was destroyed.

LAB note for 2 Peter 2:7-9

(GENESIS 13:10-11) (2 PETER 2:7) (GALATIANS 6:7) (LUKE 17:32) (2 CORINTHIANS 6:14, 17) (EPHESIANS 5:7-8, 10-11) (2 PETER 1:6, 8)

March 29

Holy, holy, holy is the Lord God Almighty.

The praises of Israel surround your throne. ▪ "Do not come any closer," God told him. "Take off your sandals, for you are standing on holy ground." Then he said, "I am the God of your ancestors—the God of Abraham, the God of Isaac, and the God of Jacob." When Moses heard this, he hid his face in his hands because he was afraid to look at God. ▪ "To whom will you compare me? Who is my equal?" asks the Holy One. ▪ I am the LORD, your God, the Holy One of Israel, your Savior. There is no other God.

Now you must be holy in everything you do, just as God—who chose you to be his children—is holy. For he himself has said, "You must be holy because I am holy." ▪ Don't you know that your body is the temple of the Holy Spirit, who lives in you and was given to you by God? You do not belong to yourself.

And so . . . I plead with you to give your bodies to God. Let them be a living and holy sacrifice—the kind he will accept. When you think of what he has done for you, is this too much to ask?

God is our friend, but he is also our sovereign Lord. To approach him frivolously shows a lack of respect and sincerity. When you come to God in worship, do you approach him casually, or do you come as though you were an invited guest before a king? *LAB note for Exodus 3:5-6*

(REVELATION 4:8) (PSALM 22:3) (EXODUS 3:5-6) (ISAIAH 40:25) (ISAIAH 43:3, 10) (1 PETER 1:15-16) (1 CORINTHIANS 6:19) (ROMANS 12:1)

March 30

I will never fail you. I will never forsake you.

That is why we can say with confidence, "The Lord is my helper, so I will not be afraid. What can mere mortals do to me?"

I will be with you, and I will protect you wherever you go. I will someday bring you safely back to this land. I will be with you constantly until I have finished giving you everything I have promised. ▩ Be strong and courageous! Do not be afraid of them! The LORD your God will go ahead of you. He will neither fail you nor forsake you.

Demas has deserted me because he loves the things of this life. The first time I was brought before the judge, no one was with me. Everyone had abandoned me. I hope it will not be counted against them. But the Lord stood with me and gave me strength, that I might preach the Good News in all its fullness for all the Gentiles to hear. ▩ Even if my father and mother abandon me, the LORD will hold me close.

I am with you always, even to the end of the age. ▩ I am the living one who died. Look, I am alive forever and ever! ▩ I will not abandon you as orphans—I will come to you. ▩ I am leaving you with a gift—peace of mind and heart.

When Jesus said, "I will come to you," he meant it. Although Jesus ascended to heaven, he sent the Holy Spirit to live in believers, and to have the Holy Spirit is to have Jesus himself. *LAB note for John 14:18*

(HEBREWS 13:5) (HEBREWS 13:6) (GENESIS 28:15) (DEUTERONOMY 31:6) (2 TIMOTHY 4:10, 16–17) (PSALM 27:10) (MATTHEW 28:20) (REVELATION 1:18) (JOHN 14:18) (JOHN 14:27)

March 31

The Kingdom of Heaven can be illustrated by the story of a man going on a trip. He called together his servants and gave them money to invest for him while he was gone . . . dividing it in proportion to their abilities.

Don't you realize that whatever you choose to obey becomes your master? You can choose sin, which leads to death, or you can choose to obey God and receive his approval.

It is the one and only Holy Spirit who distributes these gifts. He alone decides which gift each person should have. A spiritual gift is given to each of us as a means of helping the entire church. ▩ God has given gifts to each of you from his great variety of spiritual gifts. Manage them well so that God's generosity can flow through you. ▩ A person who is put in charge as a manager must be faithful. ▩ Much is required from those to whom much is given, and much more is required from those to whom much more is given.

Who is adequate for such a task as this? ▩ I can do everything with the help of Christ who gives me the strength I need.

God gives us time, gifts, and other resources according to our abilities, and he expects us to invest them wisely until he returns. We are responsible to use well what God has given us. The issue is not how much we have but how well we use what we have. *LAB note for Matthew 25:15*

(Matthew 25:14-15) (Romans 6:16) (1 Corinthians 12:11, 7) (1 Peter 4:10) (1 Corinthians 4:2) (Luke 12:48) (2 Corinthians 2:16) (Philippians 4:13)

April

One Sunday Morning

One of a kind, timeless significance
From devastating tragedy to extraordinary blessing
No other day means more than this one.

This Easter season may you gain a fresh awareness of God's wondrous plan offered for you! Such enormous grace shown to imperfect people—that is treasure beyond words.

April 1

When the Holy Spirit controls our lives, he will produce . . . love.

We know how much God loves us, and we have put our trust in him. ▩ How dearly God loves us, because he has given us the Holy Spirit to fill our hearts with his love. ▩ He is very precious to you who believe. ▩ We love each other as a result of his loving us first. ▩ Whatever we do, it is because Christ's love controls us. Since we believe that Christ died for everyone, we also believe that we have all died to the old life we used to live. He died for everyone so that those who receive his new life will no longer live to please themselves. Instead, they will live to please Christ, who died and was raised for them.

God himself has taught you to love one another. ▩ I command you to love each other in the same way that I love you. ▩ Most important of all, continue to show deep love for each other, for love covers a multitude of sins. ▩ Live a life filled with love for others, following the example of Christ, who loved you and gave himself as a sacrifice to take away your sins. And God was pleased, because that sacrifice was like sweet perfume to him.

Since Christ's love controls our lives and he died for us, we are dead to our old life. We should no longer live to please ourselves; we should spend our life pleasing Christ, who died for us and rose again from the grave. *LAB note for 2 Corinthians 5:13–15*

(Galatians 5:22) (1 John 4:16) (Romans 5:5) (1 Peter 2:7) (1 John 4:19) (2 Corinthians 5:14–15) (1 Thessalonians 4:9) (John 15:12) (1 Peter 4:8) (Ephesians 5:2)

April 2

The reward of the godly will last.

After a long time their master returned from his trip and called them to give an account of how they had used his money. The servant to whom he had entrusted the five bags of gold said, "Sir, you gave me five bags of gold to invest, and I have doubled the amount." The master was full of praise. "Well done, my good and faithful servant. You have been faithful in handling this small amount, so now I will give you many more responsibilities. Let's celebrate together!"

We must all stand before Christ to be judged. We will each receive whatever we deserve for the good or evil we have done in our bodies.

I have fought a good fight, I have finished the race, and I have remained faithful. And now the prize awaits me—the crown of righteousness that the Lord, the righteous Judge, will give me on that great day of his return. And the prize is not just for me but for all who eagerly look forward to his glorious return.

I am coming quickly. Hold on to what you have, so that no one will take away your crown.

While eternal life is a free gift given on the basis of God's grace, each of us will still be judged by Christ. All Christians must give account on the day of judgment, and Christ will reward us for how we have lived.

LAB note for 2 Corinthians 5:9-10

(PROVERBS 11:18) (MATTHEW 25:19-21) (2 CORINTHIANS 5:10)
(2 TIMOTHY 4:7-8) (REVELATION 3:11)

April 3

God is faithful.

God is not a man, that he should lie. He is not a human, that he should change his mind. . . . Has he ever promised and not carried it through? ▩ The Lord has taken an oath and will not break his vow.

God also bound himself with an oath, so that those who received the promise could be perfectly sure that he would never change his mind. So God has given us both his promise and his oath. These two things are unchangeable because it is impossible for God to lie. Therefore, we who have fled to him for refuge can take new courage, for we can hold on to his promise with confidence. ▩ So if you are suffering according to God's will, keep on doing what is right, and trust yourself to the God who made you, for he will never fail you.

I know the one in whom I trust, and I am sure that he is able to guard what I have entrusted to him until the day of his return. ▩ God, who calls you, is faithful; he will do this. ▩ All of God's promises have been fulfilled in him. That is why we say "Amen" when we give glory to God through Christ.

All of God's promises of what the Messiah would be like are fulfilled in Christ. Jesus was completely faithful in his ministry; he never sinned; he faithfully died for us; and now he faithfully intercedes for us.

LAB note for 2 Corinthians 1:19–20

(1 Corinthians 10:13) (Numbers 23:19) (Hebrews 7:21) (Hebrews 6:17–18) (1 Peter 4:19) (2 Timothy 1:12) (1 Thessalonians 5:24) (2 Corinthians 1:20)

April 4

Be strong and courageous!

The LORD is my light and my salvation—so why should I be afraid? ▩ He gives power to those who are tired and worn out; he offers strength to the weak. Even youths will become exhausted, and young men will give up. But those who wait on the LORD will find new strength. They will fly high on wings like eagles. They will run and not grow weary. They will walk and not faint. ▩ My health may fail, and my spirit may grow weak, but God remains the strength of my heart; he is mine forever.

What can we say about such wonderful things as these? If God is for us, who can ever be against us? Since God did not spare even his own Son but gave him up for us all, won't God, who gave us Christ, also give us everything else? ▩ The LORD is for me, so I will not be afraid. What can mere mortals do to me? ▩ Only by your power can we push back our enemies; only in your name can we trample our foes. ▩ Overwhelming victory is ours through Christ, who loved us.

May the LORD be with you and give you success. Be strong and courageous; do not be afraid or lose heart!

When God commissioned Joshua, he was told three times to be strong and courageous! Apparently he took God's message to heart. The next time you are afraid to do what you know is right, remember that strength and courage are readily available from God. *LAB note for Joshua 1:18*

(JOSHUA 1:18) (PSALM 27:1) (ISAIAH 40:29-31) (PSALM 73:26) (ROMANS 8:31-32) (PSALM 118:6) (PSALM 44:5) (ROMANS 8:37) (1 CHRONICLES 22:11, 13)

April 5

Riches don't last forever, and the crown might not be secure for the next generation.

We are merely moving shadows, and all our busy rushing ends in nothing. We heap up wealth for someone else to spend. ▪ Let heaven fill your thoughts. Do not think only about things down here on earth. ▪ Don't store up treasures here on earth, where they can be eaten by moths and get rusty, and where thieves break in and steal. Store your treasures in heaven, where they will never become moth-eaten or rusty and where they will be safe from thieves. Wherever your treasure is, there your heart and thoughts will be also.

All athletes practice strict self-control. They do it to win a prize that will fade away, but we do it for an eternal prize. ▪ So we don't look at the troubles we can see right now; rather, we look forward to what we have not yet seen. ▪ The reward of the godly will last. ▪ Now the prize awaits me—the crown of righteousness that the Lord, the righteous Judge, will give me on that great day of his return. And the prize is not just for me but for all who eagerly look forward to his glorious return. ▪ Your reward will be a never-ending share in his glory and honor.

Because life is uncertain, we should be all the more diligent in preparing for the future. We should act with foresight, giving responsible attention to our home, our family, and our career. Thinking ahead is a duty, not an option, for God's people. *LAB note for Proverbs 27:23-27*

(Proverbs 27:24) (Psalm 39:6) (Colossians 3:2) (Matthew 6:19-21) (1 Corinthians 9:25) (2 Corinthians 4:18) (Proverbs 11:18) (2 Timothy 4:8) (1 Peter 5:4)

April 6

Isaac . . . was taking a walk out in the fields, meditating.

May the words of my mouth and the thoughts of my heart be pleasing to you, O LORD, my rock and my redeemer.

When I look at the night sky and see the work of your fingers—the moon and the stars you have set in place—what are mortals that you should think of us, mere humans that you should care for us? ▩ I will thank the LORD with all my heart as I meet with his godly people. How amazing are the deeds of the LORD! All who delight in him should ponder them.

Oh, the joys of those who do not follow the advice of the wicked, or stand around with sinners, or join in with scoffers. But they delight in doing everything the LORD wants; day and night they think about his law. ▩ Study this Book of the Law continually. Meditate on it day and night so you may be sure to obey all that is written in it. ▩ I will praise you with songs of joy. I lie awake thinking of you, meditating on you through the night. I think how much you have helped me; I sing for joy in the shadow of your protecting wings. I follow close behind you; your strong right hand holds me securely.

Would you change the way you live if you knew that every word and thought would be examined by God first? As you begin each day, determine that God's love will guide what you say and how you think.

LAB note for Psalm 19:14

(GENESIS 24:62-63) (PSALM 19:14) (PSALM 8:3-4) (PSALM 111:1-2) (PSALM 1:1-2) (JOSHUA 1:8) (PSALM 63:5-8)

April 7

O LORD, how long will you forget me? Forever? How long will you look the other way?

Whatever is good and perfect comes to us from God above, who created all heaven's lights. Unlike them, he never changes or casts shifting shadows. ▪ Yet Jerusalem says, "The LORD has deserted us; the Lord has forgotten us." "Never! Can a mother forget her nursing child? Can she feel no love for a child she has borne? But even if that were possible, I would not forget you!"

I will not forget to help you. I have swept away your sins like the morning mists.

Although Jesus loved Martha, Mary, and Lazarus, he stayed where he was for the next two days and did not go to them. ▪ A Gentile woman . . . came to him, pleading, "Have mercy on me, O Lord, Son of David! . . ." But Jesus gave her no reply—not even a word.

These trials are only to test your faith, to show that it is strong and pure. It is being tested as fire tests and purifies gold—and your faith is far more precious to God than mere gold. So if your faith remains strong after being tried by fiery trials, it will bring you much praise and glory and honor on the day when Jesus Christ is revealed to the whole world.

Why is God sometimes slow to act? Why does he allow evil and suffering to go seemingly unchecked? The psalmist David affirmed that he would continue to trust God, no matter how long he had to wait for God's justice to be realized. When you feel impatient, remember David's steadfast faith in God's unfailing love. *LAB note for Psalm 13:1-5*

(PSALM 13:1) (JAMES 1:17) (ISAIAH 49:14-15) (ISAIAH 44:21-22) (JOHN 11:5-6) (MATTHEW 15:22-23) (1 PETER 1:7)

April 8

This same God who takes care of me will supply all your needs from his glorious riches, which have been given to us in Christ Jesus.

Your heavenly Father already knows all your needs, and he will give you all you need from day to day if you live for him and make the Kingdom of God your primary concern. ▪ Since God did not spare even his own Son but gave him up for us all, won't God, who gave us Christ, also give us everything else? ▪ Everything belongs to you: . . . the whole world and life and death; the present and the future. Everything belongs to you, and you belong to Christ, and Christ belongs to God. ▪ We own nothing, and yet we have everything.

The LORD is my shepherd; I have everything I need. ▪ For the LORD God is our light and protector. He gives us grace and glory. No good thing will the LORD withhold from those who do what is right. ▪ The living God . . . richly gives us all we need for our enjoyment. ▪ God will generously provide all you need. Then you will always have everything you need and plenty left over to share with others.

God will always meet our needs. However, there is a difference between wants and needs. Most people want to feel good and avoid pain. We may not get all that we want. But by trusting in Christ, our attitudes and appetites can change from wanting everything to accepting his provision and power to live in him. *LAB note for Philippians 4:19*

(PHILIPPIANS 4:19) (MATTHEW 6:32-33) (ROMANS 8:32) (1 CORINTHIANS 3:21-23) (2 CORINTHIANS 6:10) (PSALM 23:1) (PSALM 84:11) (1 TIMOTHY 6:17) (2 CORINTHIANS 9:8)

April 9

How can goodness be a partner with wickedness?

They loved the darkness more than the light, for their actions were evil. ▩ You are all children of the light and of the day; we don't belong to darkness and night.

Your word is a lamp for my feet and a light for my path.

The land is full of darkness and violence! ▩ Love comes from God. Anyone who loves is born of God and knows God. But anyone who does not love does not know God—for God is love.

The way of the wicked is like complete darkness. The way of the righteous is like the first gleam of dawn, which shines ever brighter until the full light of day.

I have come as a light to shine in this dark world, so that all who put their trust in me will no longer remain in the darkness. ▩ Though your hearts were once full of darkness, now you are full of light from the Lord, and your behavior should show it! For this light within you produces only what is good and right and true. Try to find out what is pleasing to the Lord.

For those who have discovered God's light, there can be no fellowship or compromise with darkness. Does your behavior shine like a light in the darkness, or is it being obscured by the darkness around you?

LAB note for 2 Corinthians 6:14-15

(2 Corinthians 6:14) (John 3:19) (1 Thessalonians 5:5) (Psalm 119:105) (Psalm 74:20) (1 John 4:7-8) (Proverbs 4:19, 18) (John 12:46) (Ephesians 5:8-10)

April 10

If you are really serious about wanting to return to the LORD, get rid of your foreign gods and your images of Ashtoreth. Determine to obey only the LORD.

Dear children, keep away from anything that might take God's place in your hearts. ▪ Therefore come out from them and separate yourselves from them, says the Lord. Don't touch their filthy things, and I will welcome you. And I will be your Father, and you will be my sons and daughters, says the Lord Almighty. ▪ You cannot serve both God and money.

You must worship no other gods, but only the LORD, for he is a God who is passionate about his relationship with you. ▪ Worship and serve him with your whole heart and with a willing mind. For the LORD sees every heart and understands and knows every plan and thought.

You desire honesty from the heart, so you can teach me to be wise in my inmost being. ▪ People judge by outward appearance, but the LORD looks at a person's thoughts and intentions. ▪ Dear friends, if our conscience is clear, we can come to God with bold confidence. ▪ Cling tightly to your faith in Christ, and always keep your conscience clear.

Do you ever feel as if God has abandoned you? Check to see if there is anything he has already told you to do. You may not receive new guidance from God until you have acted on his previous directions. How easy it is for us to complain about our problems, even to God, while we refuse to act, change, and do what he requires! *LAB note for 1 Samuel 7:2-3*

(1 SAMUEL 7:3) (1 JOHN 5:21) (2 CORINTHIANS 6:17-18) (MATTHEW 6:24) (EXODUS 34:14) (1 CHRONICLES 28:9) (PSALM 51:6) (1 SAMUEL 16:7) (1 JOHN 3:21) (1 TIMOTHY 1:19)

April 11

You must not forget, dear friends, that a day is like a thousand years to the Lord, and a thousand years is like a day.

"My thoughts are completely different from yours," says the LORD. "And my ways are far beyond anything you could imagine. For just as the heavens are higher than the earth, so are my ways higher than your ways and my thoughts higher than your thoughts. The rain and snow come down from the heavens and stay on the ground to water the earth. . . . It is the same with my word. I send it out, and it always produces fruit. It will accomplish all I want it to, and it will prosper everywhere I send it."

God has imprisoned all people in their own disobedience so he could have mercy on everyone. Oh, what a wonderful God we have! How great are his riches and wisdom and knowledge! How impossible it is for us to understand his decisions and his methods! For who can know what the Lord is thinking? Who knows enough to be his counselor? And who could ever give him so much that he would have to pay it back? For everything comes from him; everything exists by his power and is intended for his glory. To him be glory evermore.

So be on your guard, not asleep like the others. Stay alert and be sober. No matter what happens, always be thankful, for this is God's will for you who belong to Christ Jesus.

No one has fully understood the mind of the Lord. No one has been his counselor. And God owes nothing to any one of us. God alone is the possessor of absolute power and absolute wisdom.

LAB note for Romans 11:34-35

(2 PETER 3:8) (ISAIAH 55:8-11) (ROMANS 11:32-36) (1 THESSALONIANS 5:6, 18)

April 12

Lead me to the towering rock of safety.

Don't worry about anything; instead, pray about everything. Tell God what you need, and thank him for all he has done. If you do this, you will experience God's peace, which is far more wonderful than the human mind can understand. His peace will guard your hearts and minds as you live in Christ Jesus.

I am overwhelmed, and you alone know the way I should turn. ▪ He knows where I am going. And when he has tested me like gold in a fire, he will pronounce me innocent. ▪ Lord, through all the generations you have been our home! ▪ To the poor, O LORD, you are a refuge from the storm. To the needy in distress, you are a shelter from the rain and the heat.

For who is God except the LORD? Who but our God is a solid rock? ▪ They will never perish. No one will snatch them away from me. ▪ Lord, sustain me as you promised, that I may live! Do not let my hope be crushed. ▪ This confidence is like a strong and trustworthy anchor for our souls. It leads us through the curtain of heaven into God's inner sanctuary.

God is concerned for the poor and is a refuge for them. When we are disadvantaged or oppressed, we can turn to God for comfort and help. Jesus said that the Kingdom of God belongs to the poor.

LAB note for Isaiah 25:4

(PSALM 61:2) (PHILIPPIANS 4:6-7) (PSALM 142:3) (JOB 23:10) (PSALM 90:1) (ISAIAH 25:4) (PSALM 18:31) (JOHN 10:28) (PSALM 119:116) (HEBREWS 6:19)

April 13

My future is in your hands.

Your holy ones are in your hands. ▩ Then the LORD said to Elijah, "Go to the east and hide by Kerith Brook at a place east of where it enters the Jordan River. Drink from the brook and eat what the ravens bring you, for I have commanded them to bring you food." Then the LORD said to Elijah, "Go and live in the village of Zarephath, near the city of Sidon. There is a widow there who will feed you. I have given her my instructions."

Don't worry about everyday life—whether you have enough food, drink, and clothes. Doesn't life consist of more than food and clothing? Your heavenly Father already knows all your needs, and he will give you all you need from day to day if you live for him and make the Kingdom of God your primary concern. So don't worry about tomorrow, for tomorrow will bring its own worries. Today's trouble is enough for today.

Trust in the LORD with all your heart; do not depend on your own understanding. Seek his will in all you do, and he will direct your paths. ▩ Give all your worries and cares to God, for he cares about what happens to you.

In saying, "My future is in your hands," David was expressing his belief that all of life's circumstances are under God's control. Knowing that God loves and cares for us enables us to keep steady in our faith, regardless of our circumstances. *LAB note for Psalm 31:14-15*

(PSALM 31:15) (DEUTERONOMY 33:3) (1 KINGS 17:2-4, 8-9) (MATTHEW 6:25, 32-34) (PROVERBS 3:5-6) (1 PETER 5:7)

April 14

He is able, once and forever, to save everyone who comes to God through him. He lives forever to plead with God on their behalf.

Who then will condemn us? Will Christ Jesus? No, for he is the one who died for us . . . and is sitting at the place of highest honor next to God, pleading for us. ▩ Christ has entered into heaven itself to appear now before God as our Advocate.

If you do sin, there is someone to plead for you before the Father. He is Jesus Christ, the one who pleases God completely. ▩ There is only one God and one Mediator who can reconcile God and people. He is the man Christ Jesus.

We have a great High Priest who has gone to heaven, Jesus the Son of God. Let us cling to him and never stop trusting him. This High Priest of ours understands our weaknesses, for he faced all of the same temptations we do, yet he did not sin. So let us come boldly to the throne of our gracious God. There we will receive his mercy, and we will find grace to help us when we need it.

All of us . . . may come to the Father through the same Holy Spirit because of what Christ has done for us.

As our High Priest, Christ is our Advocate, the mediator between us and God. He looks after our interests and intercedes for us with God. Christ's continual presence with the Father in heaven assures us that our sins have been paid for and forgiven. *LAB note for Hebrews 7:25*

(HEBREWS 7:25) (ROMANS 8:34) (HEBREWS 9:24) (1 JOHN 2:1) (1 TIMOTHY 2:5) (HEBREWS 4:14-16) (EPHESIANS 2:18)

April 15

Those who know your name trust in you, for you, O LORD, have never abandoned anyone who searches for you.

This is his name: "The LORD Is Our Righteousness." ▩ I will praise your mighty deeds, O Sovereign LORD. I will tell everyone that you alone are just and good.

His royal titles: Wonderful Counselor. ▩ I know, LORD, that a person's life is not his own. No one is able to plan his own course.

Mighty God, Everlasting Father. ▩ I know the one in whom I trust, and I am sure that he is able to guard what I have entrusted to him until the day of his return.

Prince of Peace. ▩ Christ himself has made peace between us. ▩ Since we have been made right in God's sight by faith, we have peace with God because of what Jesus Christ our Lord has done for us.

The name of the LORD is a strong fortress; the godly run to him and are safe. ▩ Destruction is certain for those who look to Egypt for help, trusting their cavalry and chariots instead of looking to the LORD, the Holy One of Israel. ▩ There is no one like the God of Israel. He rides across the heavens to help you, across the skies in majestic splendor. The eternal God is your refuge, and his everlasting arms are under you.

God will never abandon those who seek him. God's promise does not mean that if we trust in him we will escape loss or suffering; it means that God himself will never leave us no matter what we face.

LAB note for Psalm 9:10

(PSALM 9:10) (JEREMIAH 23:6) (PSALM 71:16) (ISAIAH 9:6) (JEREMIAH 10:23) (ISAIAH 9:6) (2 TIMOTHY 1:12) (ISAIAH 9:6) (EPHESIANS 2:14) (ROMANS 5:1) (PROVERBS 18:10) (ISAIAH 31:1) (DEUTERONOMY 33:26-27)

April 16

Let us . . . work toward complete purity because we fear God.

Let us cleanse ourselves from everything that can defile our body or spirit.

You desire honesty from the heart, so you can teach me to be wise in my inmost being. ▪ We are instructed to turn from godless living and sinful pleasures. We should live in this evil world with self-control, right conduct, and devotion to God. ▪ Don't hide your light under a basket! Instead, put it on a stand and let it shine for all. In the same way, let your good deeds shine out for all to see, so that everyone will praise your heavenly Father. ▪ I don't mean to say that I have already achieved these things or that I have already reached perfection!

When he comes we will be like him, for we will see him as he really is. And all who believe this will keep themselves pure, just as Christ is pure.

God himself has prepared us for this, and as a guarantee he has given us his Holy Spirit. ▪ He is the one who gave these gifts to the church. . . . Their responsibility is to equip God's people to do his work and build up the church, the body of Christ, until we come to such unity in our faith and knowledge of God's Son that we will be mature and full grown in the Lord, measuring up to the full stature of Christ.

Cleansing is a twofold action: turning away from sin and turning toward God. Have nothing to do with paganism. Make a clean break with your past and give yourself to God alone. *LAB note for 2 Corinthians 7:1*

(2 Corinthians 7:1) (2 Corinthians 7:1) (Psalm 51:6) (Titus 2:12) (Matthew 5:15-16) (Philippians 3:12) (1 John 3:2-3) (2 Corinthians 5:5) (Ephesians 4:11-13)

April 17

He has enriched your church.

When we were utterly helpless, Christ came at just the right time and died for us sinners. ▪ Since God did not spare even his own Son but gave him up for us all, won't God, who gave us Christ, also give us everything else?

In Christ the fullness of God lives in a human body, and you are complete through your union with Christ. He is the Lord over every ruler and authority in the universe.

Remain in me, and I will remain in you. For a branch cannot produce fruit if it is severed from the vine, and you cannot be fruitful apart from me. Yes, I am the vine; you are the branches. Those who remain in me, and I in them, will produce much fruit. For apart from me you can do nothing. ▪ He has given each one of us a special gift according to the generosity of Christ.

If you stay joined to me and my words remain in you, you may ask any request you like, and it will be granted! ▪ Let the words of Christ, in all their richness, live in your hearts and make you wise.

"In Christ the fullness of God lives in a human body" means that all of God was in Christ's human body. When we have Christ, we have everything we need for salvation and right living. *LAB note for Colossians 2:9*

(1 Corinthians 1:5) (Romans 5:6) (Romans 8:32) (Colossians 2:9-10) (John 15:4-5) (Ephesians 4:7) (John 15:7) (Colossians 3:16)

April 18

I will tell of the LORD's unfailing love. I will praise the LORD for all he has done. I will rejoice in his great goodness.

He lifted me out of the pit of despair, out of the mud and the mire. He set my feet on solid ground and steadied me as I walked along. ▩ The Son of God . . . loved me and gave himself for me. ▩ Since God did not spare even his own Son but gave him up for us all, won't God, who gave us Christ, also give us everything else? ▩ God showed his great love for us by sending Christ to die for us while we were still sinners.

He has identified us as his own by placing the Holy Spirit in our hearts as the first installment of everything he will give us. ▩ The Spirit is God's guarantee that he will give us everything he promised and that he has purchased us to be his own people.

God is so rich in mercy, and he loved us so very much, that even while we were dead because of our sins, he gave us life when he raised Christ from the dead. (It is only by God's special favor that you have been saved!) For he raised us from the dead along with Christ, and we are seated with him in the heavenly realms—all because we are one with Christ Jesus.

Through faith in Christ we stand acquitted, or not guilty, before God. But God does not take us out of the world or make us robots—we will still feel like sinning, and sometimes we will sin. The difference is that before we became Christians, we were dead in sin and were slaves to our sinful nature. But now we are alive in Christ. *LAB note for Ephesians 2:4-5*

(Isaiah 63:7) (Psalm 40:2) (Galatians 2:20) (Romans 8:32) (Romans 5:8) (2 Corinthians 1:22) (Ephesians 1:14) (Ephesians 2:4-6)

April 19

Don't talk too much, for it fosters sin. Be sensible and turn off the flow!

Dear brothers and sisters, be quick to listen, slow to speak, and slow to get angry. ▩ It is better to be patient than powerful; it is better to have self-control than to conquer a city. ▩ Those who control their tongues can also control themselves in every other way. ▩ The words you say now reflect your fate then; either you will be justified by them or you will be condemned. ▩ Take control of what I say, O LORD, and keep my lips sealed.

Christ, who suffered for you, is your example. Follow in his steps. He never sinned, and he never deceived anyone. He did not retaliate when he was insulted. When he suffered, he did not threaten to get even. He left his case in the hands of God, who always judges fairly. ▩ Think about all he endured when sinful people did such terrible things to him, so that you don't become weary and give up. ▩ Gentle words bring life and health.

No falsehood can be charged against them; they are blameless.

When we talk too much and listen too little, we communicate to others that we think our ideas are much more important than theirs. Instead, reverse the process. Put a mental stopwatch on your conversations, and keep track of how much you talk and how much you listen.

LAB note for James 1:19

(PROVERBS 10:19) (JAMES 1:19) (PROVERBS 16:32) (JAMES 3:2) (MATTHEW 12:37) (PSALM 141:3) (1 PETER 2:21-23) (HEBREWS 12:3) (PROVERBS 15:4) (REVELATION 14:5)

April 20

Teach me how to live, O LORD.

The LORD says, "I will guide you along the best pathway for your life. I will advise you and watch over you." ▪ The LORD is good and does what is right; he shows the proper path to those who go astray. He leads the humble in what is right, teaching them his way.

Yes, I am the gate. Those who come in through me will be saved. Wherever they go, they will find green pastures.

Jesus told him, "I am the way, the truth, and the life. No one can come to the Father except through me." ▪ We can boldly enter heaven's Most Holy Place because of the blood of Jesus. This is the new, life-giving way that Christ has opened up for us through the sacred curtain, by means of his death for us. And since we have a great High Priest who rules over God's people, let us go right into the presence of God, with true hearts fully trusting him.

Oh, that we might know the LORD! Let us press on to know him! ▪ The LORD leads with unfailing love and faithfulness all those who keep his covenant and obey his decrees.

We are bombarded today with relentless appeals to go in various directions. Add to that the dozens of decisions we must make concerning our job, our family, our money, and our society, and we become desperate for someone to show us the right way. If you find yourself pulled in several directions, remember that God teaches the humble his way.

LAB note for Psalm 25:8–11

(PSALM 27:11) (PSALM 32:8) (PSALM 25:8–9) (JOHN 10:9) (JOHN 14:6) (HEBREWS 10:19–22) (HOSEA 6:3) (PSALM 25:10)

April 21

When God's children are in need, be the one to help them out.

One day David began wondering if anyone in Saul's family was still alive, for he had promised Jonathan that he would show kindness to them.

Come, you who are blessed by my Father, inherit the Kingdom prepared for you from the foundation of the world. For I was hungry, and you fed me. I was thirsty, and you gave me a drink. I was a stranger, and you invited me into your home. I was naked, and you gave me clothing. I was sick, and you cared for me. I was in prison, and you visited me. When you did it to one of the least of these my brothers and sisters, you were doing it to me! ▪ And if you give even a cup of cold water to one of the least of my followers, you will surely be rewarded.

Don't forget to do good and to share what you have with those in need, for such sacrifices are very pleasing to God. ▪ For God is not unfair. He will not forget how hard you have worked for him and how you have shown your love to him by caring for other Christians, as you still do. Our great desire is that you will keep right on loving others as long as life lasts, in order to make certain that what you hope for will come true.

Entertaining focuses on the host and setting; Christian hospitality focuses on the guests' needs. It can happen around a dinner table where the main dish is canned soup. Don't hesitate to offer hospitality just because you are too tired, too busy, or not wealthy enough to entertain.

LAB note for Romans 12:13

(Romans 12:13) (2 Samuel 9:1) (Matthew 25:34-36, 40) (Matthew 10:42) (Hebrews 13:16) (Hebrews 6:10-11)

April 22

Are you seeking great things for yourself? Don't do it!

Take my yoke upon you. Let me teach you, because I am humble and gentle, and you will find rest for your souls. ▩ Your attitude should be the same that Christ Jesus had. Though he was God, he did not demand and cling to his rights as God. He made himself nothing; he took the humble position of a slave and appeared in human form. And in human form he obediently humbled himself even further by dying a criminal's death on a cross.

If you refuse to take up your cross and follow me, you are not worthy of being mine. ▩ Christ, who suffered for you, is your example. Follow in his steps. ▩ Many who seem to be important now will be the least important then, and those who are considered least here will be the greatest then.

True religion with contentment is great wealth. After all, we didn't bring anything with us when we came into the world, and we certainly cannot carry anything with us when we die. So if we have enough food and clothing, let us be content. ▩ I have learned how to get along happily whether I have much or little.

It is easy to lose the joy of serving God when we take our eyes off him. The more we look away from God's purposes toward our own sacrifices, the more frustrated we will become. As you serve God, look at him rather than at yourself. *LAB note for Jeremiah 45:5*

(Jeremiah 45:5) (Matthew 11:29) (Philippians 2:5-8) (Matthew 10:38) (1 Peter 2:21) (Matthew 19:30) (1 Timothy 6:6-8) (Philippians 4:11)

April 23

Stay true to the Lord.

I have stayed in God's paths; I have followed his ways and not turned aside. ▩ The LORD loves justice, and he will never abandon the godly. ▩ The LORD keeps you from all evil and preserves your life.

A righteous person will live by faith. But I will have no pleasure in anyone who turns away. But we are not like those who turn their backs on God and seal their fate. We have faith that assures our salvation. ▩ These people left our churches because they never really belonged with us; otherwise they would have stayed with us. When they left us, it proved that they do not belong with us.

You are truly my disciples if you keep obeying my teachings. ▩ Those who endure to the end will be saved. ▩ Be on guard. Stand true to what you believe. Be courageous. Be strong. ▩ Hold on to what you have, so that no one will take away your crown. ▩ All who are victorious will be clothed in white. I will never erase their names from the Book of Life, but I will announce before my Father and his angels that they are mine.

How do we "stay true to the Lord"? The way to stay true is to keep our eyes on Christ, to remember that this world is not our home, and to focus on the fact that Christ will bring everything under his control.

LAB note for Philippians 4:1

(PHILIPPIANS 4:1) (JOB 23:11) (PSALM 37:28) (PSALM 121:7) (HEBREWS 10:38-39) (1 JOHN 2:19) (JOHN 8:31) (MATTHEW 24:13) (1 CORINTHIANS 16:13) (REVELATION 3:11) (REVELATION 3:5)

April 24

Our Lord Jesus . . . Though he was very rich, yet for your sakes he became poor, so that by his poverty he could make you rich.

For God in all his fullness was pleased to live in Christ. ▩ The Son reflects God's own glory, and everything about him represents God exactly. He sustains the universe by the mighty power of his command. After he died to cleanse us from the stain of sin, he sat down in the place of honor at the right hand of the majestic God of heaven. This shows that God's Son is far greater than the angels, just as the name God gave him is far greater than their names. ▩ Though he was God, he did not demand and cling to his rights as God. He made himself nothing; he took the humble position of a slave and appeared in human form.

Foxes have dens to live in, and birds have nests, but I, the Son of Man, have no home of my own, not even a place to lay my head.

Everything belongs to you . . . the whole world and life and death; the present and the future. Everything belongs to you, and you belong to Christ, and Christ belongs to God.

Jesus became poor by giving up his rights as God and voluntarily becoming human. In response to the Father's will, he limited his power and knowledge. Yet by doing so, he made us "rich" because we received salvation and eternal life. *LAB note for 2 Corinthians 8:9*

(2 CORINTHIANS 8:9) (COLOSSIANS 1:19) (HEBREWS 1:3-4) (PHILIPPIANS 2:6-7) (MATTHEW 8:20) (1 CORINTHIANS 3:21-23)

April 25

The time that remains is very short.

How frail is humanity! How short is life, and how full of trouble! Like a flower, we blossom for a moment and then wither. Like the shadow of a passing cloud, we quickly disappear. ▩ This world is fading away, along with everything it craves. But if you do the will of God, you will live forever. ▩ Everyone dies because all of us are related to Adam, the first man. But all who are related to Christ, the other man, will be given new life. Death is swallowed up in victory. ▩ While we live, we live to please the Lord. And when we die, we go to be with the Lord. So in life and in death, we belong to the Lord.

For to me, living is for Christ, and dying is even better.

Do not throw away this confident trust in the Lord, no matter what happens. Remember the great reward it brings you! Patient endurance is what you need now, so you will continue to do God's will. Then you will receive all that he has promised. "For in just a little while, the Coming One will come and not delay." ▩ The night is almost gone; the day of salvation will soon be here. So don't live in darkness. Get rid of your evil deeds. Shed them like dirty clothes. Clothe yourselves with the armor of right living, as those who live in the light. ▩ The end of the world is coming soon. Therefore, be earnest and disciplined in your prayers.

All believers should make the most of their time before Christ's return. Every person in every generation should have this sense of urgency about telling the Good News to others. Life is short—there's not much time!

LAB note for 1 Corinthians 7:29

(1 Corinthians 7:29) (Job 14:1-2) (1 John 2:17) (1 Corinthians 15:22, 54) (Romans 14:8) (Philippians 1:21) (Hebrews 10:35-37) (Romans 13:12) (1 Peter 4:7)

April 26

We look forward to that wonderful event when the glory of our great God and Savior, Jesus Christ, will be revealed.

This confidence is like a strong and trustworthy anchor for our souls. It leads us through the curtain of heaven into God's inner sanctuary. Jesus has already gone in there for us. He has become our eternal High Priest in the line of Melchizedek. ▩ For he must remain in heaven until the time for the final restoration of all things, as God promised long ago through his prophets. ▩ When he comes to receive glory and praise from his holy people.

We know that all creation has been groaning as in the pains of childbirth right up to the present time. And even we Christians . . . also groan to be released from pain and suffering. We, too, wait anxiously for that day when God will give us our full rights as his children, including the new bodies he has promised us. ▩ Dear friends, we are already God's children, and we can't even imagine what we will be like when Christ returns. But we do know that when he comes we will be like him, for we will see him as he really is. ▩ When Christ, who is your real life, is revealed to the whole world, you will share in all his glory.

"Yes, I am coming soon!" Amen! Come, Lord Jesus!

Christ gives us power to live for him now, and he gives us hope for the future—he will return. Christians should act now in order to be prepared for Christ's return. *LAB note for Colossians 3:4*

(TITUS 2:13) (HEBREWS 6:19-20) (ACTS 3:21) (2 THESSALONIANS 1:10) (ROMANS 8:22-23) (1 JOHN 3:2) (COLOSSIANS 3:4) (REVELATION 22:20)

April 27

Those who obey God's word really do love him.

May the God of peace, who brought again from the dead our Lord Jesus, equip you with all you need for doing his will. May he produce in you, through the power of Jesus Christ, all that is pleasing to him. Jesus is the great Shepherd of the sheep by an everlasting covenant, signed with his blood. To him be glory forever and ever. Amen.

How can we be sure that we belong to him? By obeying his commandments. ▪ All those who love me will do what I say. My Father will love them, and we will come to them and live with them. ▪ If we continue to live in him, we won't sin either. But those who keep on sinning have never known him or understood who he is. Dear children, don't let anyone deceive you about this: When people do what is right, it is because they are righteous, even as Christ is righteous.

As we live in God, our love grows more perfect. So we will not be afraid on the day of judgment, but we can face him with confidence because we are like Christ here in this world.

How can you be sure that you belong to Christ? If you do what Christ says and live as Christ wants. True Christian faith results in loving behavior; that is why the way we act can give us assurance that we belong to Christ.

LAB note for 1 John 2:3-6

(1 JOHN 2:5) (HEBREWS 13:20-21) (1 JOHN 2:3) (JOHN 14:23) (1 JOHN 3:6-7) (1 JOHN 4:17)

April 28

Those who control their anger have great understanding.

He passed in front of Moses and said, "I am the LORD, I am the LORD, the merciful and gracious God. I am slow to anger and rich in unfailing love and faithfulness."

Follow God's example in everything you do, because you are his dear children. ▩ When the Holy Spirit controls our lives, he will produce this kind of fruit in us: love, joy, peace, patience, kindness, goodness, faithfulness, gentleness, and self-control. ▩ God is pleased with you when, for the sake of your conscience, you patiently endure unfair treatment. Of course, you get no credit for being patient if you are beaten for doing wrong. But if you suffer for doing right and are patient beneath the blows, God is pleased with you. This suffering is all part of what God has called you to. Christ, who suffered for you, is your example. Follow in his steps. He never sinned, and he never deceived anyone. He did not retaliate when he was insulted. When he suffered, he did not threaten to get even. He left his case in the hands of God, who always judges fairly.

"Don't sin by letting anger gain control over you." Don't let the sun go down while you are still angry, for anger gives a mighty foothold to the Devil.

When you feel yourself getting angry, look for the cause. Are you reacting to an evil situation that you are going to set right? Or are you responding selfishly to a personal insult? Pray that God will help you control a quick temper, channeling your feelings into effective action and conquering selfish anger through humility and repentance.

LAB note for Proverbs 14:29

(PROVERBS 14:29) (EXODUS 34:6) (EPHESIANS 5:1) (GALATIANS 5:22-23) (1 PETER 2:19-23) (EPHESIANS 4:26)

April 29

The LORD is in this place.

Where two or three gather together because they are mine, I am there among them. ▧ I am with you always, even to the end of the age. ▧ I will personally go with you. . . . I will give you rest—everything will be fine for you.

I can never escape from your spirit! I can never get away from your presence! If I go up to heaven, you are there; if I go down to the place of the dead, you are there. If I ride the wings of the morning, if I dwell by the farthest oceans, even there your hand will guide me, and your strength will support me. I could ask the darkness to hide me and the light around me to become night—but even in darkness I cannot hide from you. To you the night shines as bright as day. ▧ "Am I a God who is only in one place?" asks the LORD. "Do they think I cannot see what they are doing? Can anyone hide from me? Am I not everywhere in all the heavens and earth?"

Will God really live on earth? Why, even the highest heavens cannot contain you. How much less this Temple I have built! ▧ The high and lofty one who inhabits eternity, the Holy One, says this: "I live in that high and holy place with those whose spirits are contrite and humble. I refresh the humble and give new courage to those with repentant hearts."

Jesus looked ahead to a new day when he would be present with his followers, not in body but through his Holy Spirit. In the body of believers (the church) the sincere agreement of two people in prayer is powerful because Christ's Holy Spirit is with them.

LAB note for Matthew 18:19-20

(GENESIS 28:16) (MATTHEW 18:20) (MATTHEW 28:20) (EXODUS 33:14) (PSALM 139:7-12) (JEREMIAH 23:23-24) (ISAIAH 57:15)

April 30

Keep away from anything that might take God's place in your hearts.

O my son, give me your heart. May your eyes delight in my ways of wisdom. ▩ Let heaven fill your thoughts. Do not think only about things down here on earth.

Son of man, these leaders have set up idols in their hearts. . . . Why should I let them ask me anything? ▩ Put to death the sinful, earthly things lurking within you. Have nothing to do with sexual sin, impurity, lust, and shameful desires. Don't be greedy for the good things of this life, for that is idolatry. ▩ People who long to be rich fall into temptation and are trapped by many foolish and harmful desires that plunge them into ruin and destruction. For the love of money is at the root of all kinds of evil. And some people, craving money, have wandered from the faith and pierced themselves with many sorrows. But you . . . belong to God; so run from all these evil things, and follow what is right and good. Pursue a godly life, along with faith, love, perseverance, and gentleness. ▩ Don't try to get rich by extortion or robbery. ▩ My gifts are better than the purest gold, my wages better than sterling silver!

Wherever your treasure is, there your heart and thoughts will also be. ▩ The LORD looks at a person's thoughts and intentions.

Many things can take God's place in our life. This includes anything that substitutes for the true faith, anything that robs Christ of his full deity and humanity, any human idea that claims to be more authoritative than the Bible, or any loyalty that replaces God at the center of our life.

LAB note for 1 John 5:21

(1 JOHN 5:21) (PROVERBS 23:26) (COLOSSIANS 3:2) (EZEKIEL 14:3) (COLOSSIANS 3:5) (1 TIMOTHY 6:9-11) (PSALM 62:10) (PROVERBS 8:19) (MATTHEW 6:21) (1 SAMUEL 16:7)

May

Only a Mother's Love

A mother's love is encouraging but not overbearing.
It is both sheltering and freeing.
A mother's love is a reflection of God's character.

It is often said that a mother's work is never done, and that is true. A mother never forgets her child's small victories and character-building experiences that helped mold him or her into a mature adult. May your heart be filled with the joy and peace of a mother's love.

May 1

I will comfort you there as a child is comforted by its mother.

Can a mother forget her nursing child? Can she feel no love for a child she has borne? But even if that were possible, I would not forget you!

[I give] the barren woman a home, so that she becomes a happy mother. Praise the Lord! ◆ She extends a helping hand to the poor and opens her arms to the needy. ◆ She is clothed with strength and dignity, and she laughs with no fear of the future. When she speaks, her words are wise, and kindness is the rule when she gives instructions. She carefully watches all that goes on in her household and does not have to bear the consequences of laziness.

Her children stand and bless her. Her husband praises her: "There are many virtuous and capable women in the world, but you surpass them all!"

Charm is deceptive, and beauty does not last; but a woman who fears the Lord will be greatly praised. Reward her for all she has done. Let her deeds publicly declare her praise.

God will never forget you, just as a loving mother would not forget her little child. *adapted from LAB note for Isaiah 49:15*

(Isaiah 66:13) (Isaiah 49:15) (Psalm 113:9)
(Proverbs 31:20) (Proverbs 31:25-31)

May 2

Thank you for making me so wonderfully complex!

I have stilled and quieted myself, just as a small child is quiet with its mother. Yes, like a small child is my soul within me. ▩ You have been with me from birth; from my mother's womb you have cared for me. No wonder I am always praising you! ▩ You made all the delicate, inner parts of my body and knit me together in my mother's womb. Your workmanship is marvelous—and how well I know it. ▩ You both precede and follow me. You place your hand of blessing on my head. Such knowledge is too wonderful for me, too great for me to know! I can never escape from your spirit! I can never get away from your presence! If I go up to heaven, you are there; if I go down to the place of the dead, you are there. If I ride the wings of the morning, if I dwell by the farthest oceans, even there your hand will guide me, and your strength will support me.

God's character goes into the creation of every person. When you feel worthless or even begin to hate yourself, remember that God's Spirit is ready and willing to work within you. *LAB note for Psalm 139:13–14*

(PSALM 139:14) (PSALM 131:2) (PSALM 71:6)
(PSALM 139:13-14) (PSALM 139:5-10)

May 3

Keep none of the plunder.

Come out from them and separate yourselves from them, says the Lord. Don't touch their filthy things. ▩ Dear brothers and sisters, you are foreigners and aliens here. So I warn you to keep away from evil desires because they fight against your very souls. ▩ Be careful that you aren't contaminated by their sins.

We are already God's children, and we can't even imagine what we will be like when Christ returns. But we do know that when he comes we will be like him, for we will see him as he really is. And all who believe this will keep themselves pure, just as Christ is pure. ▩ For the grace of God has been revealed, bringing salvation to all people. And we are instructed to turn from godless living and sinful pleasures. We should live in this evil world with self-control, right conduct, and devotion to God, while we look forward to that wonderful event when the glory of our great God and Savior, Jesus Christ, will be revealed. He gave his life to free us from every kind of sin, to cleanse us, and to make us his very own people, totally committed to doing what is right.

Separation from the world involves more than keeping our distance from sinners; it means staying close to God. There is no way to separate ourselves totally from all sinful influences. Nevertheless, we are to resist the sin around us, without either giving up or giving in.

LAB note for 2 Corinthians 6:17

(DEUTERONOMY 13:17) (2 CORINTHIANS 6:17) (1 PETER 2:11) (JUDE 1:23) (1 JOHN 3:2-3) (TITUS 2:11-14)

May 4

The LORD spread out a cloud above them as a covering and gave them a great fire to light the darkness.

The LORD is like a father to his children, tender and compassionate to those who fear him. For he understands how weak we are; he knows we are only dust.

The sun will not hurt you by day, nor the moon at night. ▩ It will be a shelter from daytime heat and a hiding place from storms or rain.

The LORD himself watches over you! The LORD stands beside you as your protective shade. The LORD keeps watch over you as you come and go, both now and forever. ▩ He found them in a desert land, in an empty, howling wasteland. He surrounded them and watched over them; he guarded them as his most precious possession. ▩ In your great mercy you did not abandon them to die in the wilderness. The pillar of cloud still led them forward by day, and the pillar of fire showed them the way through the night. You sent your good Spirit to instruct them, and you did not stop giving them bread from heaven or water for their thirst. For forty years you sustained them in the wilderness. They lacked nothing in all that time. Their clothes did not wear out, and their feet did not swell! ▩ With unfailing love you will lead this people whom you have ransomed. You will guide them in your strength to the place where your holiness dwells.

Jesus Christ is the same yesterday, today, and forever.

Seeing how God continued to be with his people shows that his patience is amazing! In spite of our repeated failings, pride, and stubbornness, he is always ready to pardon, and his Spirit is always ready to instruct.

LAB note for Nehemiah 9:16–21

(PSALM 105:39) (PSALM 103:13–14) (PSALM 121:6) (ISAIAH 4:6) (PSALM 121:5, 8) (DEUTERONOMY 32:10) (NEHEMIAH 9:19–21) (EXODUS 15:13) (HEBREWS 13:8)

May 5

Wars will break out near and far, but don't panic. Yes, these things must come, but the end won't follow immediately.

God is our refuge and strength, always ready to help in times of trouble. So we will not fear, even if earthquakes come and the mountains crumble into the sea. Let the oceans roar and foam. Let the mountains tremble as the waters surge! ▪ Go home, my people, and lock your doors! Hide until the LORD's anger against your enemies has passed. Look! The LORD is coming from heaven to punish the people of the earth for their sins. ▪ I will hide beneath the shadow of your wings until this violent storm is past. ▪ Your real life is hidden with Christ in God.

Happy are those who fear the LORD. Yes, happy are those who delight in doing what he commands. Such people will not be overcome by evil circumstances. Those who are righteous will be long remembered. They do not fear bad news; they confidently trust the LORD to care for them.

I have told you all this so that you may have peace in me. Here on earth you will have many trials and sorrows. But take heart, because I have overcome the world.

It seems impossible to consider the end of the world without becoming consumed by fear, but the Bible is clear—God is our refuge even in the midst of total destruction. He is not merely a temporary retreat; he is our eternal refuge and can provide strength in any circumstance.

LAB note for Psalm 46:1-3

(MATTHEW 24:6) (PSALM 46:1-3) (ISAIAH 26:20-21) (PSALM 57:1) (COLOSSIANS 3:3) (PSALM 112:1, 6-7) (JOHN 16:33)

May 6

Come to your senses and stop sinning.

You are all children of the light and of the day; we don't belong to darkness and night. So be on your guard, not asleep like the others. Stay alert and be sober.

Another reason for right living is that you know how late it is; time is running out. Wake up, for the coming of our salvation is nearer now than when we first believed. The night is almost gone; the day of salvation will soon be here. So don't live in darkness. Get rid of your evil deeds. Shed them like dirty clothes. Clothe yourselves with the armor of right living, as those who live in the light. ▪ Use every piece of God's armor to resist the enemy in the time of evil, so that after the battle you will still be standing firm. ▪ Turn from your sins! Don't let them destroy you! Put all your rebellion behind you, and get for yourselves a new heart and a new spirit. ▪ Get rid of all the filth and evil in your lives, and humbly accept the message God has planted in your hearts, for it is strong enough to save your souls.

Now, dear children, continue to live in fellowship with Christ so that when he returns, you will be full of courage and not shrink back from him in shame.

If we renounce our life's direction of sin and rebellion and turn to God, he will give us a new direction, a new love, and a new power to change. You can begin by faith, trusting in God's power to change your heart and mind. Then determine to live each day with him in control.

LAB note for Ezekiel 18:30-32

(1 CORINTHIANS 15:34) (1 THESSALONIANS 5:5-6) (ROMANS 13:11-12) (EPHESIANS 6:13) (EZEKIEL 18:30-31) (JAMES 1:21) (1 JOHN 2:28)

May 7

Their insults have broken my heart.

He's just a carpenter's son. ▩ Nazareth! . . . Can anything good come from there? ▩ He can cast out demons because he is empowered by the prince of demons. ▩ We know Jesus is a sinner. ▩ He's nothing but a fraud, deceiving the people. ▩ Blasphemy! This man talks like he is God! ▩ I, the Son of Man, feast and drink, and you say, "He's a glutton and a drunkard, and a friend of the worst sort of sinners!"

God is pleased with you when, for the sake of your conscience, you patiently endure unfair treatment. Of course, you get no credit for being patient if you are beaten for doing wrong. But if you suffer for doing right and are patient beneath the blows, God is pleased with you. This suffering is all part of what God has called you to. Christ, who suffered for you, is your example. Follow in his steps. He never sinned, and he never deceived anyone. He did not retaliate when he was insulted. When he suffered, he did not threaten to get even. He left his case in the hands of God, who always judges fairly. ▩ Be happy if you are insulted for being a Christian, for then the glorious Spirit of God will come upon you.

The student shares the teacher's fate. The servant shares the master's fate.

Good is sometimes labeled evil. If Jesus, who is perfect, was called evil, his followers should expect that similar accusations will be directed at them. But those who endure will be vindicated. *LAB note for Matthew 10:25*

(Psalm 69:20) (Matthew 13:55) (John 1:46) (Matthew 9:34) (John 9:24) (John 7:12) (Matthew 9:3) (Matthew 11:19) (1 Peter 2:19-23) (1 Peter 4:14) (Matthew 10:25)

May 8

I want men to pray with holy hands lifted up to God, free from anger and controversy.

True worshipers will worship the Father in spirit and in truth. The Father is looking for anyone who will worship him that way. For God is Spirit, so those who worship him must worship in spirit and in truth. ▪ When you call, the LORD will answer. "Yes, I am here." ▪ When you are praying, first forgive anyone you are holding a grudge against, so that your Father in heaven will forgive your sins, too.

It is impossible to please God without faith. Anyone who wants to come to him must believe that there is a God and that he rewards those who sincerely seek him. ▪ When you ask him, be sure that you really expect him to answer, for a doubtful mind is as unsettled as a wave of the sea that is driven and tossed by the wind. People like that should not expect to receive anything from the Lord.

If I had not confessed the sin in my heart, my Lord would not have listened. ▪ My dear children, I am writing this to you so that you will not sin. But if you do sin, there is someone to plead for you before the Father. He is Jesus Christ, the one who pleases God completely.

Besides displeasing God, anger and controversy make prayer difficult. That is why Jesus said that we should interrupt our prayers, if necessary, to make peace with others. God wants us to obey him immediately and thoroughly. *LAB note for 1 Timothy 2:8*

(1 TIMOTHY 2:8) (JOHN 4:23-24) (ISAIAH 58:9) (MARK 11:25) (HEBREWS 11:6) (JAMES 1:6-7) (PSALM 66:18) (1 JOHN 2:1)

May 9

My heart beats wildly, my strength fails.

O God, listen to my cry! Hear my prayer! From the ends of the earth, I will cry to you for help, for my heart is overwhelmed. Lead me to the towering rock of safety.

"My gracious favor is all you need. My power works best in your weakness." So now I am glad to boast about my weaknesses, so that the power of Christ may work through me. Since I know it is all for Christ's good, I am quite content with my weaknesses and with insults, hardships, persecutions, and calamities. For when I am weak, then I am strong.

When he [Peter] looked around at the high waves, he was terrified and began to sink. "Save me, Lord!" he shouted. Instantly Jesus reached out his hand and grabbed him. "You don't have much faith," Jesus said. "Why did you doubt me?" ▪ If you fail under pressure, your strength is not very great. ▪ He gives power to those who are tired and worn out; he offers strength to the weak. ▪ The eternal God is your refuge, and his everlasting arms are under you. ▪ We also pray that you will be strengthened with his glorious power so that you will have all the patience and endurance you need.

Even the strongest people get tired at times, but God's power and strength never diminish. He is never too tired or too busy to help and listen. When you feel all of life crushing you and you cannot go another step, remember that you can call upon God to renew your strength.

LAB note for Isaiah 40:29-31

(Psalm 38:10) (Psalm 61:1-2) (2 Corinthians 12:9-10) (Matthew 14:30-31) (Proverbs 24:10) (Isaiah 40:29) (Deuteronomy 33:27) (Colossians 1:11)

*M*ay 10

I will bless the LORD who guides me.

Wonderful Counselor. ▩ Good advice and success belong to me. Insight and strength are mine. ▩ Your word is a lamp for my feet and a light for my path. ▩ Trust in the LORD with all your heart; do not depend on your own understanding. Seek his will in all you do, and he will direct your paths.

I know, LORD, that a person's life is not his own. No one is able to plan his own course. ▩ You will hear a voice say, "This is the way; turn around and walk here." ▩ Commit your work to the LORD, and then your plans will succeed. ▩ How can we understand the road we travel? It is the LORD who directs our steps.

You will keep on guiding me with your counsel, leading me to a glorious destiny. ▩ Even when I walk through the dark valley of death, I will not be afraid, for you are close beside me. Your rod and your staff protect and comfort me. ▩ For that is what God is like. He is our God forever and ever, and he will be our guide until we die.

We must not be wise in our own eyes but be willing to listen to and be corrected by God's Word and wise counselors. Bring your decisions to God in prayer; use the Bible as your guide; and then follow God's leading. He will direct your paths by both guiding and protecting you.

LAB note for Proverbs 3:5-6

(PSALM 16:7) (ISAIAH 9:6) (PROVERBS 8:14) (PSALM 119:105) (PROVERBS 3:5-6) (JEREMIAH 10:23) (ISAIAH 30:21) (PROVERBS 16:3) (PROVERBS 20:24) (PSALM 73:24) (PSALM 23:4) (PSALM 48:14)

May 11

I am the LORD your God. . . . Follow my laws, pay attention to my instructions.

Now you must be holy in everything you do, just as God—who chose you to be his children—is holy. ▩ Those who say they live in God should live their lives as Christ did.

It is not that we think we can do anything of lasting value by ourselves. Our only power and success come from God. ▩ Remain in me, and I will remain in you. For a branch cannot produce fruit if it is severed from the vine, and you cannot be fruitful apart from me.

Be even more careful to put into action God's saving work in your lives, obeying God with deep reverence and fear. For God is working in you, giving you the desire to obey him and the power to do what pleases him. ▩ May the God of peace, who brought again from the dead our Lord Jesus, equip you with all you need for doing his will. May he produce in you, through the power of Jesus Christ, all that is pleasing to him. Jesus is the great Shepherd of the sheep by an everlasting covenant, signed with his blood.

He is a God of mercy and justice who cares personally for each of his followers. Our holy God expects us to imitate him by following his high moral standards and by being both merciful and just.

LAB note for 1 Peter 1:15

(EZEKIEL 20:19) (1 PETER 1:15) (1 JOHN 2:6) (2 CORINTHIANS 3:5) (JOHN 15:4) (PHILIPPIANS 2:12-13) (HEBREWS 13:20-21)

May 12

The Father has life in himself, and he has granted his Son to have life in himself.

Christ Jesus, our Savior . . . broke the power of death and showed us the way to everlasting life through the Good News. ▪ I am the resurrection and the life. Those who believe in me, even though they die like everyone else, will live again. ▪ I will live again, and you will, too. ▪ We will share in all that belongs to Christ. ▪ "The first man, Adam, became a living person." But the last Adam—that is, Christ—is a life-giving Spirit. But let me tell you a wonderful secret God has revealed to us. Not all of us will die, but we will all be transformed. It will happen in a moment, in the blinking of an eye, when the last trumpet is blown. For when the trumpet sounds, the Christians who have died will be raised with transformed bodies. And then we who are living will be transformed so that we will never die. For our perishable earthly bodies must be transformed into heavenly bodies that will never die.

Holy, holy, holy is the Lord God Almighty—the one who always was, who is, and who is still to come . . . the one who lives forever and ever. ▪ The blessed and only almighty God, the King of kings and Lord of lords. ▪ Glory and honor to God forever and ever. He is the eternal King, the unseen one who never dies; he alone is God. Amen.

God is the source and Creator of life, for there is no life apart from God, here or hereafter. The life in us is a gift from him. Because Jesus is eternally existent with God, the Creator, he, too, is "the life" through whom we may live eternally. *LAB note for John 5:26*

(JOHN 5:26) (2 TIMOTHY 1:10) (JOHN 11:25) (JOHN 14:19) (HEBREWS 3:14) (1 CORINTHIANS 15:45, 51-53) (REVELATION 4:8-9) (1 TIMOTHY 6:15) (1 TIMOTHY 1:17)

*M*ay 13

Let us not become conceited, or irritate one another, or be jealous of one another.

Gideon replied, ". . . I have one request. Each of you can give me an earring out of the treasures you collected from your fallen enemies." (The enemies, being Ishmaelites, all wore gold earrings.) "Gladly!" they replied. They spread out a cloak, and each one threw in a gold earring he had gathered. Gideon made a sacred ephod from the gold and put it in Ophrah, his hometown. But soon all the Israelites prostituted themselves by worshiping it, and it became a trap for Gideon and his family.

Are you seeking great things for yourself? Don't do it! ■ I have received wonderful revelations from God. But to keep me from getting puffed up, I was given a thorn in my flesh, a messenger from Satan to torment me and keep me from getting proud. Now I am glad to boast about my weaknesses, so that the power of Christ may work through me.

Don't be selfish; don't live to make a good impression on others. Be humble, thinking of others as better than yourself. ■ Love is patient and kind. Love is not jealous or boastful or proud or rude. Love does not demand its own way.

Take my yoke upon you. Let me teach you. . . . For my yoke fits perfectly.

Everyone needs a certain amount of approval from others. But those who go out of their way to secure honors or to win popularity with a lot of people become conceited. Those who look to God for approval won't need to envy others. *LAB note for Galatians 5:26*

(GALATIANS 5:26) (JUDGES 8:23-25, 27) (JEREMIAH 45:5) (2 CORINTHIANS 12:7, 9) (PHILIPPIANS 2:3) (1 CORINTHIANS 13:4-5) (MATTHEW 11:29-30)

May 14

Keep a close watch on yourself and on your teaching.

All athletes practice strict self-control. They do it to win a prize that will fade away, but we do it for an eternal prize. So I run straight to the goal with purpose in every step. I am not like a boxer who misses his punches. I discipline my body like an athlete, training it to do what it should. Otherwise, I fear that after preaching to others I myself might be disqualified.

Put on all of God's armor so that you will be able to stand firm against all strategies and tricks of the Devil. For we are not fighting against people made of flesh and blood, but against the evil rulers and the authorities of the unseen world, against those mighty powers of darkness who rule this world, and against wicked spirits in the heavenly realms.

Those who belong to Christ Jesus have nailed their passions and desires of their sinful nature to his cross and crucified them there. If we are living now by the Holy Spirit, let us follow the Holy Spirit's leading in every part of our lives.

We must be on constant guard against falling into sin, which can so easily destroy us. Yet we must watch what we believe just as closely. Wrong beliefs can quickly lead us into sin and heresy. We should be on guard against those who would persuade us that how we live is more important than what we believe. *LAB note for 1 Timothy 4:16*

(1 TIMOTHY 4:16) (1 CORINTHIANS 9:25-27) (EPHESIANS 6:11-12) (GALATIANS 5:24-25)

M a y 15

The Holy Spirit helps us in our distress.

The Counselor . . . the Holy Spirit. ■ Don't you know that your body is the temple of the Holy Spirit, who lives in you and was given to you by God? ■ God is working in you.

The Holy Spirit helps us in our distress. For we don't even know what we should pray for, nor how we should pray. But the Holy Spirit prays for us with groanings that cannot be expressed in words. And the Father who knows all hearts knows what the Spirit is saying, for the Spirit pleads for us believers in harmony with God's own will.

He knows we are only dust. ■ He will not crush those who are weak or quench the smallest hope.

Though the spirit is willing enough, the body is weak!

The LORD is my shepherd; I have everything I need. He lets me rest in green meadows; he leads me beside peaceful streams. He renews my strength. He guides me along right paths, bringing honor to his name. Even when I walk through the dark valley of death, I will not be afraid, for you are close beside me. Your rod and your staff protect and comfort me.

As a believer, you are not left to your own resources to cope with problems. Even when you don't know the right words to pray, the Holy Spirit prays with and for you, and God answers. So don't be afraid to ask the Holy Spirit to intercede for you "in harmony with God's own will."

LAB note for Romans 8:26-27

(ROMANS 8:26) (JOHN 14:26) (1 CORINTHIANS 6:19) (PHILIPPIANS 2:13) (ROMANS 8:26-27) (PSALM 103:14) (ISAIAH 42:3) (MATTHEW 26:41) (PSALM 23:1-4)

May 16

When they call on me, I will answer; I will be with them in trouble. I will rescue them and honor them.

Jabez . . . prayed to the God of Israel, "Oh, that you would bless me and extend my lands! Please be with me in all that I do, and keep me from all trouble and pain!" And God granted him his request. ▩ God appeared to Solomon in a dream and said, "What do you want? Ask, and I will give it to you!" Solomon replied to God, "You have been so faithful and kind to my father, David, and now you have made me king in his place. Give me wisdom and knowledge to rule them properly, for who is able to govern this great nation of yours?" ▩ God gave Solomon great wisdom and understanding, and knowledge too vast to be measured. In fact, his wisdom exceeded that of all the wise men of the East and the wise men of Egypt.

Asa deployed his armies for battle. . . . Then Asa cried out to the LORD his God, "O LORD, no one but you can help the powerless against the mighty! Help us, O LORD our God, for we trust in you alone. It is in your name that we have come against this vast horde. O LORD, you are our God; do not let mere men prevail against you!" So the LORD defeated the Ethiopians in the presence of Asa and the army of Judah, and the enemy fled.

You answer our prayers, and to you all people will come.

Jabez is remembered for a prayer request rather than a heroic act. When we pray for God's blessing, we should also ask him to take his rightful position as Lord over our work, our family time, and our recreation. Obeying him in daily responsibilities is heroic living.

LAB note for 1 Chronicles 4:9-10

(PSALM 91:15) (1 CHRONICLES 4:9-10) (2 CHRONICLES 1:7-8, 10)
(1 KINGS 4:29-30) (2 CHRONICLES 14:10-12) (PSALM 65:2)

*M*ay 17

Clothe yourselves with the armor of right living.

Let the Lord Jesus Christ take control of you. ▪ I have discarded everything else, counting it all as garbage, so that I may have Christ and become one with him. I no longer count on my own goodness or my ability to obey God's law, but I trust Christ to save me. For God's way of making us right with himself depends on faith. ▪ We are made right in God's sight when we trust in Jesus Christ to take away our sins. And we all can be saved in this same way, no matter who we are or what we have done.

He has dressed me with the clothing of salvation and draped me in a robe of righteousness. ▪ I will tell everyone that you alone are just and good.

For though your hearts were once full of darkness, now you are full of light from the Lord, and your behavior should show it! Take no part in the worthless deeds of evil and darkness; instead, rebuke and expose them. But when the light shines on them, it becomes clear how evil these things are. And where your light shines, it will expose their evil deeds. This is why it is said, "Awake, O sleeper, rise up from the dead, and Christ will give you light."

Attitudes are as important as actions. Just as hatred leads to murder, so jealousy leads to strife and lust to adultery. When Christ returns, he wants to find his people clean on the inside as well as on the outside.

LAB note for Romans 13:12-14

(Romans 13:12) (Romans 13:14) (Philippians 3:8-9) (Romans 3:22) (Isaiah 61:10) (Psalm 71:16) (Ephesians 5:8, 11, 13-15)

May 18

Your goodness is so great! You have stored up great blessings for those who honor you.

Since the world began, no ear has heard, and no eye has seen a God like you, who works for those who wait for him! ▧ No eye has seen, no ear has heard, and no mind has imagined what God has prepared for those who love him. But we know these things because God has revealed them to us by his Spirit, and his Spirit searches out everything and shows us even God's deep secrets. ▧ You will show me the way of life, granting me the joy of your presence and the pleasures of living with you forever.

How precious is your unfailing love, O God! All humanity finds shelter in the shadow of your wings. You feed them from the abundance of your own house, letting them drink from your rivers of delight.

Spend your time and energy in training yourself for spiritual fitness. Physical exercise has some value, but spiritual exercise is much more important, for it promises a reward in both this life and the next.

We cannot imagine all that God has in store for us, both in this life and for eternity. Knowing the wonderful and eternal future that awaits us gives us hope and courage to press on in this life, to endure hardship, and to avoid giving in to temptation. The best is yet to come.

LAB note for 1 Corinthians 2:9

(Psalm 31:19) (Isaiah 64:4) (1 Corinthians 2:9-10) (Psalm 16:11) (Psalm 36:7-8) (1 Timothy 4:7-8)

*M*ay 19

The Son of God, whose eyes are bright like flames of fire.

The human heart is most deceitful and desperately wicked. Who really knows how bad it is? But I know! I, the LORD, search all hearts and examine secret motives. I give all people their due rewards, according to what their actions deserve. ▩ You spread out our sins before you—our secret sins—and you see them all. ▩ The Lord turned and looked at Peter. . . . And Peter left the courtyard, crying bitterly.

Jesus didn't trust them, because he knew what people were really like. No one needed to tell him about human nature. ▩ He knows we are only dust. ▩ He will not crush those who are weak or quench the smallest hope.

The Lord knows those who are his. ▩ I am the good shepherd; I know my own sheep, and they know me. My sheep recognize my voice; I know them, and they follow me. I give them eternal life, and they will never perish. No one will snatch them away from me, for my Father has given them to me, and he is more powerful than anyone else. So no one can take them from me.

God makes it clear why we sin—it's a matter of the heart. Our heart is inclined toward sin from the time we are born. But we can still choose whether or not to continue in sin. We can ask God to help us resist temptation when it comes. *LAB note for Jeremiah 17:9-10*

(REVELATION 2:18) (JEREMIAH 17:9-10) (PSALM 90:8) (LUKE 22:61-62) (JOHN 2:24-25) (PSALM 103:14) (ISAIAH 42:3) (2 TIMOTHY 2:19) (JOHN 10:14, 27-29)

May 20

Jesus is the great Shepherd of the sheep.

The head Shepherd. ▩ I am the good shepherd; I know my own sheep, and they know me. My sheep recognize my voice; I know them, and they follow me. I give them eternal life, and they will never perish. No one will snatch them away from me. I have other sheep, too, that are not in this sheepfold. I must bring them also, and they will listen to my voice.

The LORD is my shepherd; I have everything I need. He lets me rest in green meadows; he leads me beside peaceful streams. He renews my strength. He guides me along right paths, bringing honor to his name.

All of us have strayed away like sheep. We have left God's paths to follow our own. Yet the LORD laid on him the guilt and sins of us all. ▩ I am the good shepherd. The good shepherd lays down his life for the sheep. ▩ I will search for my lost ones who strayed away, and I will bring them safely home again. I will bind up the injured and strengthen the weak. ▩ Once you were wandering like lost sheep. But now you have turned to your Shepherd, the Guardian of your souls.

A hired hand tends the sheep for money, while the shepherd does it out of love. The shepherd owns the sheep and is committed to them. Jesus is not merely doing a job; he is committed to love us and even lay down his life for us. *LAB note for John 10:11–12*

(HEBREWS 13:20) (1 PETER 5:4) (JOHN 10:14, 27–28, 16) (PSALM 23:1–3) (ISAIAH 53:6) (JOHN 10:11) (EZEKIEL 34:16) (1 PETER 2:25)

May 21

The city has no need of sun or moon, for the glory of God illuminates the city, and the Lamb is its light.

A light from heaven brighter than the sun shone down on me and my companions. "Who are you, sir?" I asked. And the Lord replied, "I am Jesus, the one you are persecuting." ▩ Jesus took Peter and the two brothers, James and John, and led them up a high mountain. As the men watched, Jesus' appearance changed so that his face shone like the sun, and his clothing beame dazzling white. ▩ No longer will you need the sun or moon to give you light, for the LORD your God will be your everlasting light, and he will be your glory. The sun will never set; the moon will not go down. For the LORD will be your everlasting light. Your days of mourning will come to an end.

After you have suffered a little while, he will restore, support, and strengthen you, and he will place you on a firm foundation. All power is his forever and ever. ▩ So be truly glad! There is wonderful joy ahead, even though it is necessary for you to endure many trials for a while.

The Transfiguration was a vision, a brief glimpse of the true glory of the King. This was a special revelation of Jesus' divinity to three of the disciples, and it was God's divine affirmation of everything Jesus had done and was about to do. *LAB note for Matthew 17:1ff.*

(REVELATION 21:23) (ACTS 26:13, 15) (MATTHEW 17:1-2) (ISAIAH 60:19-20) (1 PETER 5:10-11) (1 PETER 1:6)

May 22

The LORD is good. When trouble comes, he is a strong refuge. And he knows everyone who trusts in him.

Give thanks to the LORD Almighty, for the LORD is good. His faithful love endures forever! ▩ God is our refuge and strength, always ready to help in times of trouble. ▩ This I declare of the LORD: He alone is my refuge, my place of safety; he is my God, and I am trusting him. ▩ How blessed you are, O Israel! Who else is like you, a people saved by the LORD? He is your protecting shield and your triumphant sword! ▩ As for God, his way is perfect. All the LORD's promises prove true. He is a shield for all who look to him for protection. For who is God except the LORD?

The person who loves God is the one God knows and cares for. ▩ God's truth stands firm like a foundation stone with this inscription: "The Lord knows those who are his," and "Those who claim they belong to the Lord must turn away from all wickedness." ▩ The LORD watches over the path of the godly, but the path of the wicked leads to destruction. ▩ You have found favor with me, and you are my friend.

To people who refuse to believe, God's punishment is like an angry fire. To those who love him, his mercy is a refuge, providing for all their needs without diminishing his supply. The relationship we have with God is up to us. What kind of relationship will you choose?

LAB note for Nahum 1:7

(NAHUM 1:7) (JEREMIAH 33:11) (PSALM 46:1) (PSALM 91:2) (DEUTERONOMY 33:29) (2 SAMUEL 22:31-32) (1 CORINTHIANS 8:3) (2 TIMOTHY 2:19) (PSALM 1:6) (EXODUS 33:17)

May 23

I want you to be free from the concerns of this life.

Give all your worries and cares to God, for he cares about what happens to you. ▪ The eyes of the LORD search the whole earth in order to strengthen those whose hearts are fully committed to him.

Taste and see that the LORD is good. Oh, the joys of those who trust in him! Even strong young lions sometimes go hungry, but those who trust in the LORD will never lack any good thing. ▪ Don't worry about everyday life—whether you have enough food, drink, and clothes. Doesn't life consist of more than food and clothing? Look at the birds. They don't need to plant or harvest or put food in barns because your heavenly Father feeds them. And you are far more valuable to him than they are. ▪ Don't worry about anything; instead, pray about everything. Tell God what you need, and thank him for all he has done. If you do this, you will experience God's peace, which is far more wonderful than the human mind can understand. His peace will guard your hearts and minds as you live in Christ Jesus.

How many ill effects of worry are you experiencing? It damages your health, disrupts your productivity, negatively affects the way you treat others, and reduces your ability to trust in God. Here is the difference between worry and genuine concern—worry immobilizes, but concern moves you to action.

LAB note for Matthew 6:25

(1 CORINTHIANS 7:32) (1 PETER 5:7) (2 CHRONICLES 16:9) (PSALM 34:8, 10) (MATTHEW 6:25-26) (PHILIPPIANS 4:6-7)

May 24

Continue to live in fellowship with Christ.

A doubtful mind is as unsettled as a wave of the sea that is driven and tossed by the wind. People like that should not expect to receive anything from the Lord. They can't make up their minds. They waver back and forth in everything they do.

I am shocked that you are turning away so soon from God, who in his love and mercy called you to share the eternal life he gives through Christ. You are already following a different way.

If you are trying to make yourselves right with God by keeping the law, you have been cut off from Christ! You have fallen away from God's grace. You were getting along so well. Who has interfered with you to hold you back from following the truth?

Remain in me, and I will remain in you. For a branch cannot produce fruit if it is severed from the vine, and you cannot be fruitful apart from me. But if you stay joined to me and my words remain in you, you may ask any request you like, and it will be granted! ▩ For all of God's promises have been fulfilled in him. That is why we say "Amen" when we give glory to God through Christ.

Because true faith always results in good deeds, those who claim to have faith and who consistently do what is right are true believers. Good deeds cannot produce salvation, but they are necessary proof that true faith is actually present. *LAB note for 1 John 2:28–29*

(1 John 2:28) (James 1:6–8) (Galatians 1:6) (Galatians 5:4, 7) (John 15:4, 7) (2 Corinthians 1:20)

*M*ay 25

I am God Almighty; serve me faithfully and live a blameless life.

I [Paul] don't mean to say that I have already achieved these things or that I have already reached perfection! But I keep working toward that day when I will finally be all that Christ Jesus saved me for and wants me to be. No, dear brothers and sisters, I am still not all I should be, but I am focusing all my energies on this one thing: Forgetting the past and looking forward to what lies ahead, I strain to reach the end of the race and receive the prize for which God, through Christ Jesus, is calling us up to heaven.

Grow in the special favor and knowledge of our Lord and Savior Jesus Christ. ▪ All of us have had that veil removed so that we can be mirrors that brightly reflect the glory of the Lord. And as the Spirit of the Lord works within us, we become more and more like him and reflect his glory even more. ▪ The way of the righteous is like the first gleam of dawn, which shines ever brighter until the full light of day.

Jesus . . . looked up to heaven and said, ". . . I'm not asking you to take them out of the world, but to keep them safe from the evil one. I in them and you in me, all being perfected into one."

We are to obey the Lord in every respect because he is God—that is reason enough. If you don't think the benefits of obedience are worth it, consider who God is—the only one with the power and ability to meet your every need.

LAB note for Genesis 17:1

(GENESIS 17:1) (PHILIPPIANS 3:12-14) (2 PETER 3:18) (2 CORINTHIANS 3:18) (PROVERBS 4:18) (JOHN 17:1, 15, 23)

May 26

Do not bring sorrow to God's Holy Spirit by the way you live.

Love . . . given to you by the Holy Spirit. ▩ The Counselor . . . the Holy Spirit. ▩ In all their suffering he also suffered, and he personally rescued them. In his love and mercy he redeemed them. He lifted them up and carried them through all the years.

God has given us his Spirit as proof that we live in him and he in us. ▩ He identified you as his own by giving you the Holy Spirit, whom he promised long ago. The Spirit is God's guarantee that he will give us everything he promised and that he has purchased us to be his own people. This is just one more reason for us to praise our glorious God. ▩ I advise you to live according to your new life in the Holy Spirit. Then you won't be doing what your sinful nature craves. The old sinful nature loves to do evil, which is just opposite from what the Holy Spirit wants. And the Spirit gives us desires that are opposite from what the sinful nature desires.

The Holy Spirit helps us in our distress.

Are you bringing sorrow to God—or pleasing him with your attitudes and actions? Act in love toward your brothers and sisters in Christ, just as Christ acted in love by sending his Son to die for your sins.

LAB note for Ephesians 4:28-32

(EPHESIANS 4:30) (ROMANS 15:30) (JOHN 14:26) (ISAIAH 63:9) (1 JOHN 4:13) (EPHESIANS 1:13-14) (GALATIANS 5:16-17) (ROMANS 8:26)

May 27

When you obey me, you should say, "We are not worthy of praise. We are servants who have simply done our duty."

Can we boast, then, that we have done anything to be accepted by God? No, because our acquittal is not based on our good deeds. It is based on our faith. ▪ What makes you better than anyone else? What do you have that God hasn't given you? And if all you have is from God, why boast as though you have accomplished something on your own? ▪ God saved you by his special favor when you believed. And you can't take credit for this; it is a gift from God. Salvation is not a reward for the good things we have done, so none of us can boast about it. For we are God's masterpiece. He has created us anew in Christ Jesus, so that we can do the good things he planned for us long ago.

But whatever I am now, it is all because God poured out his special favor on me. ▪ For everything comes from him; everything exists by his power and is intended for his glory. ▪ Everything we have has come from you, and we give you only what you have already given us!

Do you sometimes feel you deserve extra credit for serving God? Obedience is not something extra we do; it is our duty. Jesus is not suggesting our service is meaningless or useless, nor is he advocating doing away with rewards. He is attacking unwarranted self-esteem and spiritual pride.

LAB note for Luke 17:7-10

(Luke 17:10) (Romans 3:27) (1 Corinthians 4:7) (Ephesians 2:8-10) (1 Corinthians 15:10) (Romans 11:36) (1 Chronicles 29:14)

May 28

Forgive all my sins.

"Come now, let us argue this out," says the LORD. "No matter how deep the stain of your sins, I can remove it. I can make you as clean as freshly fallen snow. Even if you are stained as red as crimson, I can make you as white as wool."

Take heart, son! Your sins are forgiven. ▩ I—yes, I alone—am the one who blots out your sins for my own sake and will never think of them again.

He is so rich in kindness that he purchased our freedom through the blood of his Son, and our sins are forgiven. ▩ He saved us, not because of the good things we did, but because of his mercy. He washed away our sins and gave us a new life through the Holy Spirit. He generously poured out the Spirit upon us because of what Jesus Christ our Savior did. ▩ He forgave all our sins. He canceled the record that contained the charges against us. He took it and destroyed it by nailing it to Christ's cross.

Praise the LORD, I tell myself. . . . He forgives all my sins.

The stain of sin seems permanent, but God can remove that stain from our life. We don't have to go through life permanently soiled. God's Word assures us that if we are willing and obedient, Christ will forgive and remove our most indelible stains. *LAB note for Isaiah 1:18*

(PSALM 25:18) (ISAIAH 1:18) (MATTHEW 9:2) (ISAIAH 43:25) (EPHESIANS 1:7) (TITUS 3:5-6) (COLOSSIANS 2:13-14) (PSALM 103:2-3)

May 29

This younger son packed all his belongings and took a trip to a distant land, and there he wasted all his money on wild living.

There was a time when some of you were just like that, but now your sins have been washed away, and you have been set apart for God. You have been made right with God because of what the Lord Jesus Christ and the Spirit of our God have done for you. ■ All of us used to live that way, following the passions and desires of our evil nature. We were born with an evil nature, and we were under God's anger just like everyone else. But God is so rich in mercy, and he loved us so very much, that even while we were dead because of our sins, he gave us life when he raised Christ from the dead. (It is only by God's special favor that you have been saved!) For he raised us from the dead along with Christ, and we are seated with him in the heavenly realms—all because we are one with Christ Jesus.

This is real love. It is not that we loved God, but that he loved us and sent his Son as a sacrifice to take away our sins. ■ God showed his great love for us by sending Christ to die for us while we were still sinners. For since we were restored to friendship with God by the death of his Son while we were still his enemies, we will certainly be delivered from eternal punishment by his life.

Nothing sinful or evil can exist in God's presence. He is absolute goodness. He cannot overlook, condone, or excuse sin as though it never happened. He loves us, but his love does not make him morally lax. If we trust in Christ, however, we will be acquitted by his atoning sacrifice.

LAB note for 1 John 4:10

(LUKE 15:13) (1 CORINTHIANS 6:11) (EPHESIANS 2:3-6)
(1 JOHN 4:10) (ROMANS 5:8, 10)

*M*ay 30

He returned home to his father. And while he was still a long distance away, his father saw him coming. Filled with love and compassion, he ran to his son, embraced him, and kissed him.

The LORD is merciful and gracious; he is slow to get angry and full of unfailing love. He will not constantly accuse us, nor remain angry forever. He has not punished us for all our sins, nor does he deal with us as we deserve. For his unfailing love toward those who fear him is as great as the height of the heavens above the earth. He has removed our rebellious acts as far away from us as the east is from the west. The LORD is like a father to his children, tender and compassionate to those who fear him.

So you should not be like cowering, fearful slaves. You should behave instead like God's very own children, adopted into his family—calling him "Father, dear Father." For his Holy Spirit speaks to us deep in our hearts and tells us that we are God's children. ▪ Now you belong to Christ Jesus. Though you once were far away from God, now you have been brought near to him because of the blood of Christ. So now you Gentiles are no longer strangers and foreigners. You are citizens along with all of God's holy people. You are members of God's family.

We are fragile, but God's care is eternal. When God examines our lives, he remembers our human condition. But our weakness should never be used as a justification for sin. His mercy takes everything into account. God will deal with you compassionately. Trust him.

LAB note for Psalm 103:13-14

(LUKE 15:20) (PSALM 103:8-13) (ROMANS 8:15-16) (EPHESIANS 2:13, 19)

*M*ay 31

Remember, the Lord forgave you, so you must forgive others.

Then Jesus told him this story: "A man loaned money to two people—five hundred pieces of silver to one and fifty pieces to the other. But neither of them could repay him, so he kindly forgave them both, canceling their debts." ▪ I forgave you that tremendous debt because you pleaded with me. Shouldn't you have mercy on your fellow servant, just as I had mercy on you?

But when you are praying, first forgive anyone you are holding a grudge against, so that your Father in heaven will forgive your sins, too. ▪ Since God chose you to be the holy people whom he loves, you must clothe yourselves with tenderhearted mercy, kindness, humility, gentleness, and patience. You must make allowance for each other's faults and forgive the person who offends you.

"Lord, how often should I forgive someone who sins against me? Seven times?" "No!" Jesus replied, "seventy times seven!"

The most important piece of clothing you must wear is love. ▪ Oh, how kind and gracious the Lord was! He filled me completely with faith and the love of Christ Jesus.

The rabbis taught that people should forgive those who offend them—but only three times. But Jesus said, "Seventy times seven," meaning we shouldn't even keep track of how many times we forgive someone. We should always forgive those who are truly repentant, no matter how many times they ask. *LAB note for Matthew 18:22*

(Colossians 3:13) (Luke 7:41-42) (Matthew 18:32-33) (Mark 11:25) (Colossians 3:12-13) (Matthew 18:21-22) (Colossians 3:14) (1 Timothy 1:14)

June

A Man among Men

Bike rides and baseball games, tree houses
and camping trips
Lighthearted fun times and spontaneous
teaching moments
One can never overestimate the importance
of a father's involvement.

A father is a wonderful balance of security and patience, wisdom and integrity, encouragement and inspiration. He has the unique and essential role of reflecting the heavenly Father's unconditional love for his children. May you be blessed by a fatherly man in your life.

June 1

I will be your Father, and you will be my sons and daughters, says the Lord Almighty.

See how very much our heavenly Father loves us, for he allows us to be called his children, and we really are! But the people who belong to this world don't know God, so they don't understand that we are his children. ▪ Everyone who believes that Jesus is the Christ is a child of God. And everyone who loves the Father loves his children, too. ▪ And because you . . . have become his children, God has sent the Spirit of his Son into your hearts, and now you can call God your dear Father. ▪ Now all of us . . . may come to the Father through the same Holy Spirit because of what Christ has done for us. ▪ He said to Jesus: "You are my Son. Today I have become your Father." And again God said, "I will be his Father, and he will be my Son."

As God's heirs, we can claim what he has provided for us—our full identity as his children. *LAB note for Galatians 4:6*

(2 Corinthians 6:18) (1 John 3:1) (1 John 5:1) (Galatians 4:6) (Ephesians 2:18) (Hebrews 1:5)

June 2

Now a word to you fathers. Don't make your children angry by the way you treat them. Rather, bring them up with the discipline and instruction approved by the Lord.

My children, listen to me. Listen to your father's instruction. Pay attention and grow wise, for I am giving you good guidance. Don't turn away from my teaching. For I, too, was once my father's son, tenderly loved by my mother as an only child.

My father told me, Take my words to heart. Follow my instructions and you will live. Learn to be wise, and develop good judgment. Don't forget or turn away from my words. ▩ Let those who are wise listen to these proverbs and become even wiser. And let those who understand receive guidance. ▩ Listen, my child, to what your father teaches you. ▩ For wisdom will enter your heart, and knowledge will fill you with joy. Wise planning will watch over you. Understanding will keep you safe. ▩ The Lord is like a father to his children, tender and compassionate to those who fear him. ▩ The Lord corrects those he loves, just as a father corrects a child in whom he delights. ▩ Now glory be to God our Father forever and ever.

The purpose of parental discipline is to help children grow, not to exasperate and provoke them to anger or discouragement. Parenting is not easy—it takes lots of patience to raise children. *LAB note for Ephesians 6:4*

(Ephesians 6:4) (Proverbs 4:1-5) (Proverbs 1:5) (Proverbs 1:8) (Proverbs 2:10-11) (Psalm 103:13) (Proverbs 3:12) (Philippians 4:20)

June 3

I am making all things new!

I assure you, unless you are born again, you can never see the Kingdom of God. ▪ Those who become Christians become new persons. They are not the same anymore, for the old life is gone. A new life has begun!

I will sprinkle clean water on you, and you will be clean. Your filth will be washed away, and you will no longer worship idols. And I will give you a new heart with new and right desires, and I will put a new spirit in you. I will take out your stony heart of sin and give you a new, obedient heart. And I will put my Spirit in you so you will obey my laws and do whatever I command. ▪ You must display a new nature because you are a new person, created in God's likeness—righteous, holy, and true.

The LORD will give you a new name. The LORD will hold you in his hands for all to see—a splendid crown in the hands of God.

I am creating new heavens and a new earth—so wonderful that no one will even think about the old ones anymore. ▪ Since everything around us is going to melt away, what holy, godly lives you should be living!

Christians are brand-new people on the inside. The Holy Spirit gives them new life, and they are not the same anymore. We are not reformed, rehabilitated, or reeducated—we are re-created (new creations), living in vital union with Christ. *LAB note for 2 Corinthians 5:17*

(REVELATION 21:5) (JOHN 3:3) (2 CORINTHIANS 5:17) (EZEKIEL 36:25-27) (EPHESIANS 4:24) (ISAIAH 62:2-3) (ISAIAH 65:17) (2 PETER 3:11)

June 4

We can be dead to sin and live for what is right.

Throw off your old evil nature and your former way of life, which is rotten through and through, full of lust and deception. Instead, there must be a spiritual renewal of your thoughts and attitudes. You must display a new nature because you are a new person, created in God's likeness—righteous, holy, and true.

You died when Christ died, and your real life is hidden with Christ in God. ▪ We died and were buried with Christ by baptism. And just as Christ was raised from the dead by the glorious power of the Father, now we also may live new lives. Our old sinful selves were crucified with Christ so that sin might lose its power in our lives. We are no longer slaves to sin. For when we died with Christ, we were set free from the power of sin. So you should consider yourselves dead to sin and able to live for the glory of God through Christ Jesus. Do not let any part of your body become a tool of wickedness, to be used for sinning. Instead, give yourselves completely to God since you have been given new life. And use your whole body as a tool to do what is right for the glory of God.

Christ died for our sins in our place, so we would not have to suffer the punishment we deserve. This is called "substitionary atonement." Since Christ has done this for us, we must choose to do right daily and to walk in his footsteps. *LAB note for 1 Peter 2:24*

(1 Peter 2:24) (Ephesians 4:22-24) (Colossians 3:3) (Romans 6:4, 6-7, 11, 13)

June 5

Remain in me, and I will remain in you.

I have been cruciified with Christ. I myself no longer live, but Christ lives in me. So I live my life in this earthly body by trusting in the Son of God, who loved me and gave himself for me.

I know I am rotten through and through so far as my old sinful nature is concerned. No matter which way I turn, I can't make myself do right. I want to, but I can't. Oh, what a miserable person I am! Who will free me from this life that is dominated by sin? Thank God! The answer is in Jesus Christ our Lord. ▪ Since Christ lives within you, even though your body will die because of sin, your spirit is alive because you have been made right with God. ▪ But you must continue to believe this truth and stand in it firmly. Don't drift away from the assurance you received when you heard the Good News.

And now, dear children, continue to live in fellowship with Christ so that when he returns, you will be full of courage and not shrink back from him in shame. ▪ Those who say they live in God should live their lives as Christ did.

In our daily life we must regularly crucify sinful desires that keep us from following Christ. And yet the focus of Christianity is not dying but living. Because we have been crucified with Christ, we have also been raised with him. *LAB note for Galatians 2:20*

(John 15:4) (Galatians 2:20) (Romans 7:18, 24-25) (Romans 8:10) (Colossians 1:23) (1 John 2:28) (1 John 2:6)

June 6

Do you believe in the Son of Man?

Who is he, sir?

The Son reflects God's own glory, and everything about him represents God exactly. ▪ The blessed and only almighty God, the King of kings and Lord of lords. He alone can never die, and he lives in light so brilliant that no human can approach him. No one has ever seen him, nor ever will. To him be honor and power forever. Amen. ▪ "I am the Alpha and the Omega—the beginning and the end," says the Lord God. "I am the one who is, who always was, and who is still to come, the Almighty One."

Yes, Lord, . . . I believe! ▪ I know the one in whom I trust, and I am sure that he is able to guard what I have entrusted to him until the day of his return. ▪ We believe because we have heard him ourselves, not just because of what you told us. He is indeed the Savior of the world.

"I am placing a stone in Jerusalem, a chosen cornerstone, and anyone who believes in him will never be disappointed." Yes, he is very precious to you who believe.

Jesus Christ is the same yesterday, today, and forever.

Alpha and omega are the first and last letters of the Greek alphabet. The Lord God is the beginning and the end. Without him you have nothing that is eternal, nothing that can change your life, nothing that can save you from sin. Is the Lord your Alpha and Omega?

LAB note for Revelation 1:8

(JOHN 9:35) (JOHN 9:36) (HEBREWS 1:3) (1 TIMOTHY 6:15-16) (REVELATION 1:8) (JOHN 9:38) (2 TIMOTHY 1:12) (JOHN 4:42) (1 PETER 2:6-7) (HEBREWS 13:8)

June 7

My dear Martha, you are so upset over all these details!

Look at the ravens. They don't need to plant or harvest or put food in barns because God feeds them. And you are far more valuable to him than any birds! Look at the lilies and how they grow. They don't work or make their clothing. And don't worry about food—what to eat or drink. Don't worry whether God will provide it for you. These things dominate the thoughts of most people, but your Father already knows your needs.

If we have enough food and clothing, let us be content. But people who long to be rich fall into temptation and are trapped by many foolish and harmful desires that plunge them into ruin and destruction. For the love of money is at the root of all kinds of evil. And some people, craving money, have wandered from the faith and pierced themselves with many sorrows.

All too quickly the message is crowded out by the cares of this life, the lure of wealth, and the desire for nice things.

Let us strip off every weight that slows us down, especially the sin that so easily hinders our progress. And let us run with endurance the race that God has set before us.

Jesus commands us not to worry because it's pointless—it can't fill any of our needs. Worry is foolish because the Creator of the universe loves us and knows what we need. He promises to meet all our real needs but not necessarily all our desires. *LAB note for Luke 12:22-34*

(LUKE 10:41) (LUKE 12:24, 27, 29-30) (1 TIMOTHY 6:8-10) (MARK 4:19) (HEBREWS 12:1)

June 8

One day Jesus told his disciples a story to illustrate their need for constant prayer and to show them that they must never give up.

Then, teaching them more about prayer, he used this illustration: "Suppose you went to a friend's house at midnight, wanting to borrow three loaves of bread. You would say to him, 'A friend of mine has just arrived for a visit, and I have nothing for him to eat.' He would call out from his bedroom, 'Don't bother me. The door is locked for the night, and we are all in bed. I can't help you this time.' But I tell you this—though he won't do it as a friend, if you keep knocking long enough, he will get up and give you what you want so his reputation won't be damaged. ▩ Pray at all times and on every occasion in the power of the Holy Spirit. Stay alert and be persistent in your prayers for all Christians everywhere.

"I will not let you go unless you bless me." "You have struggled with both God and men and have won." ▩ Devote yourselves to prayer with an alert mind and a thankful heart.

Jesus went to a mountain to pray, and he prayed to God all night.

To persist in prayer and not give up does not mean endless repetition or painfully long prayer sessions. Constant prayer means keeping our requests continually before God as we live for him day by day, believing he will answer. As we persist in prayer, we grow in character, faith, and hope. *LAB note for Luke 18:1*

(LUKE 18:1) (LUKE 11:5-8) (EPHESIANS 6:18) (GENESIS 32:26, 28) (COLOSSIANS 4:2) (LUKE 6:12)

June 9

Be careful how you live, not as fools but as those who are wise. Make the most of every opportunity for doing good in these evil days.

Be very careful to obey all the commands. . . . Love the LORD your God, walk in all his ways, obey his commands, be faithful to him, and serve him with all your heart and all your soul. ▪ Live wisely among those who are not Christians, and make the most of every opportunity. Let your conversation be gracious and effective so that you will have the right answer for everyone. ▪ Keep away from every kind of evil.

When the bridegroom was delayed, they all lay down and slept. At midnight they were roused by the shout, "Look, the bridegroom is coming! Come out and welcome him!" So stay awake and be prepared, because you do not know the day or hour of my return.

Work hard to prove that you really are among those God has called and chosen. Doing this, you will never stumble or fall away. And God will open wide the gates of heaven for you to enter into the eternal Kingdom of our Lord and Savior Jesus Christ. ▪ There will be special favor for those who are ready and waiting for his return. You must be ready all the time, for the Son of Man will come when least expected.

By referring to these days as evil, the apostle Paul was communicating his sense of urgency, due to evil's pervasiveness. We need the same sense of urgency because our days are also difficult. We must keep our standards high, act wisely, and do good whenever we can.

LAB note for Ephesians 5:15-16

(EPHESIANS 5:15-16) (JOSHUA 22:5) (COLOSSIANS 4:5-6) (1 THESSALONIANS 5:22) (MATTHEW 25:5-6, 13) (2 PETER 1:10-11) (LUKE 12:37, 40)

June 10

All of your works will thank you, LORD, and your faithful followers will bless you.

Praise the LORD, I tell myself; with my whole heart, I will praise his holy name. Praise the LORD, I tell myself, and never forget the good things he does for me. ▩ I will praise the LORD at all times. I will constantly speak his praises. I will boast only in the LORD. ▩ I will praise you, my God and King, and bless your name forever and ever. I will bless you every day, and I will praise you forever. Great is the LORD! He is most worthy of praise! His greatness is beyond discovery! Let each generation tell its children of your mighty acts. I will meditate on your majestic, glorious splendor and your wonderful miracles. Your awe-inspiring deeds will be on every tongue; I will proclaim your greatness.

Your unfailing love is better to me than life itself; how I praise you! I will honor you as long as I live, lifting up my hands to you in prayer. You satisfy me more than the richest of foods. I will praise you with songs of joy.

Oh, how I praise the Lord. How I rejoice in God my Savior!

You are worthy, O Lord our God, to receive glory and honor and power. For you created everything, and it is for your pleasure that they exist and were created.

We have plenty for which to praise God. He forgives our sins, heals our diseases, redeems us from death, crowns us with love and compassion, satisfies our desires, and gives righteousness and justice. No matter how difficult your life's journey, you can always count your blessings—past, present, and future. *LAB note for Psalm 103:1ff.*

(PSALM 145:10) (PSALM 103:1-2) (PSALM 34:1-2) (PSALM 145:1-6) (PSALM 63:3-5) (LUKE 1:46-47) (REVELATION 4:11)

June 11

Seek to live a clean and holy life, for those who are not holy will not see the Lord.

I assure you, unless you are born again, you can never see the Kingdom of God. ▩ Nothing evil will be allowed to enter—no one who practices shameful idolatry and dishonesty.

You must be holy because I, the LORD your God, am holy. ▩ Obey God because you are his children. Don't slip back into your old ways of doing evil; you didn't know any better then. But now you must be holy in everything you do, just as God—who chose you to be his children—is holy. For he himself has said, "You must be holy because I am holy." And remember the heavenly Father to whom you pray has no favorites when he judges. He will judge or reward you according to what you do. So you must live in reverent fear of him during your time as foreigners here on earth. ▩ Throw off your old evil nature and your former way of life, which is rotten through and through, full of lust and deception. Instead, there must be a spiritual renewal of your thoughts and attitudes. You must display a new nature because you are a new person, created in God's likeness—righteous, holy, and true. ▩ Long ago, even before he made the world, God loved us and chose us in Christ to be holy and without fault in his eyes.

Sin always blocks our vision of God; so if we want to see God, we must renounce sin and obey him. Holiness is coupled with living in peace. A right relationship with God leads to right relationships with fellow believers.

LAB note for Hebrews 12:14

(HEBREWS 12:14) (JOHN 3:3) (REVELATION 21:27) (LEVITICUS 19:2) (1 PETER 1:14-17) (EPHESIANS 4:22-24) (EPHESIANS 1:4)

June 12

Gold that has been purified by fire.

I assure you that everyone who has given up house or brothers or sisters or mother or father or children or property, for my sake and for the Good News, will receive now in return, a hundred times over, houses, brothers, sisters, mothers, children, and property—with persecutions. And in the world to come they will have eternal life.

Don't be surprised at the fiery trials you are going through, as if something strange were happening to you. ▪ Be truly glad! There is wonderful joy ahead, even though it is necessary for you to endure many trials for a while. These trials are only to test your faith, to show that it is strong and pure. It is being tested as fire tests and purifies gold—and your faith is far more precious to God than mere gold. So if your faith remains strong after being tried by fiery trials, it will bring you much praise and glory and honor on the day when Jesus Christ is revealed to the whole world.

After you have suffered a little while, he will restore, support, and strengthen you, and he will place you on a firm foundation. ▪ Here on earth you will have many trials and sorrows. But take heart, because I have overcome the world.

Anyone who gives up something valuable for Jesus' sake will be repaid a hundred times over in this life, although not necessarily in the same way. Along with these rewards, however, we experience persecution because the world hates God. Jesus emphasized persecution to make sure that we do not selfishly follow him only for the rewards.

LAB note for Mark 10:29-30

(REVELATION 3:18) (MARK 10:29-30) (1 PETER 4:12) (1 PETER 1:6-7) (1 PETER 5:10) (JOHN 16:33)

June 13

Christ . . . is your example. Follow in his steps.

For even I, the Son of Man, came here not to be served but to serve others, and to give my life as a ransom for many. ▪ Whoever wants to be first must be the slave of all. ▪ Though he was God, [Jesus] . . . took the humble position of a slave and appeared in human form.

Jesus went around doing good. ▪ Share each other's troubles and problems, and in this way obey the law of Christ.

I plead with the gentleness and kindness that Christ himself would use. ▪ Be humble, thinking of others as better than yourself.

Father, forgive these people, because they don't know what they are doing. ▪ Be kind to each other, tenderhearted, forgiving one another, just as God through Christ has forgiven you.

Those who say they live in God should live their lives as Christ did. ▪ We do this by keeping our eyes on Jesus, on whom our faith depends from start to finish. He was willing to die a shameful death on the cross because of the joy he knew would be his afterward. Now he is seated in the place of highest honor beside God's throne in heaven.

Businesses, organizations, and institutions measure greatness by personal achievement. In Christ's Kingdom, however, service is the way to get ahead. The desire to be on top will hinder, not help. Look for ways you can minister to the needs of others. *LAB note for Mark 10:42-45*

(1 PETER 2:21) (MARK 10:45) (MARK 10:44) (PHILIPPIANS 2:6-7) (ACTS 10:38) (GALATIANS 6:2) (2 CORINTHIANS 10:1) (PHILIPPIANS 2:3) (LUKE 23:34) (EPHESIANS 4:32) (1 JOHN 2:6) (HEBREWS 12:2)

June 14

I searched for him, but I couldn't find him anywhere. I called to him, but there was no reply.

Lord, what am I to say, now that Israel has fled from its enemies? But the LORD said to Joshua, "Get up! Why are you lying on your face like this? Israel has sinned and broken my covenant! They have stolen the things that I commanded to be set apart for me. And they have not only stolen them; they have also lied about it and hidden the things among their belongings. That is why the Israelites are running from their enemies in defeat. For now Israel has been set apart for destruction. I will not remain with you any longer unless you destroy the things among you that were set apart for destruction."

Listen! The LORD is not too weak to save you, and he is not becoming deaf. He can hear you when you call. But there is a problem—your sins have cut you off from God. Because of your sin, he has turned away and will not listen anymore.

Dear friends, if our conscience is clear, we can come to God with bold confidence. And we receive whatever we request when we obey him and do the things that please him.

God is not content with our doing what is right some of the time. He wants us to do what is right all the time. We are under his orders to eliminate any thoughts, practices, or possessions that hinder our devotion to him.

LAB note for Joshua 7:10-12

(SONG OF SONGS 5:6) (JOSHUA 7:8, 10-12) (ISAIAH 59:1-2) (1 JOHN 3:21-22)

June 15

I will ask the Father, and he will give you another Counselor, who will never leave you. He is the Holy Spirit, who leads into all truth.

It is actually best for you that I go away, because if I don't, the Counselor won't come. If I do go away, he will come because I will send him to you.

His Holy Spirit speaks to us deep in our hearts and tells us that we are God's children. ▩ So you should not be like cowering, fearful slaves. You should behave instead like God's very own children, adopted into his family—calling him "Father, dear Father." ▩ The Holy Spirit helps us in our distress. For we don't even know what we should pray for, nor how we should pray. But the Holy Spirit prays for us with groanings that cannot be expressed in words.

I pray that God, who gives you hope, will keep you happy and full of peace as you believe in him. May you overflow with hope through the power of the Holy Spirit. ▩ This expectation will not disappoint us. For we know how dearly God loves us, because he has given us the Holy Spirit to fill our hearts with his love.

The Holy Spirit is the very presence of God within us and all believers, helping us live as God wants and building Christ's church on earth. By faith we can appropriate the Spirit's power each day.

LAB note for John 14:15-16

(John 14:16-17) (John 16:7) (Romans 8:16) (Romans 8:15) (Romans 8:26) (Romans 15:13) (Romans 5:5)

June 16

Be still in the presence of the LORD, and wait patiently for him to act.

There is a special rest still waiting for the people of God. ▩ My people will live in safety, quietly at home. ▩ They will rest from all their toils and trials.

Jesus has already gone in there for us. He has become our eternal High Priest in the line of Melchizedek.

Come to me, all of you who are weary and carry heavy burdens, and I will give you rest. Take my yoke upon you. Let me teach you, because I am humble and gentle, and you will find rest for your souls. For my yoke fits perfectly, and the burden I give you is light. ▩ Only in returning to me and waiting for me will you be saved. In quietness and confidence is your strength. ▩ Look for the old, godly way, and walk in it. Travel its path, and you will find rest for your souls.

The LORD is my shepherd; I have everything I need. He lets me rest in green meadows; he leads me beside peaceful streams. ▩ Now I can rest again, for the LORD has been so good to me.

As the Lord is the good shepherd, so we are his sheep—not frightened, passive animals but obedient followers, wise enough to follow one who will lead us in the right places and in right ways. When you recognize the good shepherd, follow him! *LAB note for Psalm 23:1*

(PSALM 37:7) (HEBREWS 4:9) (ISAIAH 32:18) (REVELATION 14:13) (HEBREWS 6:20) (MATTHEW 11:28-30) (ISAIAH 30:15) (JEREMIAH 6:16) (PSALM 23:1-2) (PSALM 116:7)

June 17

Don't worry about tomorrow, for tomorrow will bring its own worries. Today's trouble is enough for today.

My future is in your hands. ▩ He subdues the nations before us, putting our enemies beneath our feet. He chose the Promised Land as our inheritance, the proud possession of Jacob's descendants, whom he loves. ▩ Lead me in the right path, O LORD. . . . Tell me clearly what to do, and show me which way to turn.

Commit everything you do to the LORD. Trust him, and he will help you. ▩ Seek his will in all you do, and he will direct your paths. ▩ You will hear a voice say, "This is the way; turn around and walk here."

The LORD is my shepherd; I have everything I need. He lets me rest in green meadows; he leads me beside peaceful streams. ▩ The LORD is like a father to his children, tender and compassionate to those who fear him. For he understands how weak we are; he knows we are only dust. ▩ Don't worry about having enough food or drink or clothing. Why be like the pagans who are so deeply concerned about these things? Your heavenly Father already knows all your needs. ▩ Give all your worries and cares to God, for he cares about what happens to you.

Planning for tomorrow is time well spent; worrying about tomorrow is time wasted. Worriers are consumed by fear and find it difficult to trust God. They let their plans interfere with their relationship with God. Don't let worries about tomorrow affect your relationship with God today.

LAB note for Matthew 6:34

(MATTHEW 6:34) (PSALM 31:15) (PSALM 47:3-4) (PSALM 5:8) (PSALM 37:5) (PROVERBS 3:6) (ISAIAH 30:21) (PSALM 23:1-2) (PSALM 103:13-14) (MATTHEW 6:31-32) (1 PETER 5:7)

June 18

When he comes we will be like him, for we will see him as he really is.

To all who believed him and accepted him, he gave the right to become children of God. ▩ And by that same mighty power, he has given us all of his rich and wonderful promises. He has promised . . . that you will share in his divine nature.

For since the world began, no ear has heard, and no eye has seen a God like you, who works for those who wait for him!

Now we see things imperfectly as in a poor mirror, but then we will see everything with perfect clarity. All that I know now is partial and imcomplete, but then I will know everything completely, just as God knows me now. ▩ Jesus Christ . . . will take these weak mortal bodies of ours and change them into glorious bodies like his own, using the same mighty power that he will use to conquer everything, everywhere. ▩ But because I have done what is right, I will see you. When I awake, I will be fully satisfied, for I will see you face to face.

The Christian life is a process of becoming more and more like Christ. The process will not be complete until we see Christ face to face, but knowing that it is our ultimate destiny should motivate us to stay pure.

LAB note for 1 John 3:2–3

(1 John 3:2) (John 1:12) (2 Peter 1:4) (Isaiah 64:4) (1 Corinthians 13:12) (Philippians 3:20–21) (Psalm 17:15)

June 19

Who will be able to survive?

Who will be able to endure it when he comes? . . . For he will be like a blazing fire that refines metal or like a strong soap that whitens clothes.

I saw a vast crowd, too great to count, from every nation and tribe and people and language, standing in front of the throne and before the Lamb. They were clothed in white and held palm branches in their hands. "These are the ones coming out of the great tribulation. They washed their robes in the blood of the Lamb and made them white. That is why they are standing in front of the throne of God, serving him day and night in his Temple. And he who sits on the throne will live among them and shelter them. They will never again be hungry or thirsty, and they will be fully protected from the scorching noontime heat. For the Lamb who stands in front of the throne will be their Shepherd. He will lead them to the springs of life-giving water. And God will wipe away all their tears."

Now there is no condemnation for those who belong to Christ Jesus. ▪ So Christ has really set us free. Now make sure that you stay free, and don't get tied up again in slavery to the law.

All who have been faithful through the ages will sing before God's throne. Their tribulations and sorrows will be over: no more tears for sin, for all sins are forgiven; no more tears for suffering, for all suffering is over; no more tears for death, for all believers will have been resurrected to die no more. *LAB note for Revelation 7:17*

(Revelation 6:17) (Malachi 3:2) (Revelation 7:9, 14-17) (Romans 8:1) (Galatians 5:1)

June 20

Don't bring your servant to trial! Compared to you, no one is perfect.

"Come now, let us argue this out," says the LORD. "No matter how deep the stain of your sins, I can remove it. I can make you as clean as freshly fallen snow. Even if you are stained as red as crimson, I can make you as white as wool."

He forgave all our sins. He canceled the record that contained the charges against us. He took it and destroyed it by nailing it to Christ's cross.

Since we have been made right in God's sight by faith, we have peace with God because of what Jesus Christ our Lord has done for us. ▩ We have believed in Christ Jesus, that we might be accepted by God because of our faith in Christ. ▩ For no one can ever be made right in God's sight by doing what his law commands. For the more we know God's law, the clearer it becomes that we aren't obeying it.

Everyone who believes in him is freed from all guilt and declared right with God. ▩ How we thank God, who gives us victory over sin and death through Jesus Christ our Lord!

Peace with God means we have been reconciled with him. There is no more hostility between us, no sin blocking our relationship. It is possible only because Jesus paid the price for our sins through his death on the cross.

LAB note for Romans 5:1

(PSALM 143:2) (ISAIAH 1:18) (COLOSSIANS 2:13-14) (ROMANS 5:1) (GALATIANS 2:16) (ROMANS 3:20) (ACTS 13:39) (1 CORINTHIANS 15:57)

June 21

The Holy Spirit tells us clearly that in the last times some will turn away from what we believe; they will follow lying spirits and teachings that come from demons.

Be sure to pay attention to what you hear. ▪ Let the words of Christ, in all their richness, live in your hearts and make you wise. ▪ In every battle you will need faith as your shield to stop the fiery arrows aimed at you by Satan.

Those who love your law have great peace and do not stumble. How sweet are your words to my taste; they are sweeter than honey. Your commandments give me understanding; no wonder I hate every false way of life.

Your word is a lamp for my feet and a light for my path. Your commands make me wiser than my enemies, for your commands are my constant guide.

Satan can disguise himself as an angel of light. ▪ Let God's curse fall on anyone, including myself, who preaches any other message than the one we told you about. Even if an angel comes from heaven and preaches any other message, let him be forever cursed.

But as for me, how good it is to be near God! I have made the Sovereign LORD my shelter, and I will tell everyone about the wonderful things you do.

It is not enough that a teacher appears to know what he is talking about, is disciplined and moral, or says that he is speaking for God. If his words contradict the Bible, his teaching is false. We must guard against any teaching that causes believers to dilute or reject any aspect of their faith.

LAB note for 1 Timothy 4:1–2

(1 TIMOTHY 4:1) (LUKE 8:18) (COLOSSIANS 3:16) (EPHESIANS 6:16) (PSALM 119:165, 103–104) (PSALM 119:105, 98) (2 CORINTHIANS 11:14) (GALATIANS 1:8) (PSALM 73:28)

June 22

Loving God means keeping his commandments.

It is my Father's will that all who see his Son and believe in him should have eternal life. ▪ We can come to God with bold confidence. And we will receive whatever we request because we obey him and do the things that please him.

Take my yoke upon you. Let me teach you, because I am humble and gentle, and you will find rest for your souls. For my yoke fits perfectly, and the burden I give you is light. ▪ If you love me, obey my commandments. Those who obey my commandments are the ones who love me. And because they love me, my Father will love them, and I will love them. And I will reveal myself to each one of them.

Happy is the person who finds wisdom and gains understanding. [Wisdom] will guide you down delightful paths; all her ways are satisfying. ▪ Those who love your law have great peace and do not stumble. ▪ I love God's law with all my heart.

And this is his commandment: We must believe in the name of his Son, Jesus Christ, and love one another. ▪ Love does no wrong to anyone, so love satisfies all of God's requirements.

Jesus never promised that obeying him would be easy. But the hard work and self-discipline of serving Christ is no burden to those who love him. And if our load starts to feel heavy, we can always trust Christ to help us bear it.

LAB note for 1 John 5:3

(1 JOHN 5:3) (JOHN 6:40) (1 JOHN 3:21-22) (MATTHEW 11:29-30) (JOHN 14:15, 21) (PROVERBS 3:13, 17) (PSALM 119:165) (ROMANS 7:22) (1 JOHN 3:23) (ROMANS 13:10)

June 23

Forgive the rebellious sins of my youth.

I have swept away your sins like the morning mists. ▩ I—yes, I alone—am the one who blots out your sins for my own sake and will never think of them again. ▩ "Come now, let us argue this out," says the LORD. "No matter how deep the stain of your sins, I can remove it. I can make you as clean as freshly fallen snow. Even if you are stained as red as crimson, I can make you as white as wool." ▩ I will forgive their wickedness and will never again remember their sins. ▩ You will trample our sins under your feet and throw them into the depths of the ocean!

Yes, it was good for me to suffer this anguish, for you have rescued me from death and have forgiven all my sins. ▩ Where is another God like you, who pardons the sins of the survivors among his people? You cannot stay angry with your people forever, because you delight in showing mercy. ▩ All praise to him who loves us and has freed us from our sins by shedding his blood for us. He has made us his kingdom and his priests who serve before God his Father. Give to him everlasting glory! He rules forever and ever! Amen!

How tempting it is to remind someone of a past offense! But when God forgives our sins, he totally forgets them. We never have to fear that he will remind us of them later. Because God forgives our sins, we need to forgive others. *LAB note for Isaiah 43:25*

(PSALM 25:7) (ISAIAH 44:22) (ISAIAH 43:25) (ISAIAH 1:18) (JEREMIAH 31:34) (MICAH 7:19) (ISAIAH 38:17) (MICAH 7:18) (REVELATION 1:5-6)

June 24

I am the one who corrects and disciplines everyone I love.

My child, don't ignore it when the Lord disciplines you, and don't be discouraged when he corrects you. For the Lord disciplines those he loves, and he punishes those he accepts as his children. ▪ The LORD corrects those he loves, just as a father corrects a child in whom he delights. ▪ For though he wounds, he also bandages. ▪ Humble yourselves under the mighty power of God, and in his good time he will honor you. ▪ I have refined you in the furnace of suffering. ▪ I am the LORD your God, who teaches you what is good and leads you along the paths you should follow.

He does not enjoy hurting people or causing them sorrow. ▪ He has not punished us for all our sins, nor does he deal with us as we deserve. For his unfailing love toward those who fear him is as great as the height of the heavens above the earth. He has removed our rebellious acts as far away from us as the east is from the west. The LORD is like a father to his children, tender and compassionate to those who fear him. For he understands how weak we are; he knows we are only dust.

Are you lukewarm in your devotion to God? God may discipline you to help you out of your uncaring attitude, but he uses only loving discipline. Just as the spark of love can be rekindled in marriage, so the Holy Spirit can reignite our zeal for God when we allow him to work in our heart.

LAB note for Revelation 3:19

(REVELATION 3:19) (HEBREWS 12:5-6) (PROVERBS 3:12) (JOB 5:18) (1 PETER 5:6) (ISAIAH 48:10) (ISAIAH 48:17) (LAMENTATIONS 3:33) (PSALM 103:10-14)

June 25

He is in heaven, and you are only here on earth. So let your words be few.

When you pray, don't babble on and on as people of other religions do. They think their prayers are answered only by repeating their words again and again. Don't be like them, because your Father knows exactly what you need even before you ask him!

They called on the name of Baal all morning, shouting, "O Baal, answer us!"

Two men went to the Temple to pray. One was a Pharisee, and the other was a dishonest tax collector. The proud Pharisee stood by himself and prayed this prayer: "I thank you, God, that I am not a sinner like everyone else, especially like that tax collector over there! For I never cheat, I don't sin, I don't commit adultery." But the tax collector stood at a distance and dared not even lift his eyes to heaven as he prayed. Instead, he beat his chest in sorrow, saying, "O God, be merciful to me, for I am a sinner." I tell you, this sinner, not the Pharisee, returned home justified before God. For the proud will be humbled, but the humble will be honored.

We don't even know what we should pray for, nor how we should pray. ❖ Lord, teach us to pray.

When we enter the house of God, we should have the attitude of being open and ready to listen to God, not to dictate to him what we think he should do.

LAB note for Ecclesiastes 5:1

(ECCLESIASTES 5:2) (MATTHEW 6:7-8) (1 KINGS 18:26) (LUKE 18:10-11, 13-14) (ROMANS 8:26) (LUKE 11:1)

June 26

Draw close to God, and God will draw close to you.

Enoch . . . enjoyed a close relationship with God. ▪ Can two people walk together without agreeing on the direction? ▪ But as for me, how good it is to be near God! I have made the Sovereign LORD my shelter, and I will tell everyone about the wonderful things you do.

The LORD will stay with you as long as you stay with him! Whenever you seek him, you will find him. But if you abandon him, he will abandon you. Whenever you were in distress and turned to the LORD, the God of Israel, and sought him out, you found him.

"I know the plans I have for you," says the LORD. "They are plans for good and not for disaster, to give you a future and a hope. In those days when you pray, I will listen. If you look for me in earnest, you will find me when you seek me."

We can boldly enter heaven's Most Holy Place because of the blood of Jesus. This is the new, life-giving way that Christ has opened up for us through the sacred curtain, by means of his death for us. And since we have a great High Priest who rules over God's people, let us go right into the presence of God, with true hearts fully trusting him.

According to God's wise plan, we are to have a future and a hope; consequently we can call upon him in confidence. If we seek him wholeheartedly, he will be found. Nothing can break our fellowship with God.

LAB note for Jeremiah 29:13

(JAMES 4:8) (GENESIS 5:24) (AMOS 3:3) (PSALM 73:28) (2 CHRONICLES 15:2, 4) (JEREMIAH 29:11-13) (HEBREWS 10:19-22)

June 27

[Jesus] went back to pray a third time.

While Jesus was here on earth, he offered prayers and pleadings, with a loud cry and tears, to the one who could deliver him out of death.

Oh, that we might know the LORD! Let us press on to know him! Then he will respond to us as surely as the arrival of dawn or the coming of rains in early spring. ▩ Be patient in trouble, and always be prayerful. ▩ Pray at all times and on every occasion in the power of the Holy Spirit. Stay alert and be persistent in your prayers for all Christians everywhere. ▩ Don't worry about anything; instead, pray about everything. Tell God what you need, and thank him for all he has done. If you do this, you will experience God's peace, which is far more wonderful than the human mind can understand. His peace will guard your hearts and minds as you live in Christ Jesus.

I want your will, not mine. ▩ We can be confident that he will listen to us whenever we ask him for anything in line with his will. ▩ Take delight in the LORD, and he will give you your heart's desires. Commit everything you do to the LORD. Trust him, and he will help you.

Have you ever felt that God didn't hear your prayers? Be sure you are praying with reverent submission, willing to do what God wants. God responds to his obedient children. *LAB note for Hebrews 5:7*

(MATTHEW 26:44) (HEBREWS 5:7) (HOSEA 6:3) (ROMANS 12:12) (EPHESIANS 6:18) (PHILIPPIANS 4:6-7) (MATTHEW 26:39) (1 JOHN 5:14) (PSALM 37:4-5)

June 28

Since we are his children, we will share his treasures—for everything God gives to his Son, Christ, is ours, too.

Now that you belong to Christ, you are the true children of Abraham. You are his heirs, and now all the promises God gave to him belong to you.

See how very much our heavenly Father loves us, for he allows us to be called his children, and we really are! ▪ Now you are no longer a slave but God's own child. And since you are his child, everything he has belongs to you. ▪ His unchanging plan has always been to adopt us into his own family by bringing us to himself through Jesus Christ. And this gave him great pleasure.

Father, I want these whom you've given me to be with me, so they can see my glory. You gave me the glory because you loved me even before the world began!

To all who are victorious, who obey me to the very end, I will give authority over all the nations. They will rule the nations with an iron rod and smash them like clay pots. ▪ I will invite everyone who is victorious to sit with me on my throne, just as I was victorious and sat with my Father on his throne.

To live as Jesus did—serving others, giving up one's rights, resisting pressures to conform to the world—always exacts a price. Nothing we suffer, however, can compare to the great price that Jesus paid to save us.

LAB note for Romans 8:17

(ROMANS 8:17) (GALATIANS 3:29) (1 JOHN 3:1) (GALATIANS 4:7) (EPHESIANS 1:5) (JOHN 17:24) (REVELATION 2:26-27) (REVELATION 3:21)

June 29

God chose things despised by the world.

How can this be? . . . These people are all from Galilee, and yet we hear them speaking the languages of the lands where we were born!

Jesus . . . saw two brothers—Simon, also called Peter, and Andrew—fishing with a net, for they were commercial fishermen. Jesus called out to them, "Come, be my disciples, and I will show you how to fish for people!" ▪ The members of the council were amazed when they saw the boldness of Peter and John, for they could see that they were ordinary men who had had no special training. They also recognized them as men who had been with Jesus.

My message and my preaching were very plain. I did not use wise and persuasive speeches, but the Holy Spirit was powerful among you.

You didn't choose me. I chose you. I appointed you to go and produce fruit that will last. Those who remain in me, and I in them, will produce much fruit. For apart from me you can do nothing. ▪ This precious treasure—this light and power that now shine within us—is held in perishable containers, that is, in our weak bodies. So everyone can see that our glorious power is from God and is not our own.

We all need to fish for souls. If we practice Christ's teachings and share the Good News with others, we will be able to draw those around us to Christ like a fisherman who pulls fish into his boat with nets.

LAB note for Matthew 4:18-20

(1 Corinthians 1:28) (Acts 2:7) (Matthew 4:18-19) (Acts 4:13)
(1 Corinthians 2:4) (John 15:16, 5) (2 Corinthians 4:7)

June 30

Don't try to act important, but enjoy the company of ordinary people.

How can you claim that you have faith in our glorious Lord Jesus Christ if you favor some people more than others? Listen to me, dear brothers and sisters. Hasn't God chosen the poor in this world to be rich in faith? Aren't they the ones who will inherit the kingdom God promised to those who love him?

Don't think only of your own good. Think of other Christians and what is best for them. ▩ If we have enough food and clothing, let us be content. But people who long to be rich fall into temptation and are trapped by many foolish and harmful desires that plunge them into ruin and destruction.

God deliberately chose things the world considers foolish in order to shame those who are powerful. God chose things despised by the world, things counted as nothing at all, and used them to bring to nothing what the world considers important, so that no one can ever boast in the presence of God.

God alone made it possible for you to be in Christ Jesus.

Are you easily impressed by status, wealth, or fame? Are you partial to the "haves" while ignoring the "have nots"? This attitude is sinful. God views all people as equals, and if he favors anyone, it is the poor and the powerless. We should follow his example.

LAB note for James 2:1–7

(ROMANS 12:16) (JAMES 2:1, 5) (1 CORINTHIANS 10:24) (1 TIMOTHY 6:8–9) (1 CORINTHIANS 1:27–29) (1 CORINTHIANS 1:30)

July

On Freedom's Wings

Courage and integrity, truth and grace
Safe boundaries without divisive barriers
These are the foundation of freedom.

Any government can offer religious freedom, but only God offers spiritual freedom. During this independence season, don't miss out on the far greater treasure that can be found only in God.

July 1

Your love for me is very great. You have rescued me from the depths of death.

Do not be afraid, for I have ransomed you. I have called you by name; you are mine. I am the LORD, and there is no other Savior. I—yes, I alone—am the one who blots out your sins for my sake and will never think of them again. ▩ They trust in their wealth and boast of great riches. Yet they cannot redeem themselves from death by paying a ransom to God. Redemption does not come so easily, for no one can pay enough. ▩ I have found a ransom for his life. ▩ God is so rich in mercy, and he loved us so very much, that even while we were dead because of our sins, he gave us life when he raised Christ from the dead.

There is salvation in no one else! There is no other name in all of heaven for people to call on to save them. ▩ God our Savior . . . wants everyone to be saved and to understand the truth. For there is only one God and one Mediator who can reconcile God and people. He is the man Christ Jesus. He gave his life to purchase freedom for everyone.

Your unfailing love will last forever. Your faithfulness is as enduring as the heavens.

God created the people of Israel, and they were special to him. God redeemed them and called them by name to be those who belong to him. He protected them in times of trouble. We are important to God, too. And if we claim to belong to God, we should never do anything that would bring shame to him. *LAB note for Isaiah 43:1-4*

(PSALM 86:13) (ISAIAH 43:1, 11, 25) (PSALM 49:6-8) (JOB 33:24) (EPHESIANS 2:4-5) (ACTS 4:12) (1 TIMOTHY 2:3-6) (PSALM 89:2)

July 2

If sinners entice you, turn your back on them! They may say, "Come and join us."

The woman was convinced . . . it would make her so wise! So she ate some of the fruit. She also gave some to her husband, who was with her. Then he ate it, too. ▪ Didn't God punish all the people of Israel when Achan, a member of the clan of Zerah, sinned by stealing the things set apart for the LORD?

Do not join a crowd that intends to do evil.

You can enter God's Kingdom only through the narrow gate. The highway to hell is broad, and its gate is wide for the many who choose the easy way.

For we are not our own masters when we live or when we die. ▪ You have been called to live in freedom—not freedom to satisfy your sinful nature, but freedom to serve one another in love. ▪ You must be careful with this freedom of yours. Do not cause a brother or sister with a weaker conscience to stumble. You are sinning against Christ when you sin against other Christians by encouraging them to do something they believe is wrong.

All of us have strayed away like sheep. We have left God's paths to follow our own. Yet the LORD laid on him the guilt and sins of us all.

Sin, even when attractive, is deadly. We must learn to make choices, not on the basis of flashy appeal or short-range pleasure, but in view of the long-range effects. Sometimes this means steering clear of people who want to entice us into activities that we know are wrong.

LAB note for Proverbs 1:10

(PROVERBS 1:10) (GENESIS 3:6) (JOSHUA 22:20) (EXODUS 23:2) (MATTHEW 7:13) (ROMANS 14:7) (GALATIANS 5:13) (1 CORINTHIANS 8:9, 12) (ISAIAH 53:6)

July 3

I am constantly aware of your unfailing love, and I have lived according to your truth.

The LORD is kind and merciful, slow to get angry, full of unfailing love. ▩ Your Father in heaven . . . gives his sunlight to both the evil and the good, and he sends rain on the just and on the unjust, too. ▩ Follow God's example in everything you do, because you are his dear children. Live a life filled with love for others, following the example of Christ, who loved you and gave himself as a sacrifice to take away your sins. And God was pleased, because that sacrifice was like sweet perfume to him. ▩ Be kind to each other, tenderhearted, forgiving one another, just as God through Christ has forgiven you. ▩ Now you can have sincere love for each other as brothers and sisters because you were cleansed from your sins when you accepted the truth of the Good News. So see to it that you really do love each other intensely with all your hearts. ▩ Whatever we do, it is because Christ's love controls us.

Love your enemies! Do good to them! Lend to them! And don't be concerned that they might not repay. Then your reward from heaven will be very great, and you will truly be acting as children of the Most High, for he is kind to the unthankful and to those who are wicked.

"Sincere" love involves selfless giving. God's love and forgiveness free you to take your eyes off yourselves and meet others' needs. By sacrificing his life, Christ showed that he truly loves you. Now you can love others by following his example and giving of yourself sacrificially.

LAB note for 1 Peter 1:22

(PSALM 26:3) (PSALM 145:8) (MATTHEW 5:45) (EPHESIANS 5:1–2) (EPHESIANS 4:32) (1 PETER 1:22) (2 CORINTHIANS 5:14) (LUKE 6:35)

July 4

Jesus was led out into the wilderness by the Holy Spirit to be tempted there by the Devil.

While Jesus was here on earth, he offered prayers and pleadings, with a loud cry and tears, to the one who could deliver him out of death. And God heard his prayers because of his reverence for God. So even though Jesus was God's Son, he learned obedience from the things he suffered. In this way, God qualified him as a perfect High Priest, and he became the source of eternal salvation for all those who obey him. ▨ This High Priest of ours understands our weaknesses, for he faced all of the same temptations we do, yet he did not sin.

The temptations that come into your life are no different from what others experience. And God is faithful. He will keep the temptation from becoming so strong that you can't stand up against it. When you are tempted, he will show you a way out so that you will not give in to it. ▨ My gracious favor is all you need. My power works best in your weakness.

A person has not shown true obedience if he or she has never had an opportunity to disobey. When God led Israel into the wilderness to humble and test them, he wanted to see whether or not they would really obey him. We, too, will be tested—and we should be alert and ready for it!

LAB note for Matthew 4:1

(Matthew 4:1) (Hebrews 5:7-9) (Hebrews 4:15)
(1 Corinthians 10:13) (2 Corinthians 12:9)

July 5

Even I, the Son of Man, came here not to be served but to serve others, and to give my life as a ransom for many.

Under the old system, the blood of goats and bulls and the ashes of a young cow could cleanse people's bodies from ritual defilement. Just think how much more the blood of Christ will purify our hearts from deeds that lead to death so that we can worship the living God. For by the power of the eternal Spirit, Christ offered himself to God as a perfect sacrifice for our sins.

He was led as a lamb to the slaughter. ▪ I lay down my life for the sheep. No one can take my life from me. I lay down my life voluntarily. For I have the right to lay it down when I want to and also the power to take it again.

The life of any creature is in its blood. I have given you the blood so you can make atonement for your sins. It is the blood, representing life, that brings you atonement. ▪ Without the shedding of blood, there is no forgiveness of sins.

God showed his great love for us by sending Christ to die for us while we were still sinners. And since we have been made right in God's sight by the blood of Christ, he will certainly save us from God's judgment.

You cannot work hard to make yourself good enough for God. Rules and rituals have never cleansed people's hearts. Only Jesus' death and what it means for you can heal your conscience and deliver you from the frustration of trying to earn God's favor. *LAB note for Hebrews 9:12-14*

(MATTHEW 20:28) (HEBREWS 9:13-14) (ISAIAH 53:7) (JOHN 10:15, 18) (LEVITICUS 17:11) (HEBREWS 9:22) (ROMANS 5:8-9)

July 6

If we confess our sins to him, he is faithful and just to forgive us and to cleanse us from every wrong.

Have mercy on me, O God, because of your unfailing love. Because of your great compassion, blot out the stain of my sins. Wash me clean from my guilt. Purify me from my sin. For I recognize my shameful deeds—they haunt me day and night. Against you, and you alone, have I sinned.

He returned home to his father. And while he was still a long distance away, his father saw him coming. Filled with love and compassion, he ran to his son, embraced him, and kissed him. ▪ I have swept away your sins like the morning mists. I have scattered your offenses like the clouds. Oh, return to me, for I have paid the price to set you free. ▪ Your sins have been forgiven because of Jesus. ▪ God through Christ has forgiven you.

I will sprinkle clean water on you, and you will be clean. . . . And I will give you a new heart with new and right desires, and I will put a new spirit in you. I will take out your stony heart of sin and give you a new, obedient heart. And I will put my Spirit in you so you will obey my laws and do whatever I command. ▪ They will walk with me in white, for they are worthy.

When we come to Christ, he forgives all the sins we have committed or will ever commit. We don't need to confess the sins of the past all over again, and we don't need to fear that God will reject us if we don't keep our slate perfectly clean. Our relationship with Christ is secure.

LAB note for 1 John 1:9

(1 John 1:9) (Psalm 51:1-4) (Luke 15:20) (Isaiah 44:22) (1 John 2:12) (Ephesians 4:32) (Ezekiel 36:25-27) (Revelation 3:4)

July 7

A student is not greater than the teacher.

You call me "Teacher" and "Lord," and you are right, because it is true.

The student shares the teacher's fate. The servant shares the master's fate. ▩ Since they persecuted me, naturally they will persecute you. And if they had listened to me, they would listen to you! ▩ I have given them your word. And the world hates them because they do not belong to the world, just as I do not.

Think about all he endured when sinful people did such terrible things to him, so that you don't become weary and give up. After all, you have not yet given your lives in your struggle against sin.

Let us run with endurance the race that God has set before us. We do this by keeping our eyes on Jesus, on whom our faith depends from start to finish. He was willing to die a shameful death on the cross because of the joy he knew would be his afterward. Now he is seated in the place of highest honor beside God's throne in heaven. ▩ Since Christ suffered physical pain, you must arm yourselves with the same attitude he had, and be ready to suffer, too.

The world hates Christians because Christians' values differ from the world's. Because Christ's followers don't cooperate with the world by joining in their sin, they are living accusations against the world's immorality. The world follows Satan's agenda. *LAB note for John 17:14*

(MATTHEW 10:24) (JOHN 13:13) (MATTHEW 10:25) (JOHN 15:20) (JOHN 17:14) (HEBREWS 12:3-4) (HEBREWS 12:1-2) (1 PETER 4:1)

July 8

My son, give me your heart.

Oh, that they would always have hearts like this, that they might fear me and obey all my commands! If they did, they and their descendants would prosper forever.

Your heart is not right before God. ▩ The sinful nature is always hostile to God. It never did obey God's laws, and it never will. That's why those who are still under the control of their sinful nature can never please God.

Their first action was to dedicate themselves to the Lord. ▩ Above all else, guard your heart, for it affects everything you do.

Work hard and cheerfully at whatever you do, as though you were working for the Lord rather than for people. ▩ Work hard, but not just to please your masters when they are watching. As slaves of Christ, do the will of God with all your heart. Work with enthusiasm, as though you were working for the Lord rather than for people.

If you will help me, I will run to follow your commands.

There is a difference between doing something because it is required and doing something because we want to. God is not interested in forced religious exercises and rule keeping. He wants our hearts and lives completely dedicated to him. *LAB note for Deuteronomy 5:29*

(PROVERBS 23:26) (DEUTERONOMY 5:29) (ACTS 8:21) (ROMANS 8:7-8) (2 CORINTHIANS 8:5) (PROVERBS 4:23) (COLOSSIANS 3:23) (EPHESIANS 6:6-7) (PSALM 119:32)

July 9

I will protect and deliver you.

Who can snatch the plunder of war from the hands of a warrior? Who can demand that a tyrant let his captives go? But the LORD says, "The captives of warriors will be released, and the plunder of tyrants will be retrieved. For I will fight those who fight you, and I will save your children. I will feed your enemies with their own flesh. They will be drunk with rivers of their own blood. All the world will know that I, the LORD, am your Savior and Redeemer, the Mighty One of Israel." ▩ Don't be afraid, for I am with you. Do not be dismayed, for I am your God. I will strengthen you. I will help you. I will uphold you with my victorious right hand.

This High Priest of ours understands our weaknesses, for he faced all of the same temptations we do, yet he did not sin. ▩ Since he himself has gone through suffering and temptation, he is able to help us when we are being tempted. ▩ The steps of the godly are directed by the LORD. He delights in every detail of their lives. Though they stumble, they will not fall, for the LORD holds them by the hand.

God proved to the world that he is God by doing the impossible—causing warriors to set their captives free and even return the plunder they had taken! Never should we doubt that God will fulfill his promises. He will even do the impossible to make them come true.

Isaiah 49:24-25

(JEREMIAH 15:20) (ISAIAH 49:24-26) (ISAIAH 41:10) (HEBREWS 4:15) (HEBREWS 2:18) (PSALM 37:23-24)

July 10

He satisfies the thirsty and fills the hungry with good things.

You have had a taste of the Lord's kindness.

O God, you are my God; I earnestly search for you. My soul thirsts for you; my whole body longs for you in this parched and weary land where there is no water. I have seen you in your sanctuary and gazed upon your power and glory. Your unfailing love is better to me than life itself; how I praise you! I will honor you as long as I live, lifting up my hands to you in prayer. ▪ I long, yes, I faint with longing to enter the courts of the LORD. ▪ I long to go and be with Christ.

When I awake, I will be fully satisfied, for I will see you face to face. ▪ They will never again be hungry or thirsty, and they will be fully protected from the scorching noontime heat. For the Lamb who stands in front of the throne will be their Shepherd. He will lead them to the springs of life-giving water. And God will wipe away all their tears. ▪ You feed them from the abundance of your own house, letting them drink from your river of delight. ▪ "I will satisfy my people with my bounty. I, the LORD, have spoken!"

Those who recognize their own lostness can receive the offer of Jesus to satisfy their needs. Jesus is the way, the bread from heaven, the living water, and the giver of rest. Have you received his life-giving offer?

LAB note for Psalm 107:4-9

(PSALM 107:9) (1 PETER 2:3) (PSALM 63:1-4) (PSALM 84:2) (PHILIPPIANS 1:23) (PSALM 17:15) (REVELATION 7:16-17) (PSALM 36:8) (JEREMIAH 31:14)

July 11

I will personally go with you. . . . I will give you rest—everything will be fine for you.

Be strong and courageous! Do not be afraid of them! The LORD your God will go ahead of you. He will neither fail you nor forsake you. ▪ I command you—be strong and courageous! Do not be afraid or discouraged. For the LORD your God is with you wherever you go. ▪ You will find favor with both God and people, and you will gain a good reputation. Trust in the LORD with all your heart; do not depend on your own understanding. Seek his will in all you do, and he will direct your paths. ▪ Happy is the person who finds wisdom and gains understanding. For the profit of wisdom is better than silver, and her wages are better than gold. Wisdom is more precious than rubies; nothing you desire can compare with her.

God has said, "I will never fail you. I will never forsake you." That is why we can say with confidence, "The Lord is my helper, so I will not be afraid. What can mere mortals do to me?" ▪ Our only power and success come from God.

I know, LORD, that a person's life is not his own. No one is able to plan his own course.

To receive God's guidance we must seek God's will in all we do. This means turning every area of life over to him. Examine your values and priorities. What is important to you? In what areas have you not acknowledged him? *LAB note for Psalm 3:6*

(EXODUS 33:14) (DEUTERONOMY 31:6, 8) (JOSHUA 1:9) (PROVERBS 3:4-6) (PROVERBS 3:13-15) (HEBREWS 13:5-6) (2 CORINTHIANS 3:5) (JEREMIAH 10:23)

July 12

Think of ways to encourage one another to outbursts of love and good deeds.

Timely advice is as lovely as golden apples in a silver basket.

Those who feared the LORD spoke with each other, and the LORD listened to what they said. In his presence, a scroll of remembrance was written to record the names of those who feared him and loved to think about him. ▪ If two of you agree down here on earth concerning anything you ask, my Father in heaven will do it for you.

The LORD God said, "It is not good for the man to be alone." ▪ Two people can accomplish more than twice as much as one; they get a better return for their labor. If one person falls, the other can reach out and help. But people who are alone when they fall are in real trouble.

Live in such a way that you will not put an obstacle in another Christian's path. If another Christian is distressed by what you eat, you are not acting in love if you eat it. Don't let your eating ruin someone for whom Christ died. Don't tear apart the work of God over what you eat. Remember, there is nothing wrong with these things in themselves. But it is wrong to eat anything if it makes another person stumble. ▪ Share each other's troubles and problems, and in this way obey the law of Christ.

God will remember those who remain faithful to him, and who love, fear, honor, and respect him. Is your name written in the scroll of remembrance? *LAB note for Malachi 3:16*

(HEBREWS 10:24) (PROVERBS 25:11) (MALACHI 3:16) (MATTHEW 18:19) (GENESIS 2:18) (ECCLESIASTES 4:9-10) (ROMANS 14:13, 15, 20) (GALATIANS 6:2)

July 13

Search the book of the LORD.

Commit yourselves completely to these words of mine. Tie them to your hands as a reminder, and wear them on your forehead. ▪ Study this Book of the Law continually. Meditate on it day and night so you may be sure to obey all that is written in it. Only then will you succeed.

The godly offer good counsel. ▪ I have followed your commands, which have kept me from going along with cruel and evil people. ▪ I had hidden your word in my heart, that I might not sin against you.

Because [we ourselves heard the voice], we have even greater confidence in the message proclaimed by the prophets. Pay close attention to what they wrote, for their words are like a light shining in a dark place—until the day Christ appears and his brilliant light shines in your hearts. ▪ Such things were written in the Scriptures long ago to teach us. They give us hope and encouragement as we wait patiently for God's promises.

Hiding (keeping) God's Word in our heart is a deterrent to sin. This alone should inspire us to memorize Scripture. But memorization alone will not keep us from sin; we must also put God's Word to work in our life, making it a vital guide for everything we do. *LAB note for Psalm 119:11*

(Isaiah 34:16) (Deuteronomy 11:18) (Joshua 1:8) (Psalm 37:30) (Psalm 17:4) (Psalm 119:11) (2 Peter 1:19) (Romans 15:4)

July 14

Whatever is in your heart determines what you say.

Let the words of Christ, in all their richness, live in your hearts and make you wise. ▪ A good person produces good words from a good heart.

Those who love to talk will experience the consequences, for the tongue can kill or nourish life. ▪ A good person produces good deeds from a good heart. . . . Whatever is in your heart determines what you say. ▪ The godly offer good counsel; they know what is right from wrong. ▪ Don't use foul or abusive language. Let everything you say be good and helpful, so that your words will be an encouragement to those who hear them.

You must give an account on judgment day of every idle word you speak. The words you say now reflect your fate then; either you will be justified by them or you will be condemned.

If anyone acknowledges me publicly here on earth, I will openly acknowledge that person before my Father in heaven. ▪ Make the most of every opportunity. Let your conversation be gracious and effective so that you will have the right answer for everyone.

Jesus reminds us that our speech and actions reveal our true underlying beliefs, attitudes, and motivations. The good impressions we try to make cannot last if our heart is deceptive. What is in your heart will come out in your speech and behavior. *LAB note for Luke 6:45*

(Matthew 12:34) (Colossians 3:16) (Matthew 12:35) (Proverbs 18:21) (Luke 6:45) (Psalm 37:30) (Ephesians 4:29) (Matthew 12:36-37) (Matthew 10:32) (Colossians 4:5-6)

July 15

We prayed to our God and guarded the city day and night to protect ourselves.

Keep alert and pray. Otherwise temptation will overpower you. ▪ Devote yourselves to prayer with an alert mind and a thankful heart. ▪ Give all your worries and cares to God, for he cares about what happens to you. Be careful! Watch out for attacks from the Devil, your great enemy. He prowls around like a roaring lion, looking for some victim to devour. Take a firm stand against him, and be strong in your faith.

Why do you call me "Lord," when you won't obey me? ▪ It is a message to obey, not just to listen to.

Then the LORD said to Moses, "Why are you crying out to me? Tell the people to get moving!"

Don't worry about anything; instead, pray about everything. Tell God what you need, and thank him for all he has done. If you do this, you will experience God's peace, which is far more wonderful than the human mind can understand. His peace will guard your hearts and minds as you live in Christ Jesus.

The way to overcome temptation is to keep alert and pray. Because temptation strikes where we are most vulnerable, we can't resist it alone. Prayer is essential because God's strength can shore up our defenses and defeat Satan's power. *LAB note for Matthew 26:40-41*

(NEHEMIAH 4:9) (MATTHEW 26:41) (COLOSSIANS 4:2) (1 PETER 5:7-9) (LUKE 6:46) (JAMES 1:22) (EXODUS 14:15) (PHILIPPIANS 4:6-7)

July 16

A gracious and compassionate God, slow to get angry and filled with unfailing love.

Please, Lord, prove that your power is as great as you have claimed it to be. For you said, "The LORD is slow to anger and rich in unfailing love, forgiving every kind of sin and rebellion. Even so he does not leave sin unpunished, but he punishes the children for the sins of their parents to the third and fourth generations."

Oh, do not hold us guilty for our former sins! Let your tenderhearted mercies quickly meet our needs, for we are brought low to the dust. Help us, O God of our salvation! Help us for the honor of your name. Oh, save us and forgive our sins. ▩ LORD, our wickedness has caught up with us. We have sinned against you. So please, help us for the sake of your own reputation. LORD, we confess our wickedness and that of our ancestors, too. ▩ Oh, don't be so angry with us, LORD. Please don't remember our sins forever. Look at us, we pray, and see that we are all your people.

LORD, if you kept a record of our sins, who, O Lord, could ever survive? But you offer forgiveness, that we might learn to fear you.

Jonah didn't want the Ninevites forgiven; he wanted them destroyed. He did not understand that the God of Israel was also the God of the whole world. Are you surprised when some unlikely person turns to God? We must not forget that in reality we do not deserve to be forgiven by God.

LAB note for Jonah 4:1-2

(JONAH 4:2) (NUMBERS 14:17-18) (PSALM 79:8-9) (JEREMIAH 14:7, 20) (ISAIAH 64:9) (PSALM 130:3-4)

July 17

She has done what she could.

This poor widow has given more than all the rest of them. ▪ If anyone gives you even a cup of water because you belong to the Messiah, I assure you, that person will be rewarded. ▪ If you are really eager to give, it isn't important how much you are able to give. God wants you to give what you have, not what you don't have.

Let us stop just saying we love each other; let us really show it by our actions. ▪ Suppose you see a brother or sister who needs food or clothing, and you say, "Well, good-bye and God bless you; stay warm and eat well"—but then you don't give that person any food or clothing. What good does that do? ▪ A farmer who plants only a few seeds will get a small crop. But the one who plants generously will get a generous crop. You must each make up your own mind as to how much you should give. Don't give reluctantly or in response to pressure. For God loves the person who gives cheerfully.

When you obey me you should say, "We are not worthy of praise. We are servants who have simply done our duty."

When we consider ourselves generous in giving a small percentage of our income to the Lord, we resemble those who gave "a tiny part of their surplus." As believers we should consider increasing our giving—whether money, time, or talents—to a point beyond mere convenience.

LAB note for Luke 21:1-4

(MARK 14:8) (LUKE 21:3) (MARK 9:41) (2 CORINTHIANS 8:12) (1 JOHN 3:18) (JAMES 2:15-16) (2 CORINTHIANS 9:6-7) (LUKE 17:10)

July 18

He, the Mighty One, is holy, and he has done great things for me.

Who else among the gods is like you, O LORD? Who is glorious in holiness like you—so awesome in splendor, performing such wonders? ▪ Nowhere among the pagan gods is there a god like you, O Lord. There are no other miracles like yours. ▪ Who will not fear, O Lord, and glorify your name? For you alone are holy. ▪ May your name be honored.

Praise the Lord, the God of Israel, because he has visited his people and redeemed them.

Who is this who comes from Edom, from the city of Bozrah, with his clothing stained red? Who is this in royal robes, marching in the greatness of his strength? "It is I, the LORD, announcing your salvation! It is I, the LORD, who is mighty to save!" ▪ For the LORD your God has arrived to live among you. He is a mighty savior. He will rejoice over you with great gladness.

Now glory be to God! By his mighty power at work within us, he is able to accomplish infinitely more than we would ever dare to ask or hope. May he be given glory in the church and in Christ Jesus forever and ever through endless ages.

The God of the Bible is unique! He is alive and able to do mighty deeds for those who love him. All human-created deities are powerless because they are merely inventions of the mind, not living beings. You need never fear that God is only one among many or that you may be worshiping the wrong God. The Lord alone is God.

LAB note for Psalm 86:8-10

(LUKE 1:49) (EXODUS 15:11) (PSALM 86:8) (REVELATION 15:4) (MATTHEW 6:9) (LUKE 1:68) (ISAIAH 63:1) (ZEPHANIAH 3:17) (EPHESIANS 3:20-21)

July 19

Whatever you do or say, let it be as a representative of the Lord Jesus.

He was despised and rejected—a man of sorrows, acquainted with bitterest grief. ▩ Here on earth you will have many trials and sorrows. But take heart, because I have overcome the world.

He is the kind of high priest we need because he is holy and blameless, unstained by sin. He has now been set apart from sinners, and he has been given the highest place of honor in heaven. ▩ No one can speak a word of blame against you. You are to live clean, innocent lives as children of God in a dark world full of crooked and perverse people.

Jesus of Nazareth . . . went around doing good and healing all who were oppressed by the Devil, for God was with him. ▩ Whenever we have the opportunity, we should do good to everyone, especially to our Christian brothers and sisters.

The one who is the true light, who gives light to everyone, was going to come into the world. ▩ You are the light of the world—like a city on a mountain, glowing in the night for all to see. Let your good deeds shine out for all to see, so that everyone will praise your heavenly Father.

As a Christian, you represent Christ at all times—wherever you go and whatever you say. What impression do people have of Christ when they see or talk with you? What changes would you make in your life in order to honor Christ?

LAB note for Colossians 3:17

(Colossians 3:17) (Isaiah 53:3) (John 16:33) (Hebrews 7:26) (Philippians 2:15) (Acts 10:38) (Galatians 6:10) (John 1:9) (Matthew 5:14, 16)

July 20

Live in such a way that God's love can bless you.

Remain in me, and I will remain in you. For a branch cannot produce fruit if it is severed from the vine, and you cannot be fruitful apart from me. Yes, I am the vine; you are the branches. Those who remain in me, and I in them, will produce much fruit. For apart from me you can do nothing.

When the Holy Spirit controls our lives, he will produce . . . love.

My true disciples produce much fruit. This brings great glory to my Father. I have loved you even as the Father has loved me. Remain in my love. When you obey me, you remain in my love, just as I obey my Father and remain in his love. ▪ Those who obey God's word really do love him.

I command you to love each other in the same way that I love you. ▪ God showed his great love for us by sending Christ to die for us while we were still sinners. ▪ We know how much God loves us, and we have put our trust in him. God is love, and all who live in love live in God, and God lives in them.

In order for God's love to bless you, you must live close to God and his people. You must not listen to false teachers—those who would try to pull you away from God. That means you should constantly check what others do and say against the Scriptures. *LAB note for Jude 1:21*

(JUDE 1:21) (JOHN 15:4-5) (GALATIANS 5:22) (JOHN 15:8-10) (1 JOHN 2:5) (JOHN 15:12) (ROMANS 5:8) (1 JOHN 4:16)

July 21

We have passed from death to eternal life.

Those who listen to my message and believe in God who sent me have eternal life. They will never be condemned for their sins, but they have already passed from death into life. ▩ Whoever has God's Son has life; whoever does not have his Son does not have life.

It is God who gives us, along with you, the ability to stand firm for Christ. He has commissioned us, and he has identified us as his own by placing the Holy Spirit in our hearts as the first installment of everything he will give us. ▩ It is by our actions that we know we are living in the truth, so we will be confident when we stand before the Lord. If our conscience is clear, we can come to God with bold confidence. ▩ We know that we are children of God.

Once you were dead, doomed forever because of your many sins. Even while we were dead because of our sins, he gave us life when he raised Christ from the dead. (It is only by God's special favor that you have been saved!) ▩ He has rescued us from the one who rules in the kingdom of darkness, and he has brought us into the Kingdom of his dear Son.

"Eternal life"—living forever with God—begins when you accept Jesus Christ as Savior. At that moment new life begins in you. It is a completed transaction. You still will face physical death, but when Christ returns again, your body will be resurrected to live forever.

LAB note for John 5:24

(1 JOHN 3:14) (JOHN 5:24) (1 JOHN 5:12) (2 CORINTHIANS 1:21-22)
(1 JOHN 3:19, 21) (1 JOHN 5:19) (EPHESIANS 2:1, 5) (COLOSSIANS 1:13)

July 22

You will show me the way of life, granting me the joy of your presence.

The LORD says: Take your choice of life or death! ▪ I will continue to teach you what is good and right. ▪ I am the way, the truth, and the life. No one can come to the Father except through me. ▪ Come.

There is a path before each person that seems right, but it ends in death. ▪ You can enter God's Kingdom only through the narrow gate. The highway to hell is broad, and its gate is wide for the many who choose the easy way. But the gateway to life is small, and the road is narrow, and only a few ever find it.

A main road will go through that once deserted land. It will be named the Highway of Holiness. Evil-hearted people will never travel on it. It will be only for those who walk in God's ways; fools will never walk there. ▪ Oh, that we might know the LORD! Let us press on to know him!

There are many rooms in my Father's home, and I am going to prepare a place for you.

As the way, Jesus is our path to the Father. As the truth, he is the reality of all God's promises. As the life, he joins his divine life to ours, both now and eternally.

LAB note for John 14:6

(PSALM 16:11) (JEREMIAH 21:8) (1 SAMUEL 12:23) (JOHN 14:6) (MATTHEW 4:19) (PROVERBS 14:12) (MATTHEW 7:13-14) (ISAIAH 35:8) (HOSEA 6:3) (JOHN 14:2)

July 23

It was by faith that Abraham obeyed when God called him to leave home and go to another land that God would give him as an inheritance.

He chose the Promised Land as our inheritance, the proud possession of Jacob's descendants, whom he loves. ▪ He found them in a desert land, in an empty, howling wasteland. He surrounded them and watched over them; he guarded them as his most precious possession. Like an eagle that rouses her chicks and hovers over her young, so he spread his wings to take them in and carried them aloft on his pinions. The LORD alone guided them; they lived without any foreign gods. He made them ride over the highlands; he let them feast on the crops of the fields.

I am the LORD your God, who teaches you what is good and leads you along the paths you should follow. ▪ Who is a teacher like him?

We live by believing and not by seeing. ▪ For this world is not our home; we are looking forward to our city in heaven, which is yet to come. ▪ Dear brothers and sisters, you are foreigners and aliens here. So I warn you to keep away from evil desires because they fight against your very souls.

Abraham's life was filled with faith. He obeyed God without question—even when it meant going to another land. Do not be surprised if God asks you to give up secure, familiar surroundings in order to carry out his will.

LAB note for Hebrews 11:8–10

(HEBREWS 11:8) (PSALM 47:4) (DEUTERONOMY 32:10–13) (ISAIAH 48:17) (JOB 36:22) (2 CORINTHIANS 5:7) (HEBREWS 13:14) (1 PETER 2:11)

July 24

May all who are godly be happy in the LORD and praise his holy name!

Even the heavens cannot be absolutely pure in his sight. How much less pure is a corrupt and sinful person with a thirst for wickedness! ▪ God is so glorious that even the moon and stars scarcely shine compared to him. How much less are mere people, who are but worms in his sight?

Who else among the gods is like you, O LORD? Who is glorious in holiness like you? ▪ Holy, holy, holy is the LORD Almighty!

Now you must be holy in everything you do, just as God—who chose you to be his children—is holy. For he himself has said, "You must be holy because I am holy." ▪ Share in his holiness.

God's temple is holy, and you Christians are that temple. ▪ What holy, godly lives you should be living! Make every effort to live a pure and blameless life. And be at peace with God.

Let everything you say be good and helpful, so that your words will be an encouragement to those who hear them. And do not bring sorrow to God's Holy Spirit by the way you live. Remember, he is the one who has identified you as his own, guaranteeing that you will be saved on the day of redemption.

The God of Israel and of the Christian church is holy—he sets the standard for morality. He is a God of mercy and justice who cares personally for each of his followers. Our holy God expects us to imitate him by following his high moral standards and by being both merciful and just.

LAB note for 1 Peter 1:14–16

(PSALM 97:12) (JOB 15:15–16) (JOB 25:5–6) (EXODUS 15:11) (ISAIAH 6:3) (1 PETER 1:15–16) (HEBREWS 12:10) (1 CORINTHIANS 3:17) (2 PETER 3:11, 14) (EPHESIANS 4:29–30)

July 25

You have armed me with strength for the battle; you have subdued my enemies under my feet.

When I am weak, then I am strong.

O LORD, no one but you can help the powerless against the mighty! Help us, O LORD our God, for we trust in you alone. It is in your name that we have come against this vast horde. O LORD, you are our God; do not let mere men prevail against you! ▩ Jehoshaphat cried out to the LORD to save him, and God helped him by turning the attack away from him.

It is better to trust the LORD than to put confidence in people. It is better to trust the LORD than to put confidence in princes. ▩ The best-equipped army cannot save a king, nor is great strength enough to save a warrior. Don't count on your warhorse to give you victory—for all its strength, it cannot save you.

For we are not fighting against people made of flesh and blood, but against the evil rulers and authorities of the unseen world, against those mighty powers of darkness who rule this world, and against wicked spirits in the heavenly realms.

We face a powerful army whose goal is to defeat Christ's church. When we believe in Christ, these beings become our enemies, and they try every device to turn us away from him and back to sin. We need supernatural power to defeat Satan, and God has provided this by giving us his Holy Spirit within us and his armor surrounding us.

LAB note for Ephesians 6:12

(PSALM 18:39) (2 CORINTHIANS 12:10) (2 CHRONICLES 14:11) (2 CHRONICLES 18:31) (PSALM 118:8-9) (PSALM 33:16-17) (EPHESIANS 6:12)

July 26

Live a life filled with love.

I am giving you a new commandment: Love each other. Just as I have loved you, you should love each other. ▪ Continue to show deep love for each other, for love covers a multitude of sins. ▪ Love covers all offenses.

When you are praying, first forgive anyone you are holding a grudge against, so that your Father in heaven will forgive your sins, too. ▪ Love your enemies! Do good to them! Lend to them! And don't be concerned that they might not repay. ▪ Do not rejoice when your enemies fall into trouble. Don't be happy when they stumble. ▪ Don't repay evil for evil. Don't retaliate when people say unkind things about you. Instead, pay them back with a blessing. That is what God wants you to do, and he will bless you for it. ▪ Do your part to live in peace with everyone, as much as possible. ▪ Be kind to each other, tenderhearted, forgiving one another, just as God through Christ has forgiven you.

Dear children, let us stop just saying we love each other; let us really show it by our actions. It is by our actions that we know we are living in the truth, so we will be confident when we stand before the Lord.

We are to love others based on Jesus' sacrificial love for us. Such love will not only bring unbelievers to Christ, it will also keep believers strong and united in a world hostile to God. Jesus was a living example of God's love, as we are to be living examples of Jesus' love.

LAB note for John 13:34

(Ephesians 5:2) (John 13:34) (1 Peter 4:8) (Proverbs 10:12) (Mark 11:25) (Luke 6:35) (Proverbs 24:17) (1 Peter 3:9) (Romans 12:18) (Ephesians 4:32) (1 John 3:18–19)

July 27

May . . . the love of God, and the fellowship of the Holy Spirit be with you all.

I will ask the Father, and he will give you another Counselor, who will never leave you. He is the Holy Spirit, who leads into all truth. The world at large cannot receive him, because it isn't looking for him and doesn't recognize him. But you do, because he lives with you now and later will be in you. ▪ He will not be presenting his own ideas; he will be telling you what he has heard. He will bring me glory by revealing to you whatever he receives from me.

We know how dearly God loves us, because he has given us the Holy Spirit to fill our hearts with his love.

The person who is joined to the Lord becomes one spirit with him. Don't you know that your body is the temple of the Holy Spirit, who lives in you and was given to you by God? You do not belong to yourself.

Do not bring sorrow to God's Holy Spirit by the way you live. Remember, he is the one who has identified you as his own, guaranteeing that you will be saved on the day of redemption. ▪ The Holy Spirit helps us in our distress. For we don't even know what we should pray for, nor how we should pray. But the Holy Spirit prays for us with groanings that cannot be expressed in words.

The Holy Spirit has been active among people from the beginning of time, but after Pentecost he came to live in all believers. Many people are unaware of the Holy Spirit's activities, but to those who hear Christ's words and understand the Spirit's power, the Spirit gives a whole new way to look at life. *LAB note for John 14:17ff.*

(2 Corinthians 13:13) (John 14:16-17) (John 16:13-14) (Romans 5:5) (1 Corinthians 6:17, 19) (Ephesians 4:30) (Romans 8:26)

July 28

The God of peace . . . produce in you, through the power of Jesus Christ, all that is pleasing to him.

Rejoice. Change your ways. Encourage each other. Live in harmony and peace.

God saved you by his special favor when you believed. And you can't take credit for this; it is a gift from God. Salvation is not a reward for the good things we have done, so none of us can boast about it. ▧ Whatever is good and perfect comes to us from God above, who created all heaven's lights. Unlike them, he never changes or casts shifting shadows.

Be even more careful to put into action God's saving work in your lives, obeying God with deep reverence and fear. For God is working in you, giving you the desire to obey him and the power to do what pleases him. ▧ Let God transform you into a new person by changing the way you think. Then you will know what God wants you to do, and you will know how good and pleasing and perfect his will really is. ▧ May you always be filled with the fruit of your salvation—those good things that are produced in your life by Jesus Christ—for this will bring much glory and praise to God.

It is not that we think we can do anything of lasting value by ourselves. Our only power and success come from God.

God works in us to make us the kind of people that would please him, and he equips us to do the kind of work that would please him. Let God change you from within and then use you to help others.

Hebrews 13:20-21

(Hebrews 13:20-21) (2 Corinthians 13:11) (Ephesians 2:8-9) (James 1:17) (Philippians 2:12-13) (Romans 12:2) (Philippians 1:11) (2 Corinthians 3:5)

July 29

The Temple of the LORD must be a magnificent structure, famous and glorious.

Now God is building you, as living stones, into his spiritual temple. ▩ Don't you realize that all of you together are the temple of God and that the Spirit of God lives in you? God will bring ruin upon anyone who ruins this temple. For God's temple is holy, and you Christians are that temple. ▩ Don't you know that your body is the temple of the Holy Spirit, who lives in you and was given to you by God? You do not belong to yourself, for God bought you with a high price. So you must honor God with your body. ▩ What union can there be between God's temple and idols? For we are the temple of the living God. ▩ You are members of God's family. We are his house, built on the foundation of the apostles and the prophets. And the cornerstone is Christ Jesus himself. We who believe are carefully joined together, becoming a holy temple for the Lord. Through him you Gentiles are also joined together as part of this dwelling where God lives by his Spirit.

Just as our bodies are the "temple of the Holy Spirit," the local church or Christian community is God's temple. Just as the Jews' Temple in Jerusalem was not to be destroyed, the church is not to be spoiled and ruined by divisions, controversy, or other sins as members come together to worship God. *LAB note for 1 Corinthians 3:16-17*

(1 CHRONICLES 22:5) (1 PETER 2:5) (1 CORINTHIANS 3:16-17)
(1 CORINTHIANS 6:19-20) (2 CORINTHIANS 6:16) (EPHESIANS 2:19-22)

July 30

God did not abandon us.

Dear friends, don't be surprised at the fiery trials you are going through, as if something strange were happening to you. ▪ As you endure this divine discipline, remember that God is treating you as his own children. Whoever heard of a child who was never disciplined? If God doesn't discipline you as he does all of his children, it means that you are illegitimate and are not really his children after all.

The LORD your God is testing you to see if you love him with all your heart and soul.

The LORD will not abandon his chosen people, for that would dishonor his great name. He made you a special nation for himself. ▪ Can a mother forget her nursing child? Can she feel no love for a child she has borne? But even if that were possible, I would not forget you! ▪ Happy are those who have the God of Israel as their helper, whose hope is in the LORD their God.

Don't you think God will surely give justice to his chosen people who plead with him day and night? Will he keep putting them off? I tell you, he will grant justice to them quickly!

Who loves his child more—the father who allows the child to do what will harm him, or the one who corrects, trains, and even punishes the child to help him learn what is right? It's never pleasant to be corrected and disciplined by God, but his discipline is a sign of his deep love for us.

LAB note for Hebrews 12:5–11

(EZRA 9:9) (1 PETER 4:12) (HEBREWS 12:7–8) (DEUTERONOMY 13:3) (1 SAMUEL 12:22) (ISAIAH 49:15) (PSALM 146:5) (LUKE 18:7–8)

July 31

My Father! If it is possible, let this cup of suffering be taken away from me. Yet I want your will, not mine.

Now my soul is deeply troubled. Should I pray, "Father, save me from what lies ahead"? But that is the very reason why I came!

I have come down from heaven to do the will of God who sent me, not to do what I want. ▪ He obediently humbled himself even further by dying a criminal's death on a cross. ▪ While Jesus was here on earth, he offered prayers and pleadings, with a loud cry and tears, to the one who could deliver him out of death. And God heard his prayers because of his reverence for God. So even though Jesus was God's Son, he learned obedience from the things he suffered.

Don't you realize that I could ask my Father for thousands of angels to protect us, and he would send them instantly? ▪ Yes, it was written long ago that the Messiah must suffer and die and rise again from the dead on the third day. With my authority, take this message of repentance to all the nations, beginning in Jerusalem: "There is forgiveness of sins for all who turn to me."

Jesus was not rebelling against his Father's will when he asked that the cup be taken away. In fact, he reaffirmed his desire to do God's will. Instead, his prayer reveals his terrible suffering. His agony was worse than death because he paid for all our sin by being separated from God.

LAB note for Matthew 26:39

(MATTHEW 26:39) (JOHN 12:27) (JOHN 6:38) (PHILIPPIANS 2:8) (HEBREWS 5:7-8) (MATTHEW 26:53) (LUKE 24:46-47)

August

Summer's Goodness

Bright sunny days and clear star-filled nights
Nurturing mornings in the garden and
lazy afternoons at the beach
There's nothing quite like a perfect summer day.

Summer is the time to break from the normal rush of work and busyness. It's the season for refreshment and relaxation. Make your summer days events to remember and celebrate the whole year!

August 1

When the Holy Spirit controls our lives, he will produce . . . goodness.

Follow God's example in everything you do, because you are his dear children. ▪ Love your enemies! Pray for those who persecute you! In that way, you will be acting as true children of your Father in heaven. For he gives his sunlight to both the evil and the good, and he sends rain on the just and on the unjust. ▪ You must be compassionate, just as your Father is compassionate.

For this light within you produces only what is good and right and true.

Then God our Savior showed us his kindness and love. He saved us, not because of the good things we did, but because of his mercy. He washed away our sins and gave us a new life through the Holy Spirit. He generously poured out the Spirit upon us because of what Jesus Christ our Savior did. ▪ The LORD is good to everyone. He showers compassion on all his creation. ▪ Since God did not spare even his own Son but gave him up for us all, won't God, who gave us Christ, also give us everything else?

By telling us not to retaliate, Jesus keeps us from taking the law into our own hands. By loving and praying for our enemies, we can overcome evil with good. If you love your enemies and treat them well, you will truly show that Jesus is Lord of your life. *LAB note for Matthew 5:43-44*

(GALATIANS 5:22) (EPHESIANS 5:1) (MATTHEW 5:44-45) (LUKE 6:36) (EPHESIANS 5:9) (TITUS 3:4-6) (PSALM 145:9) (ROMANS 8:32)

August 2

You have given me an inheritance reserved for those who fear your name.

No weapon turned against you will succeed. And everyone who tells lies in court will be brought to justice. These benefits are enjoyed by the servants of the LORD; their vindication will come from me. I, the LORD, have spoken! ▩ The angel of the LORD guards all who fear him, and he rescues them. Taste and see that the LORD is good. Oh, the joys of those who trust in him! Let the LORD's people show him reverence, for those who honor him will have all they need. Even strong young lions sometimes go hungry, but those who trust in the LORD will never lack any good thing. ▩ The land you have given me is a pleasant land. What a wonderful inheritance!

For you who fear my name, the Sun of Righteousness will rise with healing in his wings. And you will go free, leaping with joy like calves let out to pasture. ▩ Since God did not spare even his own Son but gave him up for us all, won't God, who gave us Christ, also give us everything else?

If you feel you don't have everything you need, ask: (1) Is this really a need? (2) Is this good for me? (3) Is this the best time for me to have that desire? Even if you answer yes to all three questions, God may want you to learn that you need him more than you need your immediate desires met.

LAB note for Psalm 34:9-10

(PSALM 61:5) (ISAIAH 54:17) (PSALM 34:7-10) (PSALM 16:6)
(MALACHI 4:2) (ROMANS 8:32)

August 3

I will praise you with songs of joy.

How precious are your thoughts about me, O God! They are innumerable! I can't even count them; they outnumber the grains of sand! And when I wake up in the morning, you are still with me! ■ How sweet are your words to my taste; they are sweeter than honey. ■ Your love is sweeter than wine.

Your unfailing love, O LORD, is as vast as the heavens; your faithfulness reaches beyond the clouds. Your righteousness is like the mighty mountains, your justice like the ocean depths. You care for people and animals alike, O LORD. How precious is your unfailing love, O God! All humanity finds shelter in the shadow of your wings. You feed them from the abundance of your own house, letting them drink from your rivers of delight. ■ Whom have I in heaven but you? I desire you more than anything on earth. ■ You will show me the way of life, granting me the joy of your presence and the pleasures of living with you forever.

Oh, what a wonderful God we have! How great are his riches and wisdom and knowledge! How impossible it is for us to understand his decisions and his methods! For everything comes from him; everything exists by his power and is intended for his glory.

God is faithful, righteous, and just. His love is as vast as the heavens; his faithfulness reaches beyond the clouds; his righteousness is as solid as mighty mountains; his judgments are as full of wisdom as the oceans are with water. We need not fear evil people because we know God loves us, judges evil, and will care for us throughout eternity.

LAB note for Psalm 36:5-8

(PSALM 63:5) (PSALM 139:17-18) (PSALM 119:103) (SONG OF SONGS 1:2) (PSALM 36:5-8) (PSALM 73:25) (PSALM 16:11) (ROMANS 11:33, 36)

August 4

Nicodemus, the leader who had met with Jesus earlier.

Peter was following far behind. ▩ Many people, including some of the Jewish leaders, believed in him. But they wouldn't admit it to anyone because of their fear that the Pharisees would expel them from the synagogue. For they loved human praise more than the praise of God. ▩ Fearing people is a dangerous trap, but to trust the LORD means safety.

Those the Father has given me will come to me, and I will never reject them. ▩ He will not crush those who are weak or quench the smallest hope. ▩ Faith as small as a mustard seed.

God has not given us a spirit of fear and timidity, but of power, love, and self-discipline. So you must never be ashamed to tell others about our Lord. ▩ And now, dear children, continue to live in fellowship with Christ so that when he returns, you will be full of courage and not shrink back from him in shame. ▩ If anyone acknowledges me publicly here on earth, I will openly acknowledge that person before my Father in heaven.

Since most of the Pharisees hated Jesus and wanted to kill him, Nicodemus risked his reputation and high position when he spoke up for Jesus. His statement was bold, and the Pharisees immediately became suspicious. After Jesus' death Nicodemus brought spices for his body.

LAB note for John 7:50–52

(JOHN 7:50) (MATTHEW 26:58) (JOHN 12:42–43) (PROVERBS 29:25) (JOHN 6:37) (ISAIAH 42:3) (MATTHEW 17:20) (2 TIMOTHY 1:7–8) (1 JOHN 2:28) (MATTHEW 10:32)

August 5

Endure suffering along with me, as a good soldier of Christ Jesus.

Jesus, on whom our faith depends from start to finish. He was willing to die a shameful death on the cross. ▩ It was only right that God—who made everything and for whom everything was made—should bring his many children into glory. Through the suffering of Jesus, God made him a perfect leader, one fit to bring them into their salvation. ▩ They must enter into the Kingdom of God through many tribulations.

For we are not fighting against people made of flesh and blood, but against the evil rulers and authorities of the unseen world, against those mighty powers of darkness who rule this world, and against wicked spirits in the heavenly realms. Use every piece of God's armor. ▩ We are human, but we don't wage war with human plans and methods. We use God's mighty weapons, not mere worldly weapons, to knock down the Devil's strongholds.

In his kindness God called you to his eternal glory by means of Jesus Christ. After you have suffered a little while, he will restore, support, and strengthen you, and he will place you on a firm foundation.

Despite suffering, we must keep going because of the thought of victory, the vision of winning, and the hope of harvest. We will see that our suffering is worthwhile when we achieve our goal of glorifying God, winning people to Christ, and one day living eternally with him.

LAB note for 2 Timothy 2:3-7

(2 TIMOTHY 2:3) (HEBREWS 12:2) (HEBREWS 2:10) (ACTS 14:22) (EPHESIANS 6:12-13) (2 CORINTHIANS 10:3-4) (1 PETER 5:10)

August 6

The Lord . . . is full of tenderness and mercy.

The LORD is like a father to his children, tender and compassionate to those who fear him. ▩ Who can forget the wonders he performs? How gracious and merciful is our LORD! He gives food to those who trust him; he always remembers his covenant.

He will not let you stumble and fall; the one who watches over you will not sleep. Indeed, he who watches over Israel never tires and never sleeps. ▩ Like an eagle that rouses her chicks and hovers over her young, so he spread his wings to take them in and carried them aloft on his pinions.

The unfailing love of the LORD never ends! By his mercies we have been kept from complete destruction. Great is his faithfulness; his mercies begin afresh each day.

A vast crowd was there as he [Jesus] stepped from the boat, and he had compassion on them and healed their sick. ▩ Jesus Christ is the same yesterday, today, and forever.

Not even a sparrow, worth only half a penny, can fall to the ground without your Father knowing it. And the very hairs on your head are all numbered. So don't be afraid; you are more valuable to him than a whole flock of sparrows.

Perhaps there is some sin in your life that you think God will not forgive. But God willingly responds with help when we ask. His steadfast love and mercy are greater than any sin, and he promises forgiveness.

LAB note for Lamentations 3:21-23

(JAMES 5:11) (PSALM 103:13) (PSALM 111:4-5) (PSALM 121:3-4) (DEUTERONOMY 32:11) (LAMENTATIONS 3:22-23) (MATTHEW 14:14) (HEBREWS 13:8) (MATTHEW 10:29-31)

August 7

I have trodden the winepress alone.

Who else among the gods is like you, O LORD? Who is glorious in holiness like you—so awesome in splendor, performing such wonders? ▩ He was amazed to see that no one intervened to help the oppressed. So he himself stepped in to save them with his mighty power and justice. ▩ He personally carried away our sins in his own body on the cross so we can be dead to sin and live for what is right. You have been healed by his wounds!

Sing a new song to the LORD, for he has done wonderful deeds. He has won a mighty victory by his power and holiness. ▩ God disarmed the evil rulers and authorities. He shamed them publicly by his victory over them on the cross of Christ. ▩ When he sees all that is accomplished by his anguish, he will be satisfied. And because of what he has experienced, my righteous servant will make it possible for many to be counted righteous, for he will bear all their sins.

March on, my soul, with courage! ▩ Overwhelming victory is ours through Christ, who loved us.

Because redemption is an impossible task for any human, God himself, as the Messiah, personally stepped in to help. Whether we sin once or many times, out of rebellion or out of ignorance, our sin separates us from God and will continue to separate us until God forgives us and removes it. *LAB note for Isaiah 59:16-17*

(ISAIAH 63:3) (EXODUS 15:11) (ISAIAH 59:16) (1 PETER 2:24) (PSALM 98:1) (COLOSSIANS 2:15) (ISAIAH 53:11) (JUDGES 5:21) (ROMANS 8:37)

August 8

For the LORD corrects those he loves, just as a father corrects a child in whom he delights.

There is no god other than me! I am the one who kills and gives life; I am the one who wounds and heals; no one delivers from my power! ▩ "For I know the plans I have for you," says the LORD. "They are plans for good and not for disaster, to give you a future and a hope." ▩ "My thoughts are completely different from yours," says the LORD. "And my ways are far beyond anything you could imagine."

But then I will win her back once again. I will lead her out into the desert and speak tenderly to her there. ▩ So you should realize that just as a parent disciplines a child, the LORD your God disciplines you to help you. ▩ For the Lord disciplines those he loves, and he punishes those he accepts as his children. ▩ No discipline is enjoyable while it is happening—it is painful! But afterward there will be a quiet harvest of right living for those who are trained in this way. ▩ Humble yourselves under the mighty power of God, and in his good time he will honor you.

I know, O LORD, that your decisions are fair; you disciplined me because I needed it.

God doesn't punish us because he enjoys inflicting pain but because he is deeply concerned about our development. He knows that in order to become morally strong and good, we must learn the difference between right and wrong. His loving discipline enables us to do that.

LAB note for Proverbs 3:11-12

(PROVERBS 3:12) (DEUTERONOMY 32:39) (JEREMIAH 29:11) (ISAIAH 55:8) (HOSEA 2:14) (DEUTERONOMY 8:5) (HEBREWS 12:6) (HEBREWS 12:11) (1 PETER 5:6) (PSALM 119:75)

August 9

The earth is the LORD's, and everything in it. The world and all its people belong to him.

She doesn't realize that it was I who gave her everything she has—the grain, the wine, the olive oil. Even the gold and silver she used in worshiping the god Baal were gifts from me! But now I will take back the wine and ripened grain I generously provided each harvest season. I will take away the linen and wool clothing I gave her to cover her nakedness.

Everything we have has come from you, and we give you only what you have already given us! We are here for only a moment, visitors and strangers in the land as our ancestors were before us. Our days on earth are like a shadow, gone so soon without a trace. O LORD our God, even these materials that we have gathered . . . come from you! It all belongs to you! ✻ For everything comes from him; everything exists by his power and is intended for his glory. To him be glory evermore. Amen.

[Our] trust should be in the living God, who richly gives us all we need for our enjoyment.

This same God who takes care of me will supply all your needs from his glorious riches, which have been given to us in Christ Jesus.

Because "the earth is the LORD's," all of us are stewards, or caretakers. We should be committed to the proper management of this world and its resources, but we are not to become devoted to anything created or act as sole proprietors, because this world will pass away.

LAB note for Psalm 24:1

(PSALM 24:1) (HOSEA 2:8-9) (1 CHRONICLES 29:14-16) (ROMANS 11:36) (1 TIMOTHY 6:17) (PHILIPPIANS 4:19)

August 10

Cracked cisterns that can hold no water at all!

They began to talk about construction projects. "Let's build a great city with a tower that reaches to the skies—a monument to our greatness!" The LORD scattered them all over the earth; and that ended the building of the city. ▪ I worked hard to distinguish wisdom from foolishness. But now I realize that even this was like chasing the wind. For the greater my wisdom, the greater my grief. To increase knowledge only increases sorrow. ▪ I also tried to find meaning by building huge homes for myself and by planting beautiful vineyards. I made gardens and parks, filling them with all kinds of fruit trees. I built reservoirs to collect the water to irrigate my many flourishing groves. I collected great sums of silver and gold, the treasure of many kings and provinces. But as I looked at everything I had worked so hard to accomplish, it was all so meaningless. It was like chasing the wind. There was nothing really worthwhile anywhere.

If you are thirsty, come to me! ▪ For he satisfies the thirsty and fills the hungry with good things.

Let heaven fill your thoughts. Do not think only about things down here on earth.

Who would set aside a fountain of living water for a cracked cistern, a pit that collected rainwater but could not hold it? Why should we cling to the broken promises of unstable "cisterns" (money, power, religious systems, or whatever transitory thing we are putting in place of God) when God promises to constantly refresh us with living water?

LAB note for Jeremiah 2:13

(JEREMIAH 2:13) (GENESIS 11:3-4, 8) (ECCLESIASTES 1:17-18) (ECCLESIASTES 2:4-6, 8, 11) (JOHN 7:37) (PSALM 107:9) (COLOSSIANS 3:2)

August 11

I'm not asking you to take them out of the world, but to keep them safe from the evil one.

Live clean, innocent lives as children of God in a dark world full of crooked and perverse people. Let your lives shine brightly before them. ▪ You are the salt of the earth. . . . You are the light of the world. Let your good deeds shine out for all to see, so that everyone will praise your heavenly Father.

I kept you from sinning against me. ▪ The temptations that come into your life are no different from what others experience. And God is faithful. He will keep the temptation from becoming so strong that you can't stand up against it. When you are tempted, he will show you a way out so that you will not give in to it.

The Lord is faithful; he will make you strong and guard you from the evil one. ▪ He died for our sins, just as God our Father planned, in order to rescue us from this evil world in which we live. ▪ And now, all glory to God, who is able to keep you from stumbling, and who will bring you into his glorious presence innocent of sin and with great joy. All glory to him, who alone is God our Savior, through Jesus Christ our Lord. Yes, glory, majesty, power, and authority belong to him, in the beginning, now, and forevermore. Amen.

Belief in Christ should unite those who trust him. If your church has some members who are always complaining and arguing, it lacks the unifying power of Jesus Christ. If we stop arguing with other Christians or complaining about people and conditions within the church, the world will see Christ.

LAB note for Philippians 2:14–16

(John 17:15) (Philippians 2:15) (Matthew 5:13–14, 16) (Genesis 20:6) (1 Corinthians 10:13) (2 Thessalonians 3:3) (Galatians 1:4) (Jude 1:24–25)

August 12

To trust the LORD means safety.

The LORD is very great and lives in heaven. ▪ The LORD is high above the nations; his glory is far greater than the heavens. Far below him are the heavens and the earth. He stoops to look, and he lifts the poor from the dirt and the needy from the garbage dump. He sets them among princes.

But God is so rich in mercy, and he loved us so very much, that even while we were dead because of our sins, he gave us life when he raised Christ from the dead. (It is only by God's special favor that you have been saved!) For he raised us from the dead along with Christ, and we are seated with him in the heavenly realms—all because we are one with Christ Jesus.

Since God did not spare even his own Son but gave him up for us all, won't God, who gave us Christ, also give us everything else? And I am convinced that nothing can ever separate us from his love. Death can't, and life can't. The angels can't, and the demons can't. Our fears for today, our worries about tomorrow, and even the powers of hell can't keep God's love away. Whether we are high above the sky or in the deepest ocean, nothing in all creation will ever be able to separate us from the love of God that is revealed in Christ Jesus our Lord.

Fear of people can hamper everything you try to do. By contrast, fear of God—respect, reverence, and trust—is liberating. Why fear people who can do no eternal harm? Instead, trust God who can turn the harm intended by others into good for those who trust him.

LAB note from Proverbs 29:25

(PROVERBS 29:25) (ISAIAH 33:5) (PSALM 113:4, 6-8)
(EPHESIANS 2:4-6) (ROMANS 8:32, 38-39)

August 13

God deliberately chose things the world considers foolish in order to shame those who think they are wise.

When Israel cried out to the LORD for help, the LORD raised up a man to rescue them. His name was Ehud son of Gera, of the tribe of Benjamin, who was left-handed. After Ehud, Shamgar son of Anath rescued Israel. He killed six hundred Philistines with an ox goad.

Then the LORD turned to him [Gideon] and said, "Go with the strength you have and rescue Israel from the Midianites. I am sending you!" "But Lord," Gideon replied, "how can I rescue Israel? My clan is the weakest in the whole tribe of Manasseh, and I am the least in my entire family!"

The LORD said to Gideon, "You have too many warriors with you. If I let all of you fight the Midianites, the Israelites will boast to me that they saved themselves by their own strength."

"It is not by force nor by strength, but by my Spirit," says the LORD Almighty. ▩ Be strong with the Lord's mighty power.

Is Christianity against rational thinking? Christians clearly do believe in using their minds to weigh the evidence and make wise choices. But no amount of human knowledge can replace or bypass Christ's work on the cross. *LAB note for 1 Corinthians 1:27*

(1 CORINTHIANS 1:27) (JUDGES 3:15, 31) (JUDGES 6:14–15) (JUDGES 7:2) (ZECHARIAH 4:6) (EPHESIANS 6:10)

August 14

The joy of the LORD is your strength.

Sing for joy, O heavens! Rejoice, O earth! Burst into song, O mountains! For the LORD has comforted his people and will have compassion on them in their sorrow. ▩ God has come to save me. I will trust in him and not be afraid. The LORD God is my strength and my song; he has become my salvation. ▩ The LORD is my strength, my shield from every danger. I trust in him with all my heart. He helps me, and my heart is filled with joy. I burst out in songs of thanksgiving.

Now we can rejoice in our wonderful new relationship with God—all because of what our Lord Jesus Christ has done for us in making us friends of God. ▩ Even though the fig trees have no blossoms, and there are no grapes on the vine; even though the olive crop fails, and the fields lie empty and barren; even though the flocks die in the fields, and the cattle barns are empty, yet I will rejoice in the LORD! I will be joyful in the God of my salvation. The Sovereign LORD is my strength! He will make me as surefooted as a deer and bring me safely over the mountains.

Celebration is not to be self-centered (just when we feel like it). Often when we celebrate and give to others (even when we don't feel like it), we are strengthened spiritually and filled with joy. Enter into celebrations that honor God, and allow him to fill you with his joy!

LAB note for Nehemiah 8:9-10

(NEHEMIAH 8:10) (ISAIAH 49:13) (ISAIAH 12:2) (PSALM 28:7)
(ROMANS 5:11) (HABAKKUK 3:17-19)

August 15

He existed before everything else began.

The faithful and true witness, the ruler of God's creation. ▪ Christ is the Head of the church, which is his body. He is the first of all who will rise from the dead, so he is first in everything.

The LORD formed me from the beginning, before he created anything else. I was appointed in ages past, at the very first, before the earth began. I was there when he established the heavens, when he drew the horizon on the oceans. I was there when he set the clouds above, when he established the deep fountains of the earth. I was there when he set the limits of the seas, so they would not spread beyond their boundaries. And when he marked off the earth's foundations, I was the architect at his side. I was his constant delight, rejoicing always in his presence. ▪ From eternity to eternity I am God.

Jesus, on whom our faith depends from start to finish. He was willing to die a shameful death on the cross because of the joy he knew would be his afterward. Now he is seated in the place of highest honor beside God's throne in heaven.

God is not only the creator of the world but also its sustainer. Because Christ is the sustainer of all life, none of us is independent from him. We are all his servants who must daily trust him to protect us, care for us, and sustain us. *LAB note for Colossians 1:17*

(COLOSSIANS 1:17) (REVELATION 3:14) (COLOSSIANS 1:18) (PROVERBS 8:22-23, 27-30) (ISAIAH 43:13) (HEBREWS 12:2)

August 16

Is there any god in heaven or on earth who can perform such great deeds as yours?

Who in all of heaven can compare with the LORD? What mightiest angel is anything like the LORD? O LORD God Almighty! Where is there anyone as mighty as you, LORD? Faithfulness is your very character. ▩ Nowhere among the pagan gods is there a god like you, O Lord. There are no other miracles like yours. ▩ All heaven will praise your miracles, LORD; myriads of angels will praise you for your faithfulness. ▩ For the sake of your promise and according to your will, you have done all these great things and have shown them to me. How great you are, O Sovereign LORD! . . . We have never even heard of another god like you!

"No eye has seen, no ear has heard, and no mind has imagined what God has prepared for those who love him." But we know these things because God has revealed them to us by his Spirit, and his Spirit searches out everything and shows us even God's deep secrets.

Have you never heard or understood? Don't you know that the LORD is the everlasting God, the Creator of all the earth? He never grows faint or weary.

In the courts of heaven, a host of angels praise the Lord. The scene is one of such majesty and grandeur to show that our God is beyond compare. His power and purity place him high above nature and angels.

LAB note for Psalm 89:5

(DEUTERONOMY 3:24) (PSALM 89:6, 8) (PSALM 86:8) (PSALM 89:5) (2 SAMUEL 7:21-22) (1 CORINTHIANS 2:9-10) (ISAIAH 40:28)

August 17

The person who wishes to boast should boast only of what the Lord has done.

Let not the wise man gloat in his wisdom, or the mighty man in his might, or the rich man in his riches. Let them boast in this alone: that they truly know me and understand that I am the LORD.

Everything else is worthless when compared with the priceless gain of knowing Christ Jesus my Lord. I have discarded everything else, counting it all as garbage, so that I may have Christ. ▪ His unchanging plan has always been to adopt us into his own family by bringing us to himself through Jesus Christ. ▪ I am not ashamed of this Good News about Christ. It is the power of God at work, saving everyone who believes—Jews first and also Gentiles.

Whom have I in heaven but you? I desire you more than anything on earth. ▪ My heart rejoices in the LORD!

Not to us, O LORD, but to you goes all the glory for your unfailing love and faithfulness. ▪ He must become greater and greater, and I must become less and less.

People tend to admire three things about others: wisdom, power (might), and riches. But God puts a higher priority on knowing him personally and living a life that reflects his justice and righteousness. What do you want people to admire most about you? *LAB note for Jeremiah 9:23-24*

(1 CORINTHIANS 1:31) (JEREMIAH 9:23-24) (PHILIPPIANS 3:8) (EPHESIANS 1:5) (ROMANS 1:16) (PSALM 73:25) (1 SAMUEL 2:1) (PSALM 115:1) (JOHN 3:30)

August 18

LORD, you are mine!

Everything belongs to you . . . and you belong to Christ, and Christ belongs to God. ▩ Jesus Christ . . . gave his life to free us from every kind of sin, to cleanse us, and to make us his very own people, totally committed to doing what is right. ▩ God has put all things under the authority of Christ, and he gave him this authority for the benefit of the church. ▩ Christ . . . gave up his life for her [the church]. He did this to present her to himself as a glorious church without a spot or wrinkle or any other blemish. Instead, she will be holy and without fault.

I will boast only in the LORD. ▩ I am overwhelmed with joy in the LORD my God! For he has dressed me with the clothing of salvation and draped me in a robe of righteousness.

Whom have I in heaven but you? I desire you more than anything on earth. My health may fail, and my spirit may grow weak, but God remains the strength of my heart; he is mine forever. ▩ I said to the LORD, "You are my Master! All the good things I have are from you." LORD, you alone are my inheritance, my cup of blessing. You guard all that is mine. The land you have given me is a pleasant land. What a wonderful inheritance!

As Christians we can be confident that God has won the final victory and is in control of everything. We need not fear any dictator or nation or even death or Satan himself. The contract has been signed and sealed; we are waiting just a short while for delivery.

LAB note for Ephesians 1:20-22

(PSALM 119:57) (1 CORINTHIANS 3:21, 23) (TITUS 2:13-14) (EPHESIANS 1:22) (EPHESIANS 5:25, 27) (PSALM 34:2) (ISAIAH 61:10) (PSALM 73:25-26) (PSALM 16:2, 5-6)

August 19

There is a path before each person that seems right, but it ends in death.

Trusting oneself is foolish, but those who walk in wisdom are safe.

Your word is a lamp for my feet and a light for my path. ▪ I have followed your commands, which have kept me from going along with cruel and evil people.

Suppose there are prophets among you, or those who have dreams about the future, and they promise you signs or miracles, and the predicted signs or miracles take place. If the prophets then say, "Come, let us worship the gods of foreign nations," do not listen to them. The LORD your God is testing you to see if you love him with all your heart and soul. Serve only the LORD your God and fear him alone. Obey his commands, listen to his voice, and cling to him.

The LORD says, "I will guide you along the best pathway for your life. I will advise you and watch over you. Do not be like a senseless horse or mule that needs a bit and bridle to keep it under control." Many sorrows come to the wicked, but unfailing love surrounds those who trust the LORD. So rejoice in the LORD and be glad, all you who obey him! Shout for joy, all you whose hearts are pure!

The "path . . . that seems right" may offer many options and require few sacrifices. But easy choices merit a second look. Is this solution attractive because it allows you to be lazy or not change your lifestyle? because it requires no moral restraints? The right choice often requires hard work and self-sacrifice. *LAB note for Proverbs 14:12*

(PROVERBS 14:12) (PROVERBS 28:26) (PSALM 119:105) (PSALM 17:4) (DEUTERONOMY 13:1-4) (PSALM 32:8-11)

August 20

God gave Solomon great wisdom and understanding.

Now someone greater than Solomon is here. ▪ Prince of Peace.

No one is likely to die for a good person, though someone might be willing to die for a person who is especially good. But God showed his great love for us in sending Christ to die for us while we were still sinners. ▪ Though [Jesus] was God, he did not demand and cling to his rights as God. He made himself nothing; he took the humble position of a slave and appeared in human form. And in human form he obediently humbled himself even further by dying a criminal's death on a cross. ▪ May you experience the love of Christ, though it is so great you will never fully understand it.

Christ is the mighty power of God and the wonderful wisdom of God. ▪ In him lie hidden all the treasures of wisdom and knowledge. ▪ The endless treasures available . . . in Christ. ▪ God alone made it possible for you to be in Christ Jesus. For our benefit God made Christ to be wisdom itself. He is the one who made us acceptable to God. He made us pure and holy, and he gave himself to purchase our freedom.

Even the queen of Sheba recognized the truth about God when it was presented to her—unlike Israel's religious leaders, who ignored the truth even though it stared them in the face. How have you responded to the evidence and truth that you have? *LAB note for Matthew 12:41-42*

(1 Kings 4:29) (Matthew 12:42) (Isaiah 9:6) (Romans 5:7-8) (Philippians 2:5-8) (Ephesians 3:19) (1 Corinthians 1:24) (Colossians 2:3) (Ephesians 3:8) (1 Corinthians 1:30)

August 21

I made you, and I will care for you.

But now, O Israel, the LORD who created you says: "Do not be afraid, for I have ransomed you. I have called you by name; you are mine. When you go through deep waters and great trouble, I will be with you. When you go through rivers of difficulty, you will not drown! When you walk through the fire of oppression, you will not be burned up; the flames will not consume you." ▪ I will be your God throughout your lifetime—until your hair is white with age.

Like an eagle that rouses her chicks and hovers over her young, so he spread his wings to take them in and carried them aloft on his pinions. The LORD alone guided them. ▪ In his love and mercy he redeemed them. He lifted them up and carried them through all the years.

Jesus Christ is the same yesterday, today, and forever. ▪ I am convinced that nothing can ever separate us from . . . the love of God that is revealed in Christ Jesus our Lord.

Can a mother forget her nursing child? Can she feel no love for a child she has borne? But even if that were possible, I would not forget you!

Our great God created us and cares for us. His love is so enduring that he will care for us throughout our lifetime and even through death. Then, if you have accepted Christ as your Savior, you will go to heaven to spend eternity with him! *LAB note for Isaiah 46:1-4*

(ISAIAH 46:4) (ISAIAH 43:1-2) (ISAIAH 46:4) (DEUTERONOMY 32:11-12) (ISAIAH 63:9) (HEBREWS 13:8) (ROMANS 8:38-39) (ISAIAH 49:15)

August 22

Consider the quarry from which you were mined, the rock from which you were cut!

I was born a sinner—yes, from the moment my mother conceived me. ▩ No one had the slightest interest in you; no one pitied you or cared for you. On the day you were born, you were dumped in a field and left to die, unwanted. But I came by and saw you there, helplessly kicking about in your own blood. As you lay there, I said, "Live!" And I helped you to thrive like a plant in the field.

He lifted me out of the pit of despair, out of the mud and the mire. He set my feet on solid ground and steadied me as I walked along. He has given me a new song to sing, a hymn of praise to our God.

When we were utterly helpless, Christ came at just the right time and died for us sinners. Now, no one is likely to die for a good person, though someone might be willing to die for a person who is especially good. But God showed his great love for us by sending Christ to die for us while we were still sinners. ▩ God is so rich in mercy, and he loved us so very much, that even while we were dead because of our sins, he gave us life when he raised Christ from the dead.

The faithful remnant may have felt alone because they were few. But God reminded them of their spiritual heritage: Abraham was only one person, but much came from his faithfulness. If we Christians, even a faithful few, remain faithful, think what God can do through us!

LAB note for Isaiah 51:1-2

(Isaiah 51:1) (Psalm 51:5) (Ezekiel 16:5-6) (Psalm 40:2-3)
(Romans 5:6-8) (Ephesians 2:4-5)

August 23

I am overwhelmed with joy in the LORD my God!

I will praise the LORD at all times. I will constantly speak his praises. I will boast only in the LORD; let all who are discouraged take heart. Come, let us tell of the LORD's greatness; let us exalt his name together. ▩ The LORD our God is our light and protector. He gives us grace and glory. No good thing will the LORD withhold from those who do what is right. O LORD Almighty, happy are those who trust in you. ▩ With my whole heart, I will praise his holy name.

Those who have reason to be thankful should continually sing praises to the Lord. ▩ Let the Holy Spirit fill and control you. Then you will sing psalms and hymns and spiritual songs among yourselves, making music to the Lord in your hearts. And you will always give thanks for everything to God the Father in the name of our Lord Jesus Christ. ▩ Sing psalms and hymns and spiritual songs to God with thankful hearts.

Around midnight, Paul and Silas were praying and singing hymns to God. ▩ Always be full of joy in the Lord. I say it again—rejoice!

God promises great blessings to his people, but many of them require our active participation: We must seek him, cry out to him, trust him, fear him, reverence him, refrain from lying, turn from evil, do good, seek peace, be brokenhearted, and serve him. *LAB note for Psalm 34:1ff.*

(ISAIAH 61:10) (PSALM 34:1-3) (PSALM 84:11-12) (PSALM 103:1) (JAMES 5:13) (EPHESIANS 5:18-20) (COLOSSIANS 3:16) (ACTS 16:25) (PHILIPPIANS 4:4)

August 24

My cup overflows with blessings!

Taste and see that the LORD is good. Oh, the joys of those who trust in him! Let the LORD's people show him reverence, for those who honor him will have all they need. Even strong young lions sometimes go hungry, but those who trust in the LORD will never lack any good thing. ▩ The unfailing love of the LORD never ends! . . . Great is his faithfulness; his mercies begin afresh each day.

LORD, you alone are my inheritance, my cup of blessing. You guard all that is mine. The land you have given me is a pleasant land. What a wonderful inheritance! ▩ The whole world and life and death; the present and the future. Everything belongs to you. ▩ How we praise God, the Father of our Lord Jesus Christ, who has blessed us with every spiritual blessing in the heavenly realms because we belong to Christ.

I have learned how to get along happily whether I have much or little. ▩ True religion with contentment is great wealth. ▩ God . . . will supply all your needs from his glorious riches, which have been given to us in Christ Jesus.

You say you belong to the Lord, but do you show reverence to him? To revere the Lord means to show deep respect and honor to him. We demonstrate true reverence by our humble attitude and genuine worship. *LAB note for Psalm 34:9*

(PSALM 23:5) (PSALM 34:8-10) (LAMENTATIONS 3:22-23) (PSALM 16:5-6) (1 CORINTHIANS 3:22) (EPHESIANS 1:3) (PHILIPPIANS 4:11) (1 TIMOTHY 6:6) (PHILIPPIANS 4:19)

August 25

Your word is a lamp for my feet and a light for my path.

Wherever you walk, their counsel can lead you. When you sleep, they will protect you. When you wake up in the morning, they will advise you. For these commands and this teaching are a lamp to light the way ahead of you. The correction of discipline is the way to life. ▩ You will hear a voice say, "This is the way; turn around and walk here."

I am the light of the world. If you follow me, you won't be stumbling through the darkness, because you will have the light that leads to life. ▩ We have . . . confidence in the message proclaimed by the prophets. Pay close attention to what they wrote, for their words are like a light shining in a dark place—until the day Christ appears and his brilliant light shines in your hearts. ▩ Now we see things imperfectly as in a poor mirror, but then we will see everything with perfect clarity. All that I know now is partial and incomplete, but then I will know everything completely, just as God knows me now.

In this life we walk through a dark forest of evil. But the Bible can be our light to show us the way ahead so we won't stumble as we walk. It reveals the entangling roots of false values and philosophies. Study the Bible so you will be able to see your way clear enough to stay on the right path.

LAB note for Psalm 119:105

(PSALM 119:105) (PROVERBS 6:22-23) (ISAIAH 30:21)
(JOHN 8:12) (2 PETER 1:19) (1 CORINTHIANS 13:12)

August 26

Those who trust the LORD will be happy.

Abraham never wavered in believing God's promise. In fact, his faith grew stronger, and in this he brought glory to God. He was absolutely convinced that God was able to do anything he promised. ▩ Judah defeated Israel because they trusted in the LORD, the God of their ancestors.

God is our refuge and strength, always ready to help in times of trouble. So we will not fear, even if earthquakes come and the mountains crumble into the sea. ▩ It is better to trust the LORD than to put confidence in people. It is better to trust the LORD than to put confidence in princes. ▩ The steps of the godly are directed by the LORD. He delights in every detail of their lives. Though they stumble, they will not fall, for the LORD holds them by the hand.

Taste and see that the LORD is good. Oh, the joys of those who trust in him! Let the LORD's people show him reverence, for those who honor him will have all they need.

"Taste and see" does not mean "check out God's credentials." Instead, it is a warm invitation: "Try this: I know you'll like it." When we take that first step of obedience in following God, we cannot help discovering that he is good and kind. *LAB note for Psalm 34:8*

(PROVERBS 16:20) (ROMANS 4:20-21) (2 CHRONICLES 13:18) (PSALM 46:1-2) (PSALM 118:8-9) (PSALM 37:23-24) (PSALM 34:8-9)

August 27

I will lie down in peace and sleep, for you alone, O LORD, will keep me safe.

Do not be afraid of the terrors of the night, nor fear the dangers of the day, nor dread the plague that stalks in darkness, nor the disaster that strikes at midday. He will shield you with his wings. He will shelter you with his feathers. His faithful promises are your armor and protection. ▩ He will not let you stumble and fall; the one who watches over you will not sleep. Indeed, he who watches over Israel never tires and never sleeps. The LORD himself watches over you! The LORD stands beside you as your protective shade. The sun will not hurt you by day, nor the moon at night. The LORD keeps you from all evil and preserves your life. The LORD keeps watch over you as you come and go, both now and forever.

Let me live forever in your sanctuary, safe beneath the shelter of your wings! ▩ Even in darkness I cannot hide from you. To you the night shines as bright as day. Darkness and light are both alike to you.

Since God did not spare even his own Son but gave him up for us all, won't God, who gave us Christ, also give us everything else? ▩ You belong to Christ, and Christ belongs to God. ▩ I will trust in him and not be afraid.

Do you ever think that because you aren't good enough for God, he will not save you? Because Christ gave his life for you, God isn't going to hold back the gift of salvation! He will not condemn you. And he will not withhold anything you need to live for him. *LAB note for Romans 8:31-34*

(PSALM 4:8) (PSALM 91:5-6, 4) (PSALM 121:3-8) (PSALM 61:4) (PSALM 139:12) (ROMANS 8:32) (1 CORINTHIANS 3:23) (ISAIAH 12:2)

August 28

If any of you wants to be my follower, you must put aside your selfish ambition, shoulder your cross daily, and follow me.

We serve God whether people honor us or despise us, whether they slander us or praise us. ▩ Everyone who wants to live a godly life in Christ Jesus will suffer persecution. ▩ The fact that I am still being persecuted proves that I am still preaching salvation through the cross of Christ alone.

Be happy if you are insulted for being a Christian, for then the glorious Spirit of God will come upon you. If you suffer, however, it must not be for murder, stealing, making trouble, or prying into other people's affairs. But it is no shame to suffer for being a Christian. Praise God for the privilege of being called by his wonderful name! So if you are suffering according to God's will, keep on doing what is right, and trust yourself to the God who made you.

For you have been given not only the privilege of trusting in Christ but also the privilege of suffering for him. ▩ If we endure hardship, we will reign with him.

Christians follow their Lord by imitating his life and obeying his commands. We must deny our selfish desires to use our time and money our own way and choose our own direction. Following Christ in this life may be costly, but in the long run, it is well worth the pain and effort.

LAB note for Luke 9:23

(LUKE 9:23) (2 CORINTHIANS 6:8) (2 TIMOTHY 3:12) (GALATIANS 5:11) (1 PETER 4:14-16, 19) (PHILIPPIANS 1:29) (2 TIMOTHY 2:12)

August 29

Wait patiently for the LORD. Be brave and courageous. Yes, wait patiently for the LORD.

Have you never heard or understood? Don't you know that the LORD is the everlasting God, the Creator of all the earth? He never grows faint or weary. . . . He gives power to those who are tired and worn out; he offers strength to the weak. ▪ Don't be afraid, for I am with you. Do not be dismayed, for I am your God. I will strengthen you. I will help you. I will uphold you with my victorious right hand. ▪ To the poor, O LORD, you are a refuge from the storm. To the needy in distress, you are a shelter from the rain and the heat. For the oppressive acts of ruthless people are like a storm beating against a wall.

When your faith is tested, your endurance has a chance to grow. So let it grow, for when your endurance is fully developed, you will be strong in character and ready for anything. ▪ Do not throw away this confident trust in the Lord, no matter what happens. Remember the great reward it brings you! Patient endurance is what you need now, so you will continue to do God's will. Then you will receive all that he has promised. "For in just a little while, the Coming One will come and not delay."

Waiting for God is not easy. Often it seems he isn't answering our prayers or doesn't understand the urgency of our situation. But that kind of thinking implies God is not in control or not fair. God is worth waiting for—and he often uses our times of waiting to refresh, renew, and teach us.

LAB note for Psalm 27:14

(PSALM 27:14) (ISAIAH 40:28-29) (ISAIAH 41:10) (ISAIAH 25:4) (JAMES 1:3-4) (HEBREWS 10:35-37)

August 30

You don't understand now why I am doing it; someday you will.

Remember how the LORD your God led you through the wilderness for forty years, humbling you and testing you to prove your character, and to find out whether or not you would really obey his commands.

I made a covenant with you, says the Sovereign LORD, and you became mine. ▩ The Lord disciplines those he loves.

Dear friends, don't be surprised at the fiery trials you are going through, as if something strange were happening to you. Instead, be very glad—because these trials will make you partners with Christ in his suffering, and afterward you will have the wonderful joy of sharing his glory when it is displayed to all the world. ▩ Our present troubles are quite small and won't last very long. Yet they produce for us an immeasurably great glory that will last forever! So we don't look at the troubles we can see right now; rather, we look forward to what we have not yet seen. For the troubles we see will soon be over, but the joys to come will last forever.

Imagine being Peter and watching Jesus wash the others' feet, all the while moving closer to you. Seeing his Master behave like a slave must have confused Peter. He still did not understand Jesus' teaching that to be a leader, a person must be a servant. How do you treat those who work under you?

LAB note for John 13:6-7

(JOHN 13:7) (DEUTERONOMY 8:2) (EZEKIEL 16:8) (HEBREWS 12:6)
(1 PETER 4:12-13) (2 CORINTHIANS 4:17-18)

August 31

Let us lift our hearts and hands to God in heaven.

Who can be compared with the LORD our God, who is enthroned on high? Far below him are the heavens and the earth. He stoops to look, and he lifts the poor from the dirt and the needy from the garbage dump. He sets them among princes. ■ To you, O LORD, I lift up my soul. ■ I reach out for you. I thirst for you as parched land thirsts for rain. Come quickly, LORD, and answer me, for my depression deepens. Don't turn away from me, or I will die. Let me hear of your unfailing love to me in the morning, for I am trusting you. Show me where to walk, for I have come to you in prayer.

Your unfailing love is better to me than life itself; how I praise you! I will honor you as long as I live, lifting up my hands to you in prayer. ■ Give me happiness, O Lord, for my life depends on you. O Lord, you are so good, so ready to forgive, so full of unfailing love for all who ask your aid. Listen closely to my prayer, O LORD; hear my urgent cry. I will call to you whenever trouble strikes, and you will answer me.

If our conscience is clear, we can come to God with bold confidence. And we will receive whatever we request because we obey him and do the things that please him.

Sometimes our trouble or pain is so great that all we can do is cry out to God for protection. And often when there is no relief in sight, all we can do is acknowledge the greatness of God and wait for better days. The conviction that God answers prayer will sustain us in such difficult times.

LAB note for Psalm 86:7

(LAMENTATIONS 3:41) (PSALM 113:5-8) (PSALM 25:1) (PSALM 143:6-8) (PSALM 63:3-4) (PSALM 86:4-7) (1 JOHN 3:21-22)

September

Teachable Moments

Playpens and classrooms

Offices and family rooms

Learning can happen anywhere.

Although September is the traditional month for school to begin each year, learning is a year-round activity and a lifelong endeavor. If learning ceases, growth ends. What has life been teaching you lately?

September 1

I will give them one heart and mind to worship me forever, for their own good and for the good of all their descendants.

I will give you a new heart with new and right desires, and I will put a new spirit in you. I will take out your stony heart of sin and give you a new, obedient heart. ▩ The LORD is good and does what is right; he shows the proper path to those who go astray. He leads the humble in what is right, teaching them his way. The LORD leads with unfailing love and faithfulness all those who keep his covenant and obey his decrees.

That they will be one, just as you and I are one, Father—that just as you are in me and I am in you, so they will be in us, and the world will believe you sent me.

Lead a life worthy of your calling, for you have been called by God. Be humble and gentle. Be patient with each other, making allowance for each other's faults because of your love. Always keep yourselves united in the Holy Spirit, and bind yourselves together with peace. We are all one body, we have the same Spirit, and we have all been called to the same glorious future. There is only one Lord, one faith, one baptism, and there is only one God and Father, who is over us all and in us all and living through us all.

God uses his power to accomplish his purposes through his people. God doesn't give you power to be all you want to be, but the power to be all he wants you to be. We must develop "one heart" toward him, loving God above everything else. *LAB note for Jeremiah 32:36-42*

(JEREMIAH 32:39) (EZEKIEL 36:26) (PSALM 25:8-10)
(JOHN 17:21) (EPHESIANS 4:1-6)

September 2

Watchman . . . when will the night be over?

Time is running out. Wake up, for the coming of our salvation is nearer now than when we first believed. The night is almost gone; the day of salvation will soon be here. So don't live in darkness. Get rid of your evil deeds. Shed them like dirty clothes. Clothe yourselves with the armor of right living, as those who live in the light.

Now learn a lesson from the fig tree. When its buds become tender and its leaves begin to sprout, you know without being told that summer is near. Just so, when you see the events I've described beginning to happen, you can know his return is very near, right at the door. Heaven and earth will disappear, but my words will remain forever.

I am counting on the LORD; yes, I am counting on him. I have put my hope in his word. I long for the Lord more than sentries long for the dawn, yes, more than sentries long for the dawn.

He who is the faithful witness to all these things says, "Yes, I am coming soon!" Amen! Come, Lord Jesus!

So stay awake and be prepared, because you do not know the day or hour of my return.

We don't know the day or the hour, but Jesus is coming soon and unexpectedly. This is good news to those who trust him but a terrible message for those who have rejected him. Soon means "at any moment," and we must be ready for him. *LAB note for Revelation 22:20*

(ISAIAH 21:11) (ROMANS 13:11-12) (MATTHEW 24:32-33, 35) (PSALM 130:5-6) (REVELATION 22:20) (MATTHEW 25:13)

September 3

Don't copy the behavior and customs of this world, but let God transform you into a new person by changing the way you think.

Don't you realize that friendship with this world makes you an enemy of God? I say it again, that if your aim is to enjoy this world, you can't be a friend of God.

Don't team up with those who are unbelievers. How can goodness be a partner with wickedness? How can light live with darkness? What harmony can there be between Christ and the Devil? How can a believer be a partner with an unbeliever? ▪ Stop loving this evil world and all that it offers you, for when you love the world, you show that you do not have the love of the Father in you. This world is fading away, along with everything it craves. But if you do the will of God, you will live forever.

You used to live just like the rest of the world, full of sin, obeying Satan, the mighty prince of the power of the air. ▪ That isn't what you were taught when you learned about Christ. Since you have heard all about him and have learned the truth that is in Jesus, throw off your old evil nature.

God has good, pleasing, and perfect plans for his children. He wants us to be transformed people with renewed minds, living to honor and obey him. Because he wants only what is best for us and gave his Son to make our new life possible, we should joyfully give ourselves as living sacrifices for his service. *LAB note for Romans 12:1-2*

(ROMANS 12:2) (JAMES 4:4) (2 CORINTHIANS 6:14-15) (1 JOHN 2:15, 17) (EPHESIANS 2:2) (EPHESIANS 4:20-22)

September 4

The Lord is thinking about me right now.

"For I know the plans I have for you," says the LORD. "They are plans for good and not for disaster, to give you a future and a hope." ▩ "My thoughts are completely different from yours," says the LORD. "And my ways are far beyond anything you could imagine. For just as the heavens are higher than the earth, so are my ways higher than your ways and my thoughts higher than your thoughts."

How precious are your thoughts about me, O God! They are innumerable! I can't even count them; they outnumber the grains of sand! And when I wake up in the morning, you are still with me! ▩ O LORD, what great miracles you do! And how deep are your thoughts. ▩ O LORD my God, you have done many miracles for us. Your plans for us are too numerous to list.

Few of you were wise in the world's eyes, or powerful, or wealthy when God called you. ▩ Hasn't God chosen the poor in this world to be rich in faith? Aren't they the ones who will inherit the kingdom God promised to those who love him? ▩ Our hearts ache, but we always have joy. ▩ The endless treasures available . . . in Christ.

God knows the future, and his plans for us are good and full of hope. As long as God, who knows the future, provides our agenda, and goes with us as we fulfill his mission, we can have boundless hope—even in times of pain, suffering, or hardship. *LAB note for Jeremiah 29:11*

(PSALM 40:17) (JEREMIAH 29:11) (ISAIAH 55:8-9) (PSALM 139:17-18) (PSALM 92:5) (PSALM 40:5) (1 CORINTHIANS 1:26) (JAMES 2:5) (2 CORINTHIANS 6:10) (EPHESIANS 3:8)

September 5

My feet were slipping, and I was almost gone.

I cried out, "I'm slipping!" and your unfailing love, O LORD, supported me. ▪ Simon, Simon, Satan has asked to have all of you, to sift you like wheat. But I have pleaded in prayer for you, Simon, that your faith should not fail.

They may trip seven times, but each time they will rise again. ▪ Though they stumble, they will not fall, for the LORD holds them by the hand.

Do not gloat over me, my enemies! For though I fall, I will rise again. Though I sit in darkness, the LORD himself will be my light.

He will rescue you again and again so that no evil can touch you.

If you do sin, there is someone to plead for you before the Father. He is Jesus Christ, the one who pleases God completely. ▪ He is able, once and forever, to save everyone who comes to God through him. He lives forever to plead with God on their behalf.

Satan wanted to crush Simon Peter and the other disciples like grains of wheat. He hoped to find only chaff and blow it away. But Jesus assured Peter that his faith, although it would falter, would not be destroyed. It would be renewed, and Peter would become a powerful leader.

LAB note for Luke 22:31-32

(PSALM 73:2) (PSALM 94:18) (LUKE 22:31-32) (PROVERBS 24:16) (PSALM 37:24) (MICAH 7:8) (JOB 5:19) (1 JOHN 2:1) (HEBREWS 7:25)

September 6

When the Holy Spirit controls our lives, he will produce . . . faithfulness.

God saved you by his special favor when you believed. And you can't take credit for this; it is a gift from God. ▩ It is impossible to please God without faith. Anyone who wants to come to him must believe that there is a God and that he rewards those who sincerely seek him. ▩ There is no judgment awaiting those who trust him. But those who do not trust him have already been judged for not believing in the only Son of God. ▩ I do believe, but help me not to doubt!

Those who obey God's word really do love him. That is the way to know whether or not we live in him.

That is why we live by believing and not by seeing. ▩ I have been crucified with Christ. I myself no longer live, but Christ lives in me. So I live my life in this earthly body by trusting in the Son of God, who loved me and gave himself for me. ▩ You love him even though you have never seen him. Though you do not see him, you trust him; and even now you are happy with a glorious, inexpressible joy.

When someone gives you a gift, do you say, "That's very nice—now how much do I owe you?" No, the appropriate response is "Thank you." Yet how often Christians feel obligated to try to work their way to God. Instead, we should respond with gratitude, praise, and joy.

LAB note for Ephesians 2:8-9

(Galatians 5:22) (Ephesians 2:8) (Hebrews 11:6) (John 3:18) (Mark 9:24) (1 John 2:5) (2 Corinthians 5:7) (Galatians 2:19-20) (1 Peter 1:8)

September 7

Those who wait on the LORD will find new strength.

When I am weak, then I am strong. ▪ My God has given me strength. ▪ "My gracious favor is all you need. My power works best in your weakness." So now I am glad to boast about my weaknesses, so that the power of Christ may work through me. ▪ Trust in the LORD always, for the LORD God is the eternal Rock.

Give your burdens to the LORD, and he will take care of you. He will not permit the godly to slip and fall. ▪ His arms were strengthened by the Mighty One of Jacob, the Shepherd, the Rock of Israel.

You come to me with sword, spear, and javelin, but I come to you in the name of the LORD Almighty—the God of the armies of Israel, whom you have defied. ▪ I will rejoice in the LORD. I will be glad because he rescues me. I will praise him from the bottom of my heart: "LORD, who can compare with you? Who else rescues the weak and helpless from the strong?"

Waiting on the Lord is the patient expectation that God will fulfill his promises in his Word and strengthen us to rise above life's difficulties. It means to completely trust in God. *LAB note for Isaiah 40*

(ISAIAH 40:31) (2 CORINTHIANS 12:10) (ISAIAH 49:5) (2 CORINTHIANS 12:9) (ISAIAH 26:4) (PSALM 55:22) (GENESIS 49:24) (1 SAMUEL 17:45) (PSALM 35:9-10)

September 8

Be glad for all God is planning for you.

You are looking forward to the joys of heaven. ▪ If we have hope in Christ only for this life, we are the most miserable people in the world. ▪ They must enter into the Kingdom of God through many tribulations. ▪ You cannot be my disciple if you do not carry your own cross and follow me. ▪ You know that such troubles are going to happen to us Christians.

Always be full of joy in the Lord. I say it again—rejoice! ▪ I pray that God, who gives you hope, will keep you happy and full of peace as you believe in him. ▪ All honor to the God and Father of our Lord Jesus Christ, for it is by his boundless mercy that God has given us the privilege of being born again. Now we live with a wonderful expectation because Jesus Christ rose again from the dead. ▪ You love him even though you have never seen him. Though you do not see him, you trust him; and even now you are happy with a glorious, inexpressible joy. ▪ Because of our faith, Christ has brought us into this place of highest privilege where we now stand, and we confidently and joyfully look forward to sharing God's glory.

When Paul says that we look forward to the joys of heaven, he is emphasizing the security of the believer. Because we know our future destination and salvation are sure, we are free to live for Christ and love others.

LAB note for Colossians 1:5

(ROMANS 12:12) (COLOSSIANS 1:5) (1 CORINTHIANS 15:19) (ACTS 14:22) (LUKE 14:27) (1 THESSALONIANS 3:3) (PHILIPPIANS 4:4) (ROMANS 15:13) (1 PETER 1:3) (1 PETER 1:8) (ROMANS 5:2)

September 9

The LORD is for me; he will help me.

In times of trouble, may the LORD respond to your cry. May the God of Israel keep you safe from all harm. May he send you help from his sanctuary and strengthen you from Jerusalem. May we shout for joy when we hear of your victory, flying banners to honor our God. May the LORD answer all your prayers. Some nations boast of their armies and weapons, but we boast in the LORD our God. Those nations will fall down and collapse, but we will rise up and stand firm.

He will come like a flood tide driven by the breath of the LORD. ▩ Remember that the temptations that come into your life are no different from what others experience. And God is faithful. He will keep the temptation from becoming so strong that you can't stand up against it. When you are tempted, he will show you a way out so that you will not give in to it.

If God is for us, who can ever be against us? ▩ The LORD is for me, so I will not be afraid. What can mere mortals do to me?

The God whom we serve is able to save us. He will rescue us from your power.

As long as there have been armies and weapons, nations have boasted of their power, but such power does not last. True might is in God's power. Because God alone can preserve a nation or an individual, be sure your confidence is in God, who gives eternal victory.

LAB note for Psalm 20:6-8

(PSALM 118:7) (PSALM 20:1-2, 5, 7-8) (ISAIAH 59:19) (1 CORINTHIANS 10:13) (ROMANS 8:31) (PSALM 118:6) (DANIEL 3:17)

September 10

You are the salt of the earth.

You should be known for the beauty that comes from within, the unfading beauty of a gentle and quiet spirit, which is so precious to God. ▩ For you have been born again. Your new life did not come from your earthly parents because the life they gave you will end in death. But this new life will last forever because it comes from the eternal, living word of God. Those who believe in me, even though they die like everyone else, will live again. ▩ They are children of God raised up to new life. ▩ The glorious, ever-living God.

(Those who do not have the Spirit of Christ living in them are not Christians at all.) Since Christ lives within you, even though your body will die because of sin, your spirit is alive because you have been made right with God. The Spirit of God, who raised Jesus from the dead, lives in you. And just as he raised Christ from the dead, he will give life to your mortal body by this same Spirit living within you. ▩ Our earthly bodies, which die and decay, will be different when they are resurrected, for they will never die.

Salt is good for seasoning. But if it loses its flavor, how do you make it salty again? You must have the qualities of salt among yourselves and live in peace with each other.

If a seasoning has no flavor, it has no value. If Christians make no effort to affect the world around them, they are of little value to God. If we are too much like the world, we are worthless. Instead, we should affect others positively, just as seasoning brings out the best flavor in food.

LAB note for Matthew 5:13

(Matthew 5:13) (1 Peter 3:4) (1 Peter 1:23) (John 11:25) (Luke 20:36) (Romans 1:23) (Romans 8:9-11) (1 Corinthians 15:42) (Mark 9:50)

September 11

I, even I, am the one who comforts you.

All praise to the God and Father of our Lord Jesus Christ. He is the source of every mercy and the God who comforts us. He comforts us in all our troubles so that we can comfort others. When others are troubled, we will be able to give them the same comfort God has given us. ▪ The LORD is like a father to his children, tender and compassionate to those who fear him. For he knows how weak we are; he knows we are only dust. ▪ I will comfort you there as a child is comforted by its mother. ▪ Give all your worries and cares to God, for he cares about what happens to you.

But you, O Lord, are a merciful and gracious God, slow to get angry, full of unfailing love and truth.

He will give you another Counselor . . . the Holy Spirit, who leads into all truth. ▪ The Holy Spirit helps us in our distress.

He will remove all of their sorrows, and there will be no more death or sorrow or crying or pain. For the old world and its evils are gone forever.

Many think that when God comforts us, our troubles should go away. But being "comforted" can also mean receiving strength, encouragement, and hope to deal with our troubles. The more we suffer, the more comfort God gives us. If you are feeling overwhelmed, allow God to comfort you. *LAB note for 2 Corinthians 1:3-5*

(ISAIAH 51:12) (2 CORINTHIANS 1:3-4) (PSALM 103:13-14) (ISAIAH 66:13) (1 PETER 5:7) (PSALM 86:15) (JOHN 14:16-17) (ROMANS 8:26) (REVELATION 21:4)

September 12

A doubtful mind is as unsettled as a wave of the sea that is driven and tossed by the wind.

Anyone who puts a hand to the plow and then looks back is not fit for the Kingdom of God.

It is impossible to please God without faith. Anyone who wants to come to him must believe that there is a God and that he rewards those who sincerely seek him. ▩ When you ask him, be sure that you really expect him to answer, for a doubtful mind is as unsettled as a wave of the sea that is driven and tossed by the wind. People like that should not expect to receive anything from the Lord. ▩ You can pray for anything, and if you believe, you will have it.

Then we will no longer be like children, forever changing our minds about what we believe because someone has told us something different or because someone has cleverly lied to us and made the lie sound like the truth. Instead, we will hold to the truth in love, becoming more and more in every way like Christ, who is the head of his body, the church.

Remain in me. ▩ Be strong and steady, always enthusiastic about the Lord's work, for you know that nothing you do for the Lord is ever useless.

Doubt leaves a person as unsettled as restless waves. If you want to stop being tossed about, rely on God to show you what is best for you. Ask him for wisdom, and trust that he will give it to you. Then your decisions will be sure and solid. *LAB note for James 1:6–8*

(JAMES 1:6) (LUKE 9:62) (HEBREWS 11:6) (JAMES 1:6–7) (MARK 11:24) (EPHESIANS 4:14–15) (JOHN 15:4) (1 CORINTHIANS 15:58)

September 13

Weeping may go on all night, but joy comes with the morning.

Such troubles are going to happen to us Christians. Even while we were with you, we warned you that troubles would soon come—and they did, as you well know. ▪ I have told you all this so that you may have peace in me. Here on earth you will have many trials and sorrows. But take heart, because I have overcome the world.

When I awake, I will be fully satisfied, for I will see you face to face. ▪ The night is almost gone; the day of salvation will soon be here.

He is like the light of the morning, like the sunrise bursting forth in a cloudless sky, like the refreshing rains that bring tender grass from the earth.

He will swallow up death forever! The Sovereign LORD will wipe away all tears. ▪ He will remove all of their sorrows, and there will be no more death or sorrow or crying or pain. For the old world and its evils are gone forever. ▪ We who are still alive and remain on the earth will be caught up in the clouds to meet the Lord in the air and remain with him forever. So comfort and encourage each other with these words.

Some think that troubles are always caused by sin or a lack of faith. Trials may be a part of God's plan for believers, building character, perseverance, and sensitivity toward others who also face trouble. Your troubles may be a sign of effective Christian living.

LAB note for 1 Thessalonians 3:1-3

(PSALM 30:5) (1 THESSALONIANS 3:3-4) (JOHN 16:33) (PSALM 17:15) (ROMANS 13:12) (2 SAMUEL 23:4) (ISAIAH 25:8) (REVELATION 21:4) (1 THESSALONIANS 4:17-18)

September 14

He will not crush those who are weak.

The sacrifice you want is a broken spirit. A broken and repentant heart, O God, you will not despise. ▩ He heals the brokenhearted, binding up their wounds. ▩ The high and lofty one who inhabits eternity, the Holy One, says this: "I live in that high and holy place with those whose spirits are contrite and humble. I refresh the humble and give new courage to those with repentant hearts. For I will not fight against you forever; I will not always show my anger. If I did, all people would pass away—all the souls I have made."

I will search for my lost ones who strayed away, and I will bring them safely home again. I will bind up the injured and strengthen the weak. ▩ When they walk through the Valley of Weeping, it will become a place of refreshing springs, where pools of blessing collect after the rains! ▩ So take a new grip with your tired hands and stand firm on your shaky legs. Mark out a straight path for your feet. Then those who follow you, though they are weak and lame, will not stumble and fall but will become strong. ▩ Your God . . . is coming to save you.

God wants a broken spirit and a broken and repentant heart. You can never please God by outward actions—no matter how good—if your heart attitude is not right. Are you sorry for your sin? Do you genuinely intend to stop? God is pleased by this kind of repentance.

LAB note for Psalm 51:17

(MATTHEW 12:20) (PSALM 51:17) (PSALM 147:3) (ISAIAH 57:15-16) (EZEKIEL 34:16) (PSALM 84:6) (HEBREWS 12:12-13) (ISAIAH 35:4)

September 15

Open my eyes to see the wonderful truths in your law.

He opened their minds to understand these many Scriptures. ▩ Then he explained to them, "You have been permitted to understand the secrets of the Kingdom of Heaven, but others have not. ▩ Then Jesus prayed this prayer: "O Father, Lord of heaven and earth, thank you for hiding the truth from those who think themselves so wise and clever, and for revealing it to the childlike. Yes, Father, it pleased you to do it this way! ▩ And God has actually given us his Spirit (not the world's spirit) so we can know the wonderful things God has freely given us. ▩ How precious are your thoughts about me, O God! They are innumerable! I can't even count them; they outnumber the grains of sand! And when I wake up in the morning, you are still with me! ▩ Oh, what a wonderful God we have! How great are his riches and wisdom and knowledge! How impossible it is for us to understand his decisions and his methods! For who can know what the Lord is thinking? Who knows enough to be his counselor? For everything comes from him; everything exists by his power and is intended for his glory. To him be glory evermore. Amen.

Have you ever wondered how to understand a difficult Bible passage? Besides reading surrounding passages, asking other people, and consulting reference works, pray that the Holy Spirit will open your mind to understand, giving you the needed insight to put God's Word into action in your life.

LAB note for Luke 24:45

(Psalm 119:18) (Luke 24:45) (Matthew 13:11) (Matthew 11:25-26) (1 Corinthians 2:12) (Psalm 139:17-18) (Romans 11:33-34, 36)

September 16

"The Spring of the One Who Cried Out."

If you only knew the gift God has for you and who I am, you would ask me, and I would give you living water. ▪ "If you are thirsty, come to me!" (When he said "living water," he was speaking of the Spirit, who would be given to everyone believing in him.)

"Bring all the tithes into the storehouse so there will be enough food in my Temple. If you do," says the LORD Almighty, "I will open the windows of heaven for you. I will pour out a blessing so great that you won't have enough room to take it in. Try it! Let me prove it to you!" ▪ If you sinful people know how to give good gifts to your children, how much more will your heavenly Father give the Holy Spirit to those who ask him. ▪ Keep on asking, and you will be given what you ask for. Keep on looking, and you will find.

Because you Gentiles have become his children, God has sent the Spirit of his Son into your hearts, and now you can call God your dear Father. ▪ So you should not be like cowering, fearful slaves. You should behave instead like God's very own children, adopted into his family—calling him "Father, dear Father."

What did Jesus mean by "living water"? God is called the fountain of living water. In saying he would bring living water that could forever quench a person's thirst for God, Jesus was claiming to be the Messiah. Only the Messiah could give this gift that satisfies the soul's desire.

LAB note for John 4:10

(JUDGES 15:19) (JOHN 4:10) (JOHN 7:37, 39) (MALACHI 3:10) (LUKE 11:13) (LUKE 11:9) (GALATIANS 4:6) (ROMANS 8:15)

September 17

In his kindness God called you to his eternal glory by means of Jesus Christ.

I will make all my goodness pass before you, and I will call out my name, "the LORD," to you. I will show kindness to anyone I choose, and I will show mercy to anyone I choose. ▩ God will be gracious and say, "Set him free. Do not make him die, for I have found a ransom for his life." ▩ Yet now God in his gracious kindness declares us not guilty. He has done this through Christ Jesus, who has freed us by taking away our sins. For God sent Jesus to take the punishment for our sins and to satisfy God's anger against us. We are made right with God when we believe that Jesus shed his blood, sacrificing his life for us. God was being entirely fair and just when he did not punish those who sinned in former times. And he is entirely fair and just in this present time when he declares sinners to be right in his sight because they believe in Jesus. ▩ God's unfailing love and faithfulness came through Jesus Christ.

God saved you by his special favor when you believed. And you can't take credit for this; it is a gift from God. ▩ May God our Father and Christ Jesus our Lord give you grace, mercy, and peace. ▩ God has given gifts to each of you from his great variety of spiritual gifts. Manage them well so that God's generosity can flow through you. ▩ He gives us more and more strength.

When a judge in a court of law declares the defendant not guilty, all the charges are removed from his record. Legally, it is as if the person had never been accused. When God forgives our sins, our record is wiped clean. From his perspective, it is as though we had never sinned.

LAB note for Romans 3:24

(1 PETER 5:10) (EXODUS 33:19) (JOB 33:24) (ROMANS 3:24–26) (JOHN 1:17) (EPHESIANS 2:8) (1 TIMOTHY 1:2) (1 PETER 4:10) (JAMES 4:6)

September 18

I look up to the mountains—does my help come from there? My help comes from the LORD, who made the heavens and the earth!

Just as the mountains surround and protect Jerusalem, so the LORD surrounds and protects his people. ▩ The sun will not hurt you by day, nor the moon at night. The LORD keeps you from all evil and preserves your life. The LORD keeps watch over you as you come and go, both now and forever.

I lift my eyes to you, O God, enthroned in heaven. We look to the LORD our God for his mercy, just as servants keep their eyes on their master, as a slave girl watches her mistress for the slightest signal. ▩ I think how much you have helped me; I sing for joy in the shadow of your protecting wings.

O our God, won't you stop them? We are powerless against this mighty army that is about to attack us. We do not know what to do, but we are looking to you for help. ▩ Help us, O LORD our God, for we trust in you alone. It is in your name that we have come against this vast horde. ▩ My eyes are always looking to the LORD for help, for he alone can rescue me from the traps of my enemies. ▩ Our help is from the LORD, who made the heavens and the earth.

If you are facing battles you feel you can't possibly win, don't give up. The secret of victory is first to admit the futility of unaided human effort and then trust God to save. His power works best through those who recognize their limitations. *LAB note for 2 Chronicles 14:11*

(PSALM 121:1-2) (PSALM 125:2) (PSALM 121:6-8) (PSALM 123:1-2) (PSALM 63:7) (2 CHRONICLES 20:12) (2 CHRONICLES 14:11) (PSALM 25:15) (PSALM 124:8)

September 19

But as for me, how good it is to be near God!

I love your sanctuary, LORD, the place where your glory shines. ▪ A single day in your courts is better than a thousand anywhere else! I would rather be a gatekeeper in the house of my God than live the good life in the homes of the wicked. ▪ What joy for those you choose to bring near, those who live in your holy courts. What joy awaits us inside your holy Temple.

The LORD is wonderfully good to those who wait for him and seek him. ▪ The LORD still waits for you to come to him so he can show you his love and compassion. For the LORD is a faithful God. Blessed are those who wait for him to help them.

And so, dear brothers and sisters, we can boldly enter heaven's Most Holy Place because of the blood of Jesus. This is the new, life-giving way that Christ has opened up for us through the sacred curtain, by means of his death for us. Let us go right into the presence of God, with true hearts fully trusting him. For our evil consciences have been sprinkled with Christ's blood to make us clean, and our bodies have been washed with pure water.

Access to God, the joy of living in the Temple courts, was a great honor. God had chosen a special group of Israelites from the tribe of Levi to serve as priests, and they were the only ones who could enter the sacred rooms where God's presence resided. Because of Jesus' death on the cross, believers today have access to God's presence in every place and at any time.

LAB note for Psalm 65:4

(PSALM 73:28) (PSALM 26:8) (PSALM 84:10) (PSALM 65:4) (LAMENTATIONS 3:25) (ISAIAH 30:18) (HEBREWS 10:19-20, 22)

September 20

Let it grow, for when your endurance is fully developed, you will be strong in character and ready for anything.

There is wonderful joy ahead, even though it is necessary for you to endure many trials for a while. These trials are only to test your faith, to show that it is strong and pure. It is being tested as fire tests and purifies gold—and your faith is far more precious to God than mere gold. So if your faith remains strong after being tried by fiery trials, it will bring you much praise and glory and honor on the day when Jesus Christ is revealed to the whole world. ▪ We can rejoice, too, when we run into problems and trials, for we know that they are good for us—they help us learn to endure. And endurance develops strength of character in us, and character strengthens our confident expectation of salvation.

It is good to wait quietly for salvation from the LORD. ▪ When all you owned was taken from you, you accepted it with joy. You knew you had better things waiting for you in eternity. Do not throw away this confident trust in the Lord, no matter what happens. Remember the great reward it brings you! Patient endurance is what you need now, so you will continue to do God's will. Then you will receive all that he has promised.

Instead of complaining about our struggles, we should see them as opportunities for growth. Thank God for promising to be with you in rough times. Ask him to help you solve your problems or to give you the strength to endure them. Then be patient. God will stay close and help you grow.

LAB note for James 1:2-4

(JAMES 1:4) (1 PETER 1:6-7) (ROMANS 5:3-4) (LAMENTATIONS 3:26) (HEBREWS 10:34-36)

September 21

Humble yourselves under the mighty power of God, and in his good time he will honor you.

The LORD despises pride; be assured that the proud will be punished.

And yet, LORD, you are our Father. We are the clay, and you are the potter. We are all formed by your hand. Oh, don't be so angry with us, LORD. Please don't remember our sins forever. Look at us, we pray, and see that we are all your people. ▪ You disciplined me severely, but I deserved it. I was like a calf that needed to be trained for the yoke and plow. Turn me again to you and restore me, for you alone are the Lord my God. I turned away from God, but then I was sorry. I kicked myself for my stupidity! I was thoroughly ashamed of all I did in my younger days. ▪ It is good for the young to submit to the yoke of his discipline. Let them sit alone in silence beneath the LORD's demands. Let them lie face down in the dust; then at last there is hope for them.

Evil does not spring from the soil, and trouble does not sprout from the earth. People are born for trouble as predictably as sparks fly upward from a fire. ▪ Though he brings grief, he also shows compassion according to the greatness of his unfailing love. For he does not enjoy hurting people or causing them sorrow.

We often worry about our position and status, hoping to get proper recognition for what we do. But God's recognition counts more than human praise. God is able and willing to bless us according to his timing. Humbly obey God regardless of present circumstances, and in his good time—either in this life or in the next—he will honor you.

LAB note for 1 Peter 5:6

(1 PETER 5:6) (PROVERBS 16:5) (ISAIAH 64:8-9) (JEREMIAH 31:18-19) (LAMENTATIONS 3:27-29) (JOB 5:6-7) (LAMENTATIONS 3:32-33)

September 22

The heavens tell of the glory of God. The skies display his marvelous craftsmanship.

From the time the world was created, people have seen the earth and sky and all that God made. They can clearly see his invisible qualities—his eternal power and divine nature. ◈ He never left himself without a witness. ◈ Day after day they continue to speak; night after night they make him known. They speak without a sound or a word; their voice is silent in the skies.

When I look at the night sky and see the work of your fingers—the moon and the stars you have set in place—what are mortals that you should think of us, mere humans that you should care for us?

The sun has one kind of glory, while the moon and stars each have another kind. And even the stars differ from each other in their beauty and brightness. It is the same way for the resurrection of the dead. Our earthly bodies, which die and decay, will be different when they are resurrected, for they will never die. ◈ Those who are wise will shine as bright as the sky, and those who turn many to righteousness will shine like stars forever.

To say that the universe happened by chance is absurd. Its design, intricacy, and orderliness point to a personally involved Creator. As you look at God's handiwork in nature and the heavens, thank him for such magnificent beauty and the truth it reveals about the Creator.

LAB note for Psalm 19:1-6

(Psalm 19:1) (Romans 1:20) (Acts 14:17) (Psalm 19:2-3) (Psalm 8:3-4) (1 Corinthians 15:41-42) (Daniel 12:3)

September 23

The Son can do nothing by himself. He does only what he sees the Father doing. Whatever the Father does, the Son also does.

The LORD grants wisdom! From his mouth come knowledge and understanding. He grants a treasure of good sense to the godly. He is their shield, protecting those who walk with integrity. He guards the paths of justice and protects those who are faithful to him. ■ I will give you the right words and such wisdom that none of your opponents will be able to reply!

Wait patiently for the LORD. Be brave and courageous. Yes, wait patiently for the LORD. ■ My gracious favor is all you need. My power works best in your weakness.

Called to live in the love of God the Father and the care of Jesus Christ. ■ Jesus and the ones he makes holy have the same Father. That is why Jesus is not ashamed to call them his brothers and sisters.

Am I not everywhere in all the heavens and earth? ■ And the church is his body; it is filled by Christ, who fills everything everywhere with his presence.

I am the LORD, and there is no other Savior. ■ He is indeed the Savior of the world.

May God the Father and Christ Jesus our Savior give you grace and peace.

Because of his unity with God, Jesus lived as God wanted him to live. Because of our identification with Jesus, we must honor him and live as he wants us to live. The questions "What would Jesus do?" and "What would Jesus have me do?" may help us make the right choices.

LAB note for John 5:19–23

(JOHN 5:19) (PROVERBS 2:6–8) (LUKE 21:15) (PSALM 27:14) (2 CORINTHIANS 12:9) (JUDE 1:1) (HEBREWS 2:11) (JEREMIAH 23:24) (EPHESIANS 1:23) (ISAIAH 43:11) (JOHN 4:42) (TITUS 1:4)

September 24

Show me the path where I should walk, O LORD; point out the right road for me to follow.

Moses said to the LORD, ". . . You call me by name and tell me I have found favor with you. Please, if this is really so, show me your intentions so I will understand you more fully and do exactly what you want me to do. . . ." And the LORD replied, "I will personally go with you, Moses. I will give you rest—everything will be fine for you." ▩ He revealed his character to Moses and his deeds to the people of Israel.

He leads the humble in what is right, teaching them his way. Who are those who fear the LORD? He will show them the path they should choose. ▩ Trust in the LORD with all your heart; do not depend on your own understanding. Seek his will in all you do, and he will direct your paths.

You will show me the way of life, granting me the joy of your presence and the pleasures of living with you forever. ▩ The LORD says, "I will guide you along the best pathway for your life. I will advise you and watch over you." ▩ The way of the righteous is like the first gleam of dawn, which shines ever brighter until the full light of day.

How do we receive God's guidance? The first step is to want to be guided and to realize that God's primary guidance system is in his Word, the Bible. By reading it and constantly learning from it, we will gain the wisdom to perceive God's direction for our lives. *LAB note for Psalm 25:4*

(PSALM 25:4) (EXODUS 33:12-14) (PSALM 103:7) (PSALM 25:9, 12) (PROVERBS 3:5-6) (PSALM 16:11) (PSALM 32:8) (PROVERBS 4:18)

September 25

What makes you better than anyone else? What do you have that God hasn't given you? And if all you have is from God, why boast as though you have accomplished something on your own?

Whatever I am now, it is all because God poured out his special favor on me—and not without results. ▩ In his goodness he chose to make us his own children by giving us his true word. ▩ Receiving God's promise is not up to us. We can't get it by choosing it or working hard for it. God will show mercy to anyone he chooses! ▩ Can we boast, then, that we have done anything to be accepted by God? No. ▩ God alone made it possible for you to be in Christ Jesus. For our benefit God made Christ to be wisdom itself. . . . "The person who wishes to boast should boast only of what the Lord has done."

Once you were dead, doomed forever because of your many sins. You used to live just like the rest of the world, full of sin, obeying Satan, the mighty prince of the power of the air. He is the spirit at work in the hearts of those who refuse to obey God. All of us used to live that way, following the passions and desires of our evil nature. We were born with an evil nature, and we were under God's anger just like everyone else. ▩ Now your sins have been washed away, and you have been set apart for God. You have been made right with God because of what the Lord Jesus Christ and the Spirit of our God have done for you.

Don't let your loyalty to church leaders cause strife, slander, or broken relationships. Make sure that your deepest loyalties are to Christ and not to his human agents. Those who spend more time in debating church leadership than in declaring Christ's message don't have the mind of Christ.

LAB note for 1 Corinthians 4:6-7

(1 CORINTHIANS 4:7) (1 CORINTHIANS 15:10) (JAMES 1:18) (ROMANS 9:16) (ROMANS 3:27) (1 CORINTHIANS 1:30-31) (EPHESIANS 2:1-3) (1 CORINTHIANS 6:11)

September 26

All praise to him who loves us and has freed us from our sins by shedding his blood for us.

Many waters cannot quench love, neither can rivers drown it. Love is as strong as death. ▩ The greatest love is shown when people lay down their lives for their friends.

He personally carried away our sins in his own body on the cross so we can be dead to sin and live for what is right. You have been healed by his wounds! ▩ He is so rich in kindness that he purchased our freedom through the blood of his Son, and our sins are forgiven.

Your sins have been washed away, and you have been set apart for God. You have been made right with God because of what the Lord Jesus Christ and the Spirit of our God have done for you. ▩ You are a chosen people. You are a kingdom of priests, God's holy nation, his very own possession. This is so you can show others the goodness of God, for he called you out of the darkness into his wonderful light. ▩ I plead with you to give your bodies to God. Let them be a living and holy sacrifice—the kind he will accept. When you think of what he has done for you, is this too much to ask?

We are to love each other as Jesus loved us, and he loved us enough to give his life for us. We may not have to die for someone, but there are other ways to practice sacrificial love: listening, helping, encouraging, giving. Think of someone in particular who needs this kind of love today—and give it! *LAB note for John 15:12-13*

(REVELATION 1:5) (SONG OF SONGS 8:7, 6) (JOHN 15:13) (1 PETER 2:24) (EPHESIANS 1:7) (1 CORINTHIANS 6:11) (1 PETER 2:9) (ROMANS 12:1)

September 27

There are different kinds of service in the church, but it is the same Lord we are serving.

Azmaveth son of Adiel was in charge of the palace treasuries. Jonathan son of Uzziah was in charge of the regional treasuries throughout the towns, villages, and fortresses of Israel. Ezri son of Kelub was in charge of the field workers who farmed the king's lands. Shimei from Ramah was in charge of the king's vineyards. Zabdi from Shepham was responsible for the grapes and the supplies of wine. All these officials were overseers of King David's property.

Here is a list of some of the members that God has placed in the body of Christ: first are apostles, second are prophets, third are teachers, then those who do miracles, those who have the gift of healing, those who can help others, those who can get others to work together, those who speak in unknown languages.

God has given gifts to each of you from his great variety of spiritual gifts. Manage them well so that God's generosity can flow through you. Are you called to be a speaker? Then speak as though God himself were speaking through you. Are you called to help others? Do it with all the strength and energy that God supplies. Then God will be given glory in everything through Jesus Christ. All glory and power belong to him forever and ever. Amen.

Some people, well aware of their abilities, believe that they have the right to use their abilities as they please. Others feel they have no special talents at all. But everyone has some gifts; find yours and use them. All our abilities should be used in serving others; none are for our own exclusive enjoyment. *LAB note for 1 Peter 4:10-11*

(1 Corinthians 12:5) (1 Chronicles 27:25-27, 31)
(1 Corinthians 12:28) (1 Peter 4:10-11)

September 28

When Moses came down the mountain carrying the stone tablets inscribed with the terms of the covenant, he wasn't aware that his face glowed because he had spoken to the LORD face to face.

To you goes all the glory for your unfailing love and faithfulness. ▪ Lord, when did we ever see you hungry and feed you? Or thirsty and give you something to drink? ▪ When you did it to one of the least of these my brothers and sisters, you were doing it to me! ▪ Be humble, thinking of others as better than yourself. ▪ Serve each other in humility.

Jesus' appearance changed so that his face shone like the sun, and his clothing became dazzling white. ▪ Everyone in the council stared at Stephen because his face became as bright as an angel's. ▪ Glorify your Son so he can give glory back to you. ▪ All of us have had that veil removed so that we can be mirrors that brightly reflect the glory of the Lord. And as the Spirit of the Lord works within us, we become more and more like him and reflect his glory even more.

You are the light of the world—like a city on a mountain, glowing in the night for all to see. Don't hide your light under a basket! ▪ Let your lives shine brightly before them. Hold tightly to the word of life.

Moses' face glowed after he spent time with God. The people could clearly see God's presence in him. How often do you spend time alone with God? Although your face may not light up a room, time spent in prayer, reading the Bible, and meditating should have such an effect on your life that people will know you have been with God.

LAB note for Exodus 34:28-35

(EXODUS 34:29) (PSALM 115:1) (MATTHEW 25:37) (MATTHEW 25:40) (PHILIPPIANS 2:3) (1 PETER 5:5) (MATTHEW 17:2) (ACTS 6:15) (JOHN 17:22) (2 CORINTHIANS 3:18) (MATTHEW 5:14-15) (PHILIPPIANS 2:15-16)

September 29

There are different ways God works in our lives, but it is the same God who does the work through all of us.

Some men from Manasseh defected from the Israelite army and joined David. They were all brave and able warriors who became commanders in his army. ▩ A spiritual gift is given to each of us as a means of helping the entire church.

From the tribe of Issachar, there were 200 leaders of the tribe with their relatives. All these men understood the temper of the times and knew the best course for Israel to take. ▩ To one person the Spirit gives the ability to give wise advice; to another he gives the gift of special knowledge.

From the tribe of Zebulun, there were 50,000 skilled warriors. They were fully armed and prepared for battle and completely loyal to David. ▩ I take joy in doing your will, my God, for your law is written on my heart.

God made our bodies with many parts, and he has put each part just where he wants it. If one part suffers, all the parts suffer with it, and if one part is honored, all the parts are glad.

One Lord, one faith, one baptism.

People are often drawn to a great cause and the brave determined people who support it. As believers, we have the greatest cause—the salvation of people. If we are brave, determined, and faithful, others will be drawn to work with us. *LAB note for 1 Chronicles 12:22*

(1 CORINTHIANS 12:6) (1 CHRONICLES 12:19, 21) (1 CORINTHIANS 12:7) (1 CHRONICLES 12:32) (1 CORINTHIANS 12:8) (1 CHRONICLES 12:33) (PSALM 40:8) (1 CORINTHIANS 12:18, 26) (EPHESIANS 4:5)

September 30

The Coming One will come and not delay.

Write my answer in large, clear letters on a tablet, so that a runner can read it and tell everyone else. But these things I plan won't happen right away. Slowly, steadily, surely, the time approaches when the vision will be fulfilled. If it seems slow, wait patiently, for it will surely take place. It will not be delayed.

You must not forget, dear friends, that a day is like a thousand years to the Lord, and a thousand years is like a day. The Lord isn't really being slow about his promise to return, as some people think. No, he is being patient for your sake. He does not want anyone to perish, so he is giving more time for everyone to repent. ▪ You, O Lord, are a merciful and gracious God, slow to get angry, full of unfailing love and truth. ▪ Oh, that you would burst from the heavens and come down! How the mountains would quake in your presence! For since the world began, no ear has heard, and no eye has seen a God like you, who works for those who wait for him!

It isn't easy to be patient when evil and injustice seem to have the upper hand in the world. But it helps to remember that God hates sin even more than we do. Punishment of sin will certainly come. We must wait patiently, trusting God even when we don't understand why events occur as they do.

LAB note for Habakkuk 2:3

(HEBREWS 10:37) (HABAKKUK 2:2-3) (2 PETER 3:8-9)
(PSALM 86:15) (ISAIAH 64:1, 4)

October

Autumn's Abundance

Apple picking and pumpkin pie
Crackling leaves and hayrides
Autumn brings a harvest of blessing.

As the crisp winds of autumn chase away summer's greenery, take time to notice the fiery display of new colors. What a creative God he is to make such a beautiful world for us!

October 1

You will always reap what you sow!

Experience shows that those who plant trouble and cultivate evil will harvest the same. ▩ They have planted the wind and will harvest the whirlwind. ▩ Those who live only to satisfy their own sinful desires will harvest the consequences of decay and death.

The reward of the godly will last. ▩ Those who live to please the Spirit will harvest everlasting life from the Spirit. So don't get tired of doing what is good. Don't get discouraged and give up, for we will reap a harvest of blessing at the appropriate time. Whenever we have the opportunity, we should do good to everyone, especially to our Christian brothers and sisters.

It is possible to give freely and become more wealthy, but those who are stingy will lose everything. The generous prosper and are satisfied; those who refresh others will themselves be refreshed. ▩ Remember this—a farmer who plants only a few seeds will get a small crop. But the one who plants generously will get a generous crop.

It would certainly be a surprise if you planted corn and pumpkins came up. It's a natural law to reap what we sow. If you plant to please your own desires, you'll reap a crop of sorrow and evil. If you plant to please God, you'll reap joy and everlasting life. What kinds of seeds are you sowing?

LAB note for Galatians 6:7-8

(GALATIANS 6:7) (JOB 4:8) (HOSEA 8:7) (GALATIANS 6:8) (PROVERBS 11:18) (GALATIANS 6:8-10) (PROVERBS 11:24-25) (2 CORINTHIANS 9:6)

October 2

Never be lazy in your work, but serve the Lord enthusiastically.

Whatever you do, do well. For when you go to the grave, there will be no work or planning or knowledge or wisdom. ▪ Work hard and cheerfully at whatever you do, as though you were working for the Lord rather than for people. Remember that the Lord will give you an inheritance as your reward, and the Master you are serving is Christ. ▪ Remember that the Lord will reward each one of us for the good we do.

All of us must quickly carry out the tasks assigned us by the one who sent me, because there is little time left before the night falls and all work comes to an end.

So, dear brothers and sisters, work hard to prove that you really are among those God has called and chosen. Doing this, you will never stumble or fall away. ▪ Our great desire is that you will keep right on loving others as long as life lasts, in order to make certain that what you hope for will come true. Then you will not become spiritually dull and indifferent. Instead, you will follow the example of those who are going to inherit God's promises because of their faith and patience. ▪ Run in such a way that you will win.

Considering the uncertainties of the future and the certainty of death, Solomon recommends enjoying life as God's gift. He may have been criticizing those who put off all present pleasures in order to accumulate wealth, much like those who get caught up in today's rat race. Enjoy God's gifts while you are able! *LAB note for Ecclesiastes 9:7-10*

(ROMANS 12:11) (ECCLESIASTES 9:10) (COLOSSIANS 3:23-24) (EPHESIANS 6:8) (JOHN 9:4) (2 PETER 1:10) (HEBREWS 6:11-12) (1 CORINTHIANS 9:24)

October 3

It is good to wait quietly for salvation from the LORD.

Has God forgotten to be kind? Has he slammed the door on his compassion? ▩ In sudden fear I had cried out, "I have been cut off from the LORD!" But you heard my cry for mercy and answered my call for help. Love the LORD, all you faithful ones! For the LORD protects those who are loyal to him, but he harshly punishes all who are arrogant. So be strong and take courage, all you who put your hope in the LORD!

Don't you think God will surely give justice to his chosen people who plead with him day and night? Will he keep putting them off? I tell you, he will grant justice to them quickly! ▩ Wait for the LORD to handle the matter. ▩ Be still in the presence of the LORD, and wait patiently for him to act. Don't worry about evil people who prosper.

You will not even need to fight. Take your positions; then stand still and watch the LORD's victory.

Don't get tired of doing what is good. Don't get discouraged and give up, for we will reap a harvest of blessing at the appropriate time. ▩ Be patient as you wait for the Lord's return. Consider the farmers who eagerly look for the rains in the fall and in the spring. They patiently wait for the precious harvest to ripen.

Asaph cried out to God for courage during a time of deep distress. But as he expressed his requests and doubts to God, his focus changed from thinking of himself to worshiping God. Only after he put aside his doubts about God's holiness and care for him did he eliminate his distress.

LAB note for Psalm 77:1-12

(LAMENTATIONS 3:26) (PSALM 77:9) (PSALM 31:22-24) (LUKE 18:7-8) (PROVERBS 20:22) (PSALM 37:7) (2 CHRONICLES 20:17) (GALATIANS 6:9) (JAMES 5:7)

October 4

The LORD's promises are pure, like silver refined in a furnace, purified seven times over.

Your promises have been thoroughly tested; that is why I love them so much. ▩ The law of the LORD is perfect, reviving the soul. The commandments of the LORD are right, bringing joy to the heart. The commands of the LORD are clear, giving insight to life. ▩ Every word of God proves true. He defends all who come to him for protection. Do not add to his words, or he may rebuke you, and you will be found a liar.

I have hidden your word in my heart, that I might not sin against you. I will study your commandments and reflect on your ways. ▩ The laws of the LORD are true; each one is fair. They are more desirable than gold, even the finest gold. They are sweeter than honey, even honey dripping from the comb. ▩ Fix your thoughts on what is true and honorable and right. Think about things that are pure and lovely and admirable. Think about things that are excellent and worthy of praise. ▩ You must crave pure spiritual milk so that you can grow into the fullness of your salvation. Cry out for this nourishment as a baby cries for milk.

As for God, his way is perfect. All the LORD's promises prove true. He is a shield for all who look to him for protection. For who is God except the LORD? Who but our God is a solid rock?

Sincerity and truth are extremely valuable because they are so rare. When we feel as though sincerity and truth have nearly gone out of existence, we have one hope—the word of God. God's words are as flawless as refined silver. So listen carefully when he speaks. *LAB note for Psalm 12:6*

(PSALM 12:6) (PSALM 119:140) (PSALM 19:7-8) (PROVERBS 30:5-6) (PSALM 119:11, 15) (PSALM 19:9-10) (PHILIPPIANS 4:8) (1 PETER 2:2) (PSALM 18:30-31)

October 5

You, O God, are my place of safety.

The LORD is my rock, my fortress, and my savior; my God is my rock, in whom I find protection. He is my shield, the strength of my salvation, and my stronghold, my high tower. ▪ The LORD is my strength, my shield from every danger. I trust in him with all my heart. He helps me, and my heart is filled with joy. I burst out in songs of thanksgiving.

They will respect and glorify the name of the LORD throughout the world. For he will come like a flood tide driven by the breath of the LORD. ▪ That is why we can say with confidence, "The Lord is my helper, so I will not be afraid. What can mere mortals do to me?"

The LORD is my light and my salvation—so why should I be afraid? The LORD protects me from danger—so why should I tremble? ▪ Though I sit in darkness, the LORD himself will be my light.

Just as the mountains surround and protect Jerusalem, so the LORD surrounds and protects his people, both now and forever. ▪ I think how much you have helped me; I sing for joy in the shadow of your protecting wings.

For the honor of your name, lead me out of this peril. ▪ Be our strength each day and our salvation in times of trouble.

We become content when we realize God's sufficiency for our needs. Christians who become materialistic are saying by their actions that God can't take care of them—or at least that he won't take care of them the way they want. The only antidote to this insecurity is to trust God to meet all our needs.

LAB note for Hebrews 13:5-6

(PSALM 59:9) (2 SAMUEL 22:2-3) (PSALM 28:7) (ISAIAH 59:19) (HEBREWS 13:6) (PSALM 27:1) (MICAH 7:8) (PSALM 125:2) (PSALM 63:7) (PSALM 31:3) (ISAIAH 33:2)

October 6

He leads the humble in what is right, teaching them his way.

God blesses those who are gentle and lowly.

I have observed something else in this world of ours. The fastest runner doesn't always win the race, and the strongest warrior doesn't always win the battle. The wise are often poor, and the skillful are not necessarily wealthy. ▩ We can make our plans, but the LORD determines our steps.

I lift my eyes to you, O God, enthroned in heaven. We look to the LORD our God for his mercy, just as servants keep their eyes on their master, as a slave girl watches her mistress for the slightest signal. ▩ Show me where to walk, for I have come to you in prayer.

O our God, won't you stop them? We are powerless against this mighty army that is about to attack us. We do not know what to do, but we are looking to you for help.

If you need wisdom—if you want to know what God wants you to do—ask him, and he will gladly tell you. He will not resent your asking.

When the Spirit of truth comes, he will guide you into all truth.

In the Kingdom of Heaven, wealth and power and authority are unimportant. Kingdom people seek different blessings and benefits, and they have different attitudes. Are your attitudes a carbon copy of the world's selfishness, pride, and lust for power, or do they reflect the humility and self-sacrifice of Jesus, your king? *LAB note for Matthew 5:3-12*

(PSALM 25:9) (MATTHEW 5:5) (ECCLESIASTES 9:11) (PROVERBS 16:9) (PSALM 123:1-2) (PSALM 143:8) (2 CHRONICLES 20:12) (JAMES 1:5) (JOHN 16:13)

October 7

Do not stay so far from me, for trouble is near.

O LORD, how long will you forget me? Forever? How long will you look the other way? How long must I struggle with anguish in my soul, with sorrow in my heart every day? ▪ Do not hide yourself from me. Do not reject your servant in anger. You have always been my helper. Don't leave me now; don't abandon me, O God of my salvation!

When they call on me, I will answer; I will be with them in trouble. I will rescue them and honor them. ▪ The LORD is close to all who call on him, yes, to all who call on him sincerely. He fulfills the desires of those who fear him; he hears their cries for help and rescues them.

I will not abandon you as orphans—I will come to you. ▪ I am with you always, even to the end of the age.

God is our refuge and strength, always ready to help in times of trouble. ▪ I wait quietly before God, for my hope is in him. He alone is my rock and my salvation, my fortress where I will not be shaken.

God's loving concern does not begin on the day we are born and conclude on the day we die. It reaches back to those days before we were born and reaches ahead along the unending path of eternity. Our only sure help comes from a God whose concern for us reaches beyond our earthly existence.

LAB note for Psalm 22:9-11

(PSALM 22:11) (PSALM 13:1-2) (PSALM 27:9) (PSALM 91:15) (PSALM 145:18-19) (JOHN 14:18) (MATTHEW 28:20) (PSALM 46:1) (PSALM 62:5-6)

October 8

I am the Alpha and the Omega—the beginning and the end.

The LORD is king! He is robed in majesty. Indeed, the LORD is robed in majesty and armed with strength. The world is firmly established; it cannot be shaken. Your throne, O LORD, has been established from time immemorial. You yourself are from the everlasting past.

He displays his power. ▩ If God is for us, who can ever be against us? ▩ The God whom we serve is able to save us. He will rescue us from your power. ▩ My Father has given them to me, and he is more powerful than anyone else. So no one can take them from me. ▩ You belong to God, my dear children. You have already won your fight with these false prophets, because the Spirit who lives in you is greater than the spirit who lives in the world.

Not to us, O LORD, but to you goes all the glory. ▩ Yours, O LORD, is the greatness, the power, the glory, the victory, and the majesty. Everything in the heavens and on earth is yours, O LORD, and this is your kingdom. We adore you as the one who is over all things. O, our God, we thank you and praise your glorious name! But who am I, and who are my people, that we could give anything to you? Everything we have has come from you, and we give you only what you have already given us!

Just as a shepherd protects his sheep, Jesus protects his people from eternal harm. While believers can expect to suffer on earth, Satan cannot harm their souls or take away their eternal life with God. If you choose to follow Jesus, he will give you everlasting safety.

LAB note for John 10:28-29

(REVELATION 1:8) (PSALM 93:1-2) (NAHUM 1:3) (ROMANS 8:31) (DANIEL 3:17) (JOHN 10:29) (1 JOHN 4:4) (PSALM 115:1) (1 CHRONICLES 29:11, 13-14)

October 9

The LORD is your security.

Human opposition only enhances your glory, for you use it as a sword of judgment. ▩ The king's heart is like a stream of water directed by the LORD; he turns it wherever he pleases. ▩ When the ways of people please the LORD, he makes even their enemies live at peace with them.

I am counting on the LORD; yes, I am counting on him. I have put my hope in his word. I long for the Lord more than sentries long for the dawn. ▩ I prayed to the LORD, and he answered me, freeing me from all my fears.

The eternal God is your refuge, and his everlasting arms are under you. He thrusts out the enemy before you; it is he who cries, "Destroy them!" ▩ Blessed are those who trust in the LORD and have made the LORD their hope and confidence. They are like trees planted along a riverbank, with roots that reach deep into the water. Such trees are not bothered by the heat or worried by long months of drought. Their leaves stay green, and they go right on producing delicious fruit.

What can we say about such wonderful things as these? If God is for us, who can ever be against us?

How can wrath bring praise to God? Hostility to God and his people gives God the opportunity to do great deeds. God turns the tables of evildoers and brings glory to himself from the foolishness of those who deny him or revolt against him. *LAB note for Psalm 76:10*

(PROVERBS 3:26) (PSALM 76:10) (PROVERBS 21:1) (PROVERBS 16:7) (PSALM 130:5-6) (PSALM 34:4) (DEUTERONOMY 33:27) (JEREMIAH 17:7-8) (ROMANS 8:31)

October 10

A servant is not greater than the master. Nor are messengers more important than the one who sends them. You know these things—now do them! That is the path of blessing.

They began to argue among themselves as to who would be the greatest in the coming Kingdom. Jesus told them, "In this world the kings and great men order their people around, and yet they are called 'friends of the people.' But among you, those who are the greatest should take the lowest rank, and the leader should be a servant. Normally the master sits at the table and is served by his servants. But not here! For I am your servant." ▪ Whoever is the least among you is the greatest. ▪ Whoever wants to be a leader among you must be your servant, and whoever wants to be first must become your slave. For even I, the Son of Man, came here not to be served but to serve others, and to give my life as a ransom for many.

He [Jesus] got up from the table, took off his robe, wrapped a towel around his waist, and poured water into a basin. Then he began to wash the disciples' feet and to wipe them with the towel he had around him.

Lead them by your good example.

Jesus did not wash his disciples' feet just to get them to be nice to each other. His far greater goal was to extend his mission on earth after he was gone. These men were to move into the world serving God, serving each other, and serving all people to whom they took the message of salvation. *LAB note for John 13:12ff.*

(John 13:16-17) (Luke 22:24-27) (Luke 9:48) (Matthew 20:26-28) (John 13:4-5) (1 Peter 5:3)

October 11

My heart is confident in you, O God; no wonder I can sing your praises!

The LORD is my light and my salvation—so why should I be afraid?

You will keep in perfect peace all who trust in you, whose thoughts are fixed on you! For those who are righteous, the path is not steep and rough. You are a God of justice, and you smooth out the road ahead of them. ▪ They do not fear bad news; they confidently trust the LORD to care for them. They are confident and fearless and can face their foes triumphantly.

But when I am afraid, I put my trust in you. ▪ He will conceal me there when troubles come; he will hide me in his sanctuary. He will place me out of reach on a high rock. . . . At his Tabernacle I will offer sacrifices with shouts of joy, singing and praising the LORD with music.

After you have suffered a little while, he will restore, support, and strengthen you, and he will place you on a firm foundation. All power is his forever and ever. Amen.

At times the "path" of the righteous doesn't seem smooth, and it isn't easy to do God's will, but we are never alone when we face tough times. God is there to help us, to comfort us, and to lead us. He gives us wisdom to make decisions and faith to trust him. *LAB note for Isaiah 26:7-8*

(PSALM 108:1) (PSALM 27:1) (ISAIAH 26:3, 7) (PSALM 112:7-8) (PSALM 56:3) (PSALM 27:5-6) (1 PETER 5:10-11)

October 12

Real life is not measured by how much we own.

It is better to be godly and have little than to be evil and possess much. ▩ It is better to have little with fear for the LORD than to have great treasure with turmoil. ▩ True religion with contentment is great wealth. So if we have enough food and clothing, let us be content. ▩ Give me neither poverty nor riches! Give me just enough to satisfy my needs. For if I grow rich, I may deny you and say, "Who is the LORD?" And if I am too poor, I may steal and thus insult God's holy name. ▩ Give us our food for today.

Don't worry about everyday life—whether you have enough food, drink, and clothes. Doesn't life consistent of more than food and clothing? ▩ "When I sent you out to preach the Good News and you did not have money, a traveler's bag, or extra clothing, did you lack anything?" "No," they replied. ▩ Stay away from the love of money; be satisfied with what you have. For God has said, "I will never fail you. I will never forsake you."

How do you respond to the constant pressure to buy? Jesus says that the good life has nothing to do with being wealthy, so be on guard against greed. Learn to tune out expensive enticements and concentrate instead on the truly fulfilled life—living in a relationship with God and doing his work. *LAB note for Luke 12:15*

(LUKE 12:15) (PSALM 37:16) (PROVERBS 15:16) (1 TIMOTHY 6:6, 8) (PROVERBS 30:8-9) (MATTHEW 6:11) (MATTHEW 6:25) (LUKE 22:35) (HEBREWS 13:5)

October 13

It is the Spirit who gives eternal life.

The Scriptures tell us, "The first man, Adam, became a living person." But the last Adam—that is, Christ—is a life-giving Spirit. ▩ Humans can reproduce only human life, but the Holy Spirit gives new life from heaven. ▩ He saved us, not because of the good things we did, but because of his mercy. He washed away our sins and gave us a new life through the Holy Spirit.

You are controlled by the Spirit if you have the Spirit of God living in you. . . . Since Christ lives within you, even though your body will die because of sin, your spirit is alive because you have been made right with God. The Spirit of God, who raised Jesus from the dead, lives in you. And just as he raised Christ from the dead, he will give life to your mortal body by this same Spirit living within you.

I have been crucified with Christ. I myself no longer live, but Christ lives in me. So I live my life in this earthly body by trusting in the Son of God, who loved me and gave himself for me. ▩ So you should consider yourselves dead to sin and able to live for the glory of God through Christ Jesus.

The Holy Spirit gives spiritual life; without the work of the Holy Spirit, we cannot even see our need for new life. All spiritual renewal begins and ends with God. He reveals truth to us, lives within us, and then enables us to respond to that truth. *LAB note for John 6:63-65*

(JOHN 6:63) (1 CORINTHIANS 15:45) (JOHN 3:6) (TITUS 3:5) (ROMANS 8:9-11) (GALATIANS 2:19-20) (ROMANS 6:11)

October 14

The end of the world is coming soon.

I saw a great white throne, and I saw the one who was sitting on it. The earth and sky fled from his presence, but they found no place to hide. ▩ God has commanded that the heavens and the earth will be consumed by fire on the day of judgment, when ungodly people will perish.

God is our refuge and strength, always ready to help in times of trouble. So we will not fear, even if earthquakes come and the mountains crumble into the sea. Let the oceans roar and foam. Let the mountains tremble as the waters surge! ▩ Wars will break out near and far, but don't panic. Yes, these things must come, but the end won't follow immediately.

We will have a home in heaven, an eternal body made for us by God himself and not by human hands. ▩ We are looking forward to the new heavens and new earth he has promised, a world where everyone is right with God. And so, dear friends, while you are waiting for these things to happen, make every effort to live a pure and blameless life. And be at peace with God.

When the disciples asked Jesus when he would come in power and what they could expect then, Jesus pointed out that they should be less concerned with knowing the exact date and more concerned with being prepared. They should live God's way consistently so that no matter when Jesus came, they would be ready. *LAB note for Matthew 24:3ff.*

(1 PETER 4:7) (REVELATION 20:11) (2 PETER 3:7) (PSALM 46:1-3) (MATTHEW 24:6) (2 CORINTHIANS 5:1) (2 PETER 3:13-14)

October 15

The LORD is king!

Do you have no respect for me? Why do you not tremble in my presence? I, the LORD, am the one who defines the ocean's sandy shoreline, an everlasting boundary that the waters cannot cross. The waves may toss and roar, but they can never pass the bounds I set. ▪ For no one on earth—from east or west, or even from the wilderness —can raise another person up. It is God alone who judges; he decides who will rise and who will fall.

He determines the course of world events; he removes kings and sets others on the throne. He gives wisdom to the wise and knowledge to the scholars. ▪ Wars will break out near and far, but don't panic. Yes, these things must come, but the end won't follow immediately.

If God is for us, who can ever be against us? ▪ Not even a sparrow, worth only half a penny, can fall to the ground without your Father knowing it. And the very hairs on your head are all numbered. So don't be afraid; you are more valuable to him than a whole flock of sparrows.

When we see evil leaders who live long and good leaders who die young, we may wonder if God is still in control. But God governs the world according to his purposes. You may be dismayed when you see evil people prosper, but God is in control. Let this knowledge give you confidence and peace no matter what happens. *LAB note for Daniel 2:21*

(PSALM 99:1) (JEREMIAH 5:22) (PSALM 75:6-7) (DANIEL 2:21) (MATTHEW 24:6) (ROMANS 8:31) (MATTHEW 10:29-31)

October 16

The enemy.

Be careful! Watch out for attacks from the Devil, your great enemy. He prowls around like a roaring lion, looking for some victim to devour. ▪ Resist the Devil, and he will flee from you.

Put on all of God's armor so that you will be able to stand firm against all strategies and tricks of the Devil. For we are not fighting against people made of flesh and blood, but against the evil rulers and authorities of the unseen world, against those mighty powers of darkness who rule this world, and against wicked spirits in the heavenly realms. Use every piece of God's armor to resist the enemy in the time of evil, so that after the battle you will still be standing firm. Stand your ground, putting on the sturdy belt of truth and the body armor of God's righteousness. For shoes, put on the peace that comes from the Good News, so that you will be fully prepared. In every battle you will need faith as your shield to stop the fiery arrows aimed at you by Satan.

Do not gloat over me, my enemies! For though I fall, I will rise again.

When you feel alone, weak, helpless, and cut off from other believers, you can become so focused on your troubles that you forget to watch for danger. That is when you are especially vulnerable to Satan's attacks. During suffering, seek other Christians for support, keep your eyes on Christ, and resist the Devil—he will flee from you!

LAB note for 1 Peter 5:8–9

(LUKE 10:19) (1 PETER 5:8) (JAMES 4:7) (EPHESIANS 6:11–16) (MICAH 7:8)

October 17

David found strength in the LORD his God.

Lord, to whom would we go? You alone have the words that give eternal life. ▪ I know the one in whom I trust, and I am sure that he is able to guard what I have entrusted to him until the day of his return.

In my distress I cried out to the LORD; yes, I prayed to my God for help. He heard me from his sanctuary; my cry reached his ears. They attacked me at a moment when I was weakest, but the LORD upheld me. He led me to a place of safety; he rescued me because he delights in me. He reached down from heaven and rescued me; he drew me out of deep waters. He delivered me from my powerful enemies, from those who hated me and were too strong for me.

I will praise the LORD at all times. I will constantly speak his praises. I will boast only in the LORD; let all who are discouraged take heart. Come, let us tell of the LORD's greatness; let us exalt his name together. I prayed to the LORD, and he answered me, freeing me from all my fears. Taste and see that the LORD is good. Oh, the joys of those who trust in him!

Faced with the tragedy of losing their families, David's soldiers began to turn against him. But David found his strength in God and began looking for a solution instead of a scapegoat. When facing problems, remember that it is useless to look for someone to blame or criticize. Instead, consider how you can help find a solution. *LAB note for 1 Samuel 30:6*

(1 SAMUEL 30:6) (JOHN 6:68) (2 TIMOTHY 1:12) (PSALM 18:6, 18-19, 16-17) (PSALM 34:1-4, 8)

October 18

He set my feet on solid ground and steadied me as I walked along.

All drank from the miraculous rock that traveled with them, and that rock was Christ. ▩ Simon Peter answered, "You are the Messiah, the Son of the living God." Upon this rock I will build my church, and all the powers of hell will not conquer it. ▩ There is salvation in no one else! There is no other name in all of heaven for people to call on to save them.

Fully trusting him . . . without wavering. ▩ A doubtful mind is as unsettled as a wave of the sea that is driven and tossed by the wind.

Can anything ever separate us from Christ's love? Does it mean he no longer loves us if we have trouble or calamity, or are persecuted, or are hungry or cold or in danger or threatened with death? No, despite all these things, overwhelming victory is ours through Christ, who loved us. And I am convinced that nothing can ever separate us from . . . the love of God that is revealed in Christ Jesus our Lord.

Waiting for God to help us is not easy, but David received four benefits from waiting: God (1) lifted him out of his despair, (2) set his feet on solid ground, (3) steadied him as he walked, and (4) put a new song of praise in his mouth. Often blessings cannot be received unless we go through the trial of waiting. *LAB note for Psalm 40:1-3*

(Psalm 40:2) (1 Corinthians 10:4) (Matthew 16:16, 18) (Acts 4:12) (Hebrews 10:22-23) (James 1:6) (Romans 8:35, 37-39)

October 19

May the words of my mouth and the thoughts of my heart be pleasing to you, O LORD, my rock and my redeemer.

How can I know all the sins lurking in my heart? Cleanse me from these hidden faults. ▩ Look after each other so that none of you will miss out on the special favor of God. Watch out that no bitter root of unbelief rises up among you, for whenever it springs up, many are corrupted by its poison.

I am sure that God, who began the good work within you, will continue his work until it is finally finished on that day when Christ Jesus comes back again. You must live in a manner worthy of the Good News about Christ. ▩ So also, the tongue is a small thing, but what enormous damage it can do. A tiny spark can set a great forest on fire. And the tongue is a flame of fire. It is full of wickedness that can ruin your whole life. It can turn the entire course of your life into a blazing flame of destruction, for it is set on fire by hell itself. No one can tame the tongue. It is an uncontrollable evil, full of deadly poison. ▩ Let your conversation be gracious and effective.

Many Christians are plagued by guilt. Guilt can play an important role in bringing us to Christ and in keeping us behaving properly, but it should not cripple us or make us fearful. God fully and completely forgives us—even for those sins we do unknowingly.

LAB note for Psalm 19:12-13

(PSALM 19:14) (PSALM 19:12) (HEBREWS 12:15) (PHILIPPIANS 1:6, 27) (JAMES 3:5-6, 8) (COLOSSIANS 4:6)

October 20

Not by force nor by strength, but by my Spirit, says the LORD Almighty.

Who is able to advise the Spirit of the LORD? Who knows enough to be his teacher or counselor?

God deliberately chose things the world considers foolish in order to shame those who think they are wise. And he chose those who are powerless to shame those who are powerful. God chose things despised by the world, things counted as nothing at all, and used them to bring to nothing what the world considers important, so that no one can ever boast in the presence of God.

Just as you can hear the wind but can't tell where it comes from or where it is going, so you can't explain how people are born of the Spirit. ▪ Reborn! This is not a physical birth resulting from human passion or plan—this rebirth comes from God.

My Spirit remains among you, just as I promised. . . . So do not be afraid. ▪ The battle is not yours, but God's.

The LORD does not need weapons to rescue his people. It is his battle, not ours.

Many people believe that to survive in this world a person must be tough, strong, unbending, and harsh. But it is only through God's Spirit that anything of lasting value is accomplished. As you live for God, determine not to trust in your own strength or abilities. Instead, depend on God and work in the power of his Spirit! *LAB note for Zechariah 4:6*

(ZECHARIAH 4:6) (ISAIAH 40:13) (1 CORINTHIANS 1:27-29) (JOHN 3:8) (JOHN 1:13) (HAGGAI 2:5) (2 CHRONICLES 20:15) (1 SAMUEL 17:47)

October 21

Always try to do good.

This suffering is all part of what God has called you to. Christ, who suffered for you, is your example. Follow in his steps. He never sinned, and he never deceived anyone. He did not retaliate when he was insulted. When he suffered, he did not threaten to get even. He left his case in the hands of God, who always judges fairly. ▪ Think about all he endured when sinful people did such terrible things to him, so that you don't become weary and give up.

Let us strip off every weight that slows us down, especially the sin that so easily hinders our progress. And let us run with endurance the race that God has set before us. We do this by keeping our eyes on Jesus, on whom our faith depends from start to finish. He was willing to die a shameful death on the cross because of the joy he knew would be his afterward. Now he is seated in the place of highest honor beside God's throne in heaven.

Let me say one more thing as I close this letter. Fix your thoughts on what is true and honorable and right. Think about things that are pure and lovely and admirable. Think about things that are excellent and worthy of praise.

Christ never sinned, and yet he suffered so that we could be set free. When we follow Christ's example and live for others, we, too, may suffer. Our goal should be to face suffering as he did—with patience, calmness, and confidence that God is in control of the future.

LAB note for 1 Peter 2:21–22

(1 Thessalonians 5:15) (1 Peter 2:21–23) (Hebrews 12:3)
(Hebrews 12:1–2) (Philippians 4:8)

October 22

The paths of the LORD are true and right, and righteous people live by walking in them. But sinners stumble and fall along the way.

He is very precious to you who believe. But for those who reject him . . . "He is the stone that makes people stumble, the rock that will make them fall." They stumble because they do not listen to God's word or obey it, and so they meet the fate that has been planned for them. ▩ The LORD protects the upright but destroys the wicked.

Anyone who is willing to hear should listen and understand! ▩ Those who are wise will take all this to heart; they will see in our history the faithful love of the LORD. ▩ A pure eye lets sunshine into your soul. ▩ Anyone who wants to do the will of God will know whether my teaching is from God or is merely my own. ▩ To those who are open to my teaching, more understanding will be given, and they will have an abundance of knowledge.

Anyone whose Father is God listens gladly to the words of God. Since you don't, it proves you aren't God's children. ▩ You refuse to come to me so that I can give you this eternal life. ▩ My sheep recognize my voice; I know them, and they follow me.

The book of Hosea closes with an appeal to listen, learn, and benefit from God's word. All readers have a choice: to listen to the message and follow God's ways or refuse to walk along the Lord's path. If you are lost, you can find the way by turning from your sin and following God.

LAB note for Hosea 14:9

(HOSEA 14:9) (1 PETER 2:7-8) (PROVERBS 10:29) (MATTHEW 11:15) (PSALM 107:43) (MATTHEW 6:22) (JOHN 7:17) (MATTHEW 13:12) (JOHN 8:47) (JOHN 5:40) (JOHN 10:27)

October 23

There is wonderful joy ahead, even though it is necessary for you to endure many trials for a while.

Dear friends, don't be surprised at the fiery trials you are going through, as if something strange were happening to you. Instead, be very glad—because these trials will make you partners with Christ in his suffering, and afterward you will have the wonderful joy of sharing his glory. ▩ Have you entirely forgotten the encouraging words God spoke to you, his children? He said, "My child, don't ignore it when the Lord disciplines you, and don't be discouraged when he corrects you." ▩ No discipline is enjoyable while it is happening—it is painful! But afterward there will be a quiet harvest of right living for those who are trained in this way.

This High Priest of ours understands our weaknesses, for he faced all of the same temptations we do, yet he did not sin. ▩ Since he himself has gone through suffering and temptation, he is able to help us when we are being tempted. ▩ Remember that the temptations that come into your life are no different from what others experience. And God is faithful. He will keep the temptation from becoming so strong that you can't stand up against it. When you are tempted, he will show you a way out so that you will not give in to it.

All believers face trials when they let their light shine into the darkness. We must accept trials as part of the refining process that burns away impurities and prepares us to meet Christ. Trials teach us patience and help us grow to be the kind of people God wants.

LAB note for 1 Peter 1:6–7

(1 Peter 1:6) (1 Peter 4:12–13) (Hebrews 12:5) (Hebrews 12:11) (Hebrews 4:15) (Hebrews 2:18) (1 Corinthians 10:13)

October 24

Praise the LORD for his great love and for all his wonderful deeds.

Taste and see that the LORD is good. Oh, the joys of those who trust in him! ■ Your goodness is so great! You have stored up great blessings for those who honor you. You have done so much for those who come to you for protection, blessing them before the watching world.

His unchanging plan has always been to adopt us into his own family by bringing us to himself through Jesus Christ. And this gave him great pleasure. So we praise God for the wonderful kindness he has poured out on us because we belong to his dearly loved Son.

How wonderful and beautiful they will be! The young men and women will thrive on the abundance of grain and new wine. ■ The LORD is good to everyone. He showers compassion on all his creation. All of your works will thank you, LORD, and your faithful followers will bless you. They will talk together about the glory of your kingdom; they will celebrate examples of your power. They will tell about your mighty deeds and about the majesty and glory of your reign.

God's "unchanging plan" is another way of saying that salvation is God's work and not our own doing. In his infinite love, God has adopted us as his own children. Through Jesus' sacrifice he has brought us into his family and made us heirs along with Jesus. *LAB note for Ephesians 1:5*

(PSALM 107:8) (PSALM 34:8) (PSALM 31:19) (EPHESIANS 1:5-6) (ZECHARIAH 9:17) (PSALM 145:9-12)

October 25

Lead me by your truth and teach me.

When the Spirit of truth comes, he will guide you into all truth. He will not be presenting his own ideas; he will be telling you what he has heard. ▩ The Holy Spirit has come upon you, and all of you know the truth.

"Check their predictions against my testimony," says the LORD. "If their predictions are different from mine, it is because there is no light or truth in them." ▩ All Scripture is inspired by God and is useful to teach us what is true and to make us realize what is wrong in our lives. It straightens us out and teaches us to do what is right. It is God's way of preparing us in every way, fully equipped for every good thing God wants us to do.

The LORD says, "I will guide you along the best pathway for your life. I will advise you and watch over you." ▩ A pure eye lets sunshine into your soul. ▩ Anyone who wants to do the will of God will know whether my teaching is from God or is merely my own. ▩ It will be only for those who walk in God's ways; fools will never walk there.

Jesus said the Holy Spirit would tell them "about the future"— the nature of their mission, the opposition they would face, and the final outcome of their efforts. They didn't fully understand these promises until the Holy Spirit came after Jesus' death and resurrection.

LAB note for John 16:13

(PSALM 25:5) (JOHN 16:13) (1 JOHN 2:20) (ISAIAH 8:20) (2 TIMOTHY 3:16–17) (PSALM 32:8) (MATTHEW 6:22) (JOHN 7:17) (ISAIAH 35:8)

October 26

We give great honor to those who endure under suffering.

We can rejoice, too, when we run into problems and trials, for we know that they are good for us—they help us learn to endure. And endurance develops strength of character in us, and character strengthens our confident expectation of salvation. And this expectation will not disappoint us. For we know how dearly God loves us, because he has given us the Holy Spirit to fill our hearts with his love.

No discipline is enjoyable while it is happening—it is painful! But afterward there will be a quiet harvest of right living for those who are trained in this way. ▩ Let it grow, for when your endurance is fully developed, you will be strong in character and ready for anything.

I am glad to boast about my weaknesses, so that the power of Christ may work through me. Since I know it is all for Christ's good, I am quite content with my weaknesses and with insults, hardships, persecutions, and calamities. For when I am weak, then I am strong.

We will experience difficulties that help us grow. We can rejoice in suffering, not because we like pain or deny its tragedy, but because we know God is using life's difficulties and Satan's attacks to build our character. Thank God for these opportunities to grow!

LAB note for Romans 5:3-4

(JAMES 5:11) (ROMANS 5:3-5) (HEBREWS 12:11) (JAMES 1:4)
(2 CORINTHIANS 12:9-10)

October 27

The way you live will always honor and please the Lord, and you will continually do good, kind things for others. All the while, you will learn to know God better and better.

Dear brothers and sisters, I plead with you to give your bodies to God. Let them be a living and holy sacrifice—the kind he will accept. When you think of what he has done for you, is this too much to ask? Don't copy the behavior and customs of this world, but let God transform you into a new person by changing the way you think. Then you will know what God wants you to do, and you will know how good and pleasing and perfect his will really is. ▪ Before, you let yourselves be slaves of impurity and lawlessness. Now you must choose to be slaves of righteousness so that you will become holy. ▪ What counts is whether we really have been changed into new and different people. May God's mercy and peace be upon all those who live by this principle. They are the new people of God.

My true disciples produce much fruit. This brings great glory to my Father. ▪ You didn't choose me. I chose you. I appointed you to go and produce fruit that will last, so that the Father will give you whatever you ask for, using my name. I command you to love each other.

Knowledge is not merely to be accumulated; it should give us direction for living. It is not a secret that only a few can discover; it is open to everyone. God wants us to learn more about him and put belief into practice by helping others. *LAB note for Colossians 1:9–14*

(Colossians 1:10) (Romans 12:1–2) (Romans 6:19) (Galatians 6:15–16) (John 15:8) (John 15:16)

October 28

I will get up now and roam the city, searching for him.

Return, O Israel, to the LORD your God, for your sins have brought you down. Bring your petitions, and return to the LORD. Say to him, "Forgive all our sins and graciously receive us, so that we may offer you the sacrifice of praise."

Remember, no one who wants to do wrong should ever say, "God is tempting me." God is never tempted to do wrong, and he never tempts anyone else either. Temptation comes from the lure of our own evil desires. These evil desires lead to evil actions, and evil actions lead to death. So don't be misled, my dear brothers and sisters. Whatever is good and perfect comes to us from God above, who created all heaven's lights. Unlike them, he never changes or casts shifting shadows.

Wait patiently for the LORD. Be brave and courageous. Yes, wait patiently for the LORD. ▪ It is good to wait quietly for salvation from the LORD. ▪ Don't you think God will surely give justice to his chosen people who plead with him day and night?

I wait quietly before God, for my salvation comes from him.

When you love someone, you will do all you can to care for his or her needs, even at a cost to your personal comfort. This is demonstrated most often in small actions—getting your spouse a glass of water, leaving work early to attend some function your child is involved in, or sacrificing time to tend to a friend's needs. *LAB note for Song of Songs 3:1–4*

(SONG OF SONGS 3:2) (HOSEA 14:1-2) (JAMES 1:13-17) (PSALM 27:14) (LAMENTATIONS 3:26) (LUKE 18:7) (PSALM 62:1)

October 29

God can use sorrow in our lives to help us turn away from sin and seek salvation.

Jesus' words flashed through Peter's mind: "Before the rooster crows, you will deny me three times." And he went away, crying bitterly. ▩ If we confess our sins to him, he is faithful and just to forgive us and to cleanse us from every wrong. ▩ The blood of Jesus, his Son, cleanses us from every sin.

Troubles surround me—too many to count! They pile up so high I can't see my way out. They are more numerous than the hairs on my head. I have lost all my courage. Please, LORD, rescue me! Come quickly, LORD, and help me.

Your sins have brought you down. ▩ Come back to your God! Act on the principles of love and justice, and always live in confident dependence on your God. ▩ Be still in the presence of the LORD, and wait patiently for him to act.

The sacrifice you want is a broken spirit. A broken and repentant heart, O God, you will not despise. ▩ He heals the brokenhearted, binding up their wounds. ▩ The LORD has already told you what is good, and this is what he requires: to do what is right, to love mercy, and to walk humbly with your God.

Sorrow for our sins can result in changed behavior. Many people are sorry only for the effects of their sins or for being caught. Compare Peter's remorse and repentance with Judas's bitterness and suicide. Both denied Christ. One repented and was restored to faith and service; the other took his own life. *LAB note for 2 Corinthians 7:10*

(2 CORINTHIANS 7:10) (MATTHEW 26:75) (1 JOHN 1:9) (1 JOHN 1:7) (PSALM 40:12-13) (HOSEA 14:1) (HOSEA 12:6) (PSALM 37:7) (PSALM 51:17) (PSALM 147:3) (MICAH 6:8)

October 30

These trials are only to test your faith, to show that it is strong and pure.

We are well known, but we are treated as unknown. We live close to death, but here we are, still alive. We have been beaten within an inch of our lives. Our hearts ache, but we always have joy. We are poor, but we give spiritual riches to others. We own nothing, and yet we have everything.

We are pressed on every side by troubles, but we are not crushed and broken. We are perplexed, but we don't give up and quit. We are hunted down, but God never abandons us. We get knocked down, but we get up again and keep going.

Though our bodies are dying, our spirits are being renewed every day. For our present troubles are quite small and won't last very long. Yet they produce for us an immeasurably great glory that will last forever!

So we don't look at the troubles we can see right now; rather, we look forward to what we have not yet seen. For the troubles we see will soon be over, but the joys to come will last forever.

As gold is heated, impurities float to the top and can be skimmed off. Steel is tempered or strengthened by heating it in fire. Likewise, our trials, struggles, and persecutions refine and strengthen our faith, making us useful to God. *LAB note for 1 Peter 1:7*

(1 Peter 1:7) (2 Corinthians 6:9-10) (2 Corinthians 4:8-9) (2 Corinthians 4:16-17) (2 Corinthians 4:18)

October 31

Love each other in the same way that I love you.

Live a life filled with love for others, following the example of Christ, who loved you and gave himself as a sacrifice to take away your sins. And God was pleased, because that sacrifice was like sweet perfume to him. ▩ This is the message we have heard from the beginning: We should love one another. ▩ Our lives are a fragrance presented by Christ to God.

You have been born again. Your new life did not come from your earthly parents because the life they gave you will end in death. But this new life will last forever because it comes from the eternal, living word of God. ▩ Make them pure and holy by teaching them your words of truth. ▩ No one can enter the Kingdom of God without being born of water and the Spirit. ▩ He saved us, not because of the good things we did, but because of his mercy. He washed away our sins and gave us a new life through the Holy Spirit. ▩ Your promise revives me.

May God, who gives this patience and encouragement, help you live in complete harmony with each other—each with the attitude of Christ Jesus toward the other.

When Christians preach the Good News, it is good news to some and repulsive news to others. Believers recognize the life-giving fragrance of the message. To unbelievers, however, it smells foul, like death—their own.

LAB note for 2 Corinthians 2:14–16

(John 15:12) (Ephesians 5:2) (1 John 3:11) (2 Corinthians 2:15) (1 Peter 1:23) (John 17:17) (John 3:5) (Titus 3:5) (Psalm 119:50) (Romans 15:5)

We Give Thanks

Daily necessities and moment-by-moment protection;
Loving guidance and heartwarming friendship;
God's generous character flows into
every area of our lives.

It's the annual season for giving thanks.
As the year nears its end, spend a few moments
appreciating the countless blessings that
are often overlooked in daily life.

November 1

With all my heart I will praise you, O Lord my God.

Giving thanks is a sacrifice that truly honors me. ▩ It is good to give thanks to the LORD, to sing praises to the Most High. It is good to proclaim your unfailing love in the morning, your faithfulness in the evening.

Let everything that lives sing praises to the LORD!

Dear brothers and sisters, I plead with you to give your bodies to God. Let them be a living and holy sacrifice—the kind he will accept. When you think of what he has done for you, is this too much to ask? ▩ As a sacrifice for sin . . . Jesus suffered and died outside the city gates in order to make his people holy by shedding his own blood. With Jesus' help, let us continually offer our sacrifice of praise to God by proclaiming the glory of his name. ▩ Always give thanks for everything to God the Father in the name of our Lord Jesus Christ.

The Lamb is worthy—the Lamb who was killed. He is worthy to receive power and riches and wisdom and strength and honor and glory and blessing.

Thanks should be on our lips every day. When thanksgiving becomes an integral part of your life, you will find that your attitude toward life will change. You will become more positive, gracious, loving, and humble.

LAB note for Psalm 92:1-2

(PSALM 86:12) (PSALM 50:23) (PSALM 92:1-2) (PSALM 150:6) (ROMANS 12:1) (HEBREWS 13:11-12, 15) (EPHESIANS 5:20) (REVELATION 5:12)

November 2

If you need wisdom—if you want to know what God wants you to do—ask him, and he will gladly tell you.

Jesus . . . said to her, "Where are your accusers? Didn't even one of them condemn you?" "No, Lord," she said. And Jesus said, "Neither do I. Go and sin no more."

What a difference between our sin and God's generous gift of forgiveness. For this one man, Adam, brought death to many through his sin. But this other man, Jesus Christ, brought forgiveness to many through God's bountiful gift. And the result of God's gracious gift is very different from the result of that one man's sin. For Adam's sin led to condemnation, but we have the free gift of being accepted by God, even though we are guilty of many sins.

God is so rich in mercy, and he loved us so very much, that even while we were dead because of our sins, he gave us life when he raised Christ from the dead. (It is only by God's special favor that you have been saved!) For he raised us from the dead along with Christ, and we are seated with him in the heavenly realms—all because we are one with Christ Jesus. And so God can always point to us as examples of the incredible wealth of his favor and kindness toward us, as shown in all he has done for us through Christ Jesus.

Since God did not spare even his own Son but gave him up for us all, won't God, who gave us Christ, also give us everything else?

Christ offers us the opportunity to be born into his spiritual family—the family line that begins with forgiveness and leads to eternal life. If we do nothing, we receive death through Adam; but if we come to God by faith, we receive life through Christ. To which family line do you now belong? *LAB note for Romans 5:15-19*

(JAMES 1:5) (JOHN 8:10-11) (ROMANS 5:15-16)
(EPHESIANS 2:4-7) (ROMANS 8:32)

November 3

Make them pure and holy by teaching them your words of truth.

You have already been pruned for greater fruitfulness by the message I have given you. ▪ Let the words of Christ, in all their richness, live in your hearts and make you wise.

How can a young person stay pure? By obeying your word and following its rules. I have tried my best to find you—don't let me wander from your commands.

For wisdom will enter your heart, and knowledge will fill you with joy. Wise planning will watch over you. Understanding will keep you safe.

I have stayed in God's paths; I have followed his ways and not turned aside. I have not departed from his commands but have treasured his word in my heart. ▪ Even perfection has its limits, but your commands have no limit. Oh, how I love your law! I think about it all day long. Your commands make me wiser than my enemies, for your commands are my constant guide. Yes, I have more insight than my teachers, for I am always thinking of your decrees. ▪ You are truly my disciples if you keep obeying my teachings. And you will know the truth, and the truth will set you free.

A follower of Christ becomes pure and holy through believing and obeying the Word of God. He or she has already accepted forgiveness through Christ's sacrificial death. But daily application of God's Word has a purifying effect on our minds and hearts. *LAB note for John 17:17*

(John 17:17) (John 15:3) (Colossians 3:16) (Psalm 119:9-10) (Proverbs 2:10-11) (Job 23:11-12) (Psalm 119:96-99) (John 8:31-32)

November 4

How deep are your thoughts.

We have continued praying for you ever since we first heard about you. We ask God to give you a complete understanding of what he wants to do in your lives, and we ask him to make you wise with spiritual wisdom. ▩ I pray that Christ will be more and more at home in your hearts as you trust in him. May your roots go down deep into the soil of God's marvelous love. And may you have the power to understand, as all God's people should, how wide, how long, how high, and how deep his love really is. May you experience the love of Christ, though it is so great you will never fully understand it. Then you will be filled with the fullness of life and power that comes from God.

Oh, what a wonderful God we have! How great are his riches and wisdom and knowledge! How impossible it is for us to understand his decisions and his methods! ▩ "My thoughts are completely different from yours," says the LORD. "And my ways are far beyond anything you could imagine. For just as the heavens are higher than the earth, so are my ways higher than your ways and my thoughts higher than your thoughts." ▩ O LORD my God, you have done many miracles for us. Your plans for us are too numerous to list. If I tried to recite all your wonderful deeds, I would never come to the end of them.

God is ultimately wise. Although his methods and means are beyond our comprehension, God himself is not arbitrary. He governs the universe and our life in perfect wisdom, justice, and love.

LAB note for Romans 11:33

(PSALM 92:5) (COLOSSIANS 1:9) (EPHESIANS 3:17-19)
(ROMANS 11:33) (ISAIAH 55:8-9) (PSALM 40:5)

November 5

When the Holy Spirit controls our lives, he will produce . . . gentleness.

The humble will be filled with fresh joy from the LORD. Those who are poor will rejoice in the Holy One of Israel.

Unless you turn from your sins and become as little children, you will never get into the Kingdom of Heaven. Therefore, anyone who becomes as humble as this little child is the greatest in the Kingdom of Heaven. ▪ You should be known for the beauty that comes from within, the unfading beauty of a gentle and quiet spirit, which is so precious to God. ▪ Love is patient and kind. Love is not jealous or boastful or proud.

Pursue a godly life, along with faith, love, perseverance, and gentleness. ▪ Take my yoke upon you. Let me teach you, because I am humble and gentle. ▪ He was oppressed and treated harshly, yet he never said a word. He was led as a lamb to the slaughter. And as a sheep is silent before the shearers, he did not open his mouth.

This suffering is all part of what God has called you to. Christ, who suffered for you, is your example. Follow in his steps. He never sinned, and he never deceived anyone. He did not retaliate when he was insulted. When he suffered, he did not threaten to get even. He left his case in the hands of God, who always judges fairly.

Jesus used a child to help his self-centered disciples get the point. We are not to be childish (like the disciples, arguing over petty issues) but childlike, with humble and sincere hearts. Are you being childlike or childish?

LAB note for Matthew 18:1-4

(GALATIANS 5:22-23) (ISAIAH 29:19) (MATTHEW 18:3-4) (1 PETER 3:4) (1 CORINTHIANS 13:4) (1 TIMOTHY 6:11) (MATTHEW 11:29) (ISAIAH 53:7) (1 PETER 2:21-23)

November 6

He has punished Israel only a little. He has exiled her from her land as though blown away in a storm from the east.

Let us fall into the hands of the LORD, for his mercy is great. Do not let me fall into human hands. ▩ I am with you and will save you, says the LORD. . . . I will not destroy you. But I must discipline you; I cannot let you go unpunished. ▩ He will not constantly accuse us, nor remain angry forever. He has not punished us for all our sins, nor does he deal with us as we deserve. He knows we are only dust. ▩ I will spare them as a father spares an obedient and dutiful child.

Remember that the temptations that come into your life are no different from what others experience. And God is faithful. He will keep the temptation from becoming so strong that you can't stand up against it. When you are tempted, he will show you a way out so that you will not give in to it. ▩ Satan has asked to have all of you, to sift you like wheat. But I have pleaded in prayer for you . . . that your faith should not fail.

To the poor, O LORD, you are a refuge from the storm. To the needy in distress, you are a shelter from the rain and the heat. For the oppressive acts of ruthless people are like a storm beating against a wall.

David wisely chose the form of punishment that came most directly from God. He knew how brutal and harsh men in war could be, and he also knew God's great mercy. When you sin greatly, turn back to God. To be punished by him is far better than to take your chances without him. *LAB note for 2 Samuel 24:12-14*

(ISAIAH 27:8) (2 SAMUEL 24:14) (JEREMIAH 30:11) (PSALM 103:9-10, 14) (MALACHI 3:17) (1 CORINTHIANS 10:13) (LUKE 22:31-32) (ISAIAH 25:4)

November 7

Though I sit in darkness, the LORD himself will be my light.

When you go through deep waters and great trouble, I will be with you. When you go through rivers of difficulty, you will not drown! When you walk through the fire of oppression, you will not be burned up; the flames will not consume you. For I am the LORD, your God, the Holy One of Israel, your Savior. ▪ I will lead blind Israel down a new path, guiding them along an unfamiliar way. I will make the darkness bright before them and smooth out the road ahead of them. ▪ Who among you fears the LORD and obeys his servant? If you are walking in darkness, without a ray of light, trust in the LORD and rely on your God.

Even when I walk through the dark valley of death, I will not be afraid, for you are close beside me. Your rod and your staff protect and comfort me. ▪ When I am afraid, I put my trust in you. O God, I praise your word. I trust in God, so why should I be afraid? What can mere mortals do to me? ▪ The LORD is my light and my salvation—so why should I be afraid?

Micah showed great faith in God as he waited on God to bring his people through tough times. We, too, can have a relationship with God that can allow us to have confidence like Micah's. It doesn't take unusual talent; it simply takes faith in God and a willingness to act on that faith.

LAB note for Micah 7:7-10

(MICAH 7:8) (ISAIAH 43:2-3) (ISAIAH 42:16) (ISAIAH 50:10) (PSALM 23:4) (PSALM 56:3-4) (PSALM 27:1)

November 8

Pray as you are directed by the Holy Spirit.

God is Spirit, so those who worship him must worship in spirit and in truth. ▪ All of us, both Jews and Gentiles, may come to the Father through the same Holy Spirit because of what Christ has done for us.

My Father! If it is possible, let this cup of suffering be taken away from me. Yet I want your will, not mine.

The Holy Spirit helps us in our distress. For we don't even know what we should pray for, nor how we should pray. But the Holy Spirit prays for us with groanings that cannot be expressed in words. And the Father who knows all hearts knows what the Spirit is saying, for the Spirit pleads for us believers in harmony with God's own will. ▪ And we can be confident that he will listen to us whenever we ask him for anything in line with his will. ▪ When the Spirit of truth comes, he will guide you into all truth.

Pray at all times and on every occasion in the power of the Holy Spirit. Stay alert and be persistent in your prayers for all Christians everywhere.

To pray as we are "directed by the Holy Spirit" means to pray in the power and strength of the Holy Spirit. He prays for us, opens our mind to Jesus, and teaches us about him. *LAB note for Jude 1:20*

(Jude 1:20) (John 4:24) (Ephesians 2:18) (Matthew 26:39) (Romans 8:26-27) (1 John 5:14) (John 16:13) (Ephesians 6:18)

November 9

If a tree is cut down, there is hope that it will sprout again and grow new branches.

He will not crush those who are weak. ▪ He renews my strength.

God can use sorrow in our lives to help us turn away from sin and seek salvation. We will never regret that kind of sorrow. But sorrow without repentance is the kind that results in death. ▪ No discipline is enjoyable while it is happening—it is painful! But afterward there will be a quiet harvest of right living for those who are trained in this way.

I used to wander off until you disciplined me; but now I closely follow your word.

Do not gloat over me, my enemies! For though I fall, I will rise again. Though I sit in darkness, the LORD himself will be my light. I will be patient as the LORD punishes me, for I have sinned against him. But after that, he will take up my case and punish my enemies for all the evil they have done to me. The LORD will bring me out of my darkness into the light, and I will see his righteousness.

Job's pessimism about death is understandable, since Jesus had not yet conquered death. What is remarkable is his budding hope: If only he could die and live again! When we must endure suffering, we have an advantage over Job. We know that the dead will rise—because Christ rose!

LAB note for Job 14:7–22

(JOB 14:7) (ISAIAH 42:3) (PSALM 23:3) (2 CORINTHIANS 7:10) (HEBREWS 12:11) (PSALM 119:67) (MICAH 7:8–9)

*N*ovember 10

My Kingdom is not of this world.

Our High Priest offered himself to God as one sacrifice for sins, good for all time. Then he sat down at the place of highest honor at God's right hand. ▩ In the future you will see me, the Son of Man, sitting at God's right hand in the place of power and coming back on the clouds of heaven.

Christ must reign until he humbles all his enemies beneath his feet.

How we thank God, who gives us victory over sin and death through Jesus Christ our Lord! ▩ This is the same mighty power that raised Christ from the dead and seated him in the place of honor at God's right hand in the heavenly realms. Now he is far above any ruler or authority or power or leader or anything else in this world or in the world to come. And God has put all things under the authority of Christ, and he gave him this authority for the benefit of the church. And the church is his body; it is filled by Christ, who fills everything everywhere with his presence. ▩ For at the right time Christ will be revealed from heaven by the blessed and only almighty God, the King of kings and Lord of lords.

Jesus declared his royalty in no uncertain terms. In saying he was the Son of Man, Jesus was claiming to be the Messiah, as his listeners well knew. He knew this declaration would be his undoing, but he did not panic. He was calm, courageous, and determined. *LAB note for Matthew 26:64*

(John 18:36) (Hebrews 10:12-13) (Matthew 26:64) (1 Corinthians 15:25) (1 Corinthians 15:57) (Ephesians 1:19-23) (1 Timothy 6:15)

*N*ovember 11

What are you doing here, Elijah?

He knows where I am going. ▩ O LORD, you have examined my heart and know everything about me. You know when I sit down or stand up. You know my every thought when far away. You chart the path ahead of me and tell me where to stop and rest. I can never escape from your spirit! I can never get away from your presence! If I ride the wings of the morning, if I dwell by the farthest oceans, even there your hand will guide me, and your strength will support me.

Elijah was as human as we are. ▩ Fearing people is a dangerous trap, but to trust the LORD means safety. ▩ Though they stumble, they will not fall, for the LORD holds them by the hand. ▩ They may trip seven times, but each time they will rise again.

Don't get tired of doing what is good. Don't get discouraged and give up, for we will reap a harvest of blessing at the appropriate time. ▩ Though the spirit is willing enough, the body is weak! ▩ The LORD is like a father to his children, tender and compassionate to those who fear him. For he understands how weak we are; he knows we are only dust.

God is omnipresent—he is present everywhere. Because this is so, you can never escape from his Spirit. This is good news to those who know and love God, because no matter what we do or where we go, we can never be far from God's comforting presence. *LAB note for Psalm 139:7*

(1 KINGS 19:9) (JOB 23:10) (PSALM 139:1-3, 7, 9-10) (JAMES 5:17) (PROVERBS 29:25) (PSALM 37:24) (PROVERBS 24:16) (GALATIANS 6:9) (MATTHEW 26:41) (PSALM 103:13-14)

November 12

Now you are free from sin, your old master, and you have become slaves to your new master, righteousness.

No one can serve two masters. . . . You cannot serve both God and money. ▩ When you were slaves of sin, you weren't concerned with doing what was right. And what was the result? It was not good, since now you are ashamed of the things you used to do, things that end in eternal doom. But now you are free from the power of sin and have become slaves of God. Now you do those things that lead to holiness and result in eternal life.

Christ has accomplished the whole purpose of the law. All who believe in him are made right with God.

All those who want to be my disciples must come and follow me, because my servants must be where I am. And if they follow me, the Father will honor them. ▩ Take my yoke upon you. Let me teach you, because I am humble and gentle, and you will find rest for your souls. For my yoke fits perfectly, and the burden I give you is light.

O LORD our God, others have ruled us, but we worship you alone. ▩ If you will help me, I will run to follow your commands.

All people have a master and pattern themselves after him. Without Jesus we would have no choice but to be enslaved to sin. But thanks to him, we can now choose God as our Master. Following him we can enjoy new life and learn how to work for him.

LAB note for Romans 6:16-18

(ROMANS 6:18) (MATTHEW 6:24) (ROMANS 6:20-22) (ROMANS 10:4) (JOHN 12:26) (MATTHEW 11:29-30) (ISAIAH 26:13) (PSALM 119:32)

November 13

Anyone who calls on the name of the Lord will be saved.

Manasseh . . . rebuilt the pagan shrines his father, Hezekiah, had destroyed. He constructed altars for Baal and set up an Asherah pole, just as King Ahab of Israel had done. He even built pagan altars in the Temple of the LORD, the place where the LORD had said his name should be honored. He built these altars for all the forces of heaven in both courtyards of the LORD's Temple. Manasseh even sacrificed his own son in the fire. He practiced sorcery and divination, and he consulted with mediums and psychics. He did much that was evil in the LORD's sight, arousing his anger. ▩ While in deep distress, Manasseh sought the LORD his God and cried out humbly to the God of his ancestors. And when he prayed, the LORD listened to him and was moved by his request for help. So the LORD let Manasseh return to Jerusalem and to his kingdom. Manasseh had finally realized that the LORD alone is God!

"Come now, let us argue this out," says the LORD. "No matter how deep the stain of your sins, I can remove it. I can make you as clean as freshly fallen snow. Even if you are stained as red as crimson, I can make you as white as wool." ▩ He does not want anyone to perish.

Today, many books, television shows, and games emphasize fortune-telling, séances, and other occult practices. Don't let desire to know the future or the belief that superstition is harmless lead you into condoning occult practices. They are counterfeits of God's power and have as their root a system of beliefs totally opposed to God.

LAB note for 2 Kings 21:6

(ACTS 2:21) (2 KINGS 21:1, 3-6) (2 CHRONICLES 33:12-13)
(ISAIAH 1:18) (2 PETER 3:9)

November 14

When the Holy Spirit controls our lives, he will produce . . . patience, kindness.

I am the LORD, I am the LORD, the merciful and gracious God. I am slow to anger and rich in unfailing love and faithfulness.

Lead a life worthy of your calling, for you have been called by God. Be humble and gentle. Be patient with each other, making allowance for each other's faults because of your love. ▪ Be kind to each other, tenderhearted, forgiving one another, just as God through Christ has forgiven you. ▪ The wisdom that comes from heaven is first of all pure. It is also peace loving, gentle at all times, and willing to yield to others. It is full of mercy and good deeds. It shows no partiality and is always sincere. ▪ Love is patient and kind.

Don't get tired of doing what is good. Don't get discouraged and give up, for we will reap a harvest of blessing at the appropriate time. ▪ Dear brothers and sisters, you must be patient as you wait for the Lord's return. Consider the farmers who eagerly look for the rains in the fall and in the spring. They patiently wait for the precious harvest to ripen. You, too, must be patient. And take courage, for the coming of the Lord is near.

No one is ever going to be perfect here on earth, so we must accept, love, and be patient with other Christians in spite of their faults. Rather than dwelling on a person's weaknesses or looking for faults, pray for him or her.

LAB note for Ephesians 4:2

(GALATIANS 5:22) (EXODUS 34:6) (EPHESIANS 4:1-2) (EPHESIANS 4:32) (JAMES 3:17) (1 CORINTHIANS 13:4) (GALATIANS 6:9) (JAMES 5:7-8)

November 15

Just as the body is dead without a spirit, so also faith is dead without good deeds.

Not all people who sound religious are really godly. They may refer to me as "Lord," but they still won't enter the Kingdom of Heaven. The decisive issue is whether they obey my Father in heaven.

Seek to live a clean and holy life, for those who are not holy will not see the Lord. ▩ Make every effort to apply the benefits of these promises to your life. Then your faith will produce a life of moral excellence. A life of moral excellence leads to knowing God better. Knowing God leads to self-control. Self-control leads to patient endurance, and patient endurance leads to godliness. Godliness leads to love for other Christians, and finally you will grow to have genuine love for everyone. The more you grow like this, the more you will become productive and useful in your knowledge of our Lord Jesus Christ. But those who fail to develop these virtues are blind or, at least, very shortsighted. They have already forgotten that God has cleansed them from their old life of sin. So, dear brothers and sisters, work hard to prove that you really are among those God has called and chosen. Doing this, you will never stumble or fall away.

Salvation is not a reward for the good things we have done, so none of us can boast about it.

Jesus is more concerned about our walk than our talk. He wants us to do right, not just say the right words. You can only withstand the storms of life if you do what is right instead of just talking about it. What you do cannot be separated from what you believe. *LAB note for Matthew 7:21*

(JAMES 2:26) (MATTHEW 7:21) (HEBREWS 12:14)
(2 PETER 1:5-10) (EPHESIANS 2:9)

November 16

Do you . . . believe?

What's the use of saying you have faith if you don't prove it by your actions? That kind of faith can't save anyone. It isn't enough just to have faith. Faith that doesn't show itself by good deeds is no faith at all—it is dead and useless.

It was by faith that Abraham offered Isaac as a sacrifice when God was testing him. Abraham, who had received God's promises, was ready to sacrifice his only son, Isaac, though God had promised him, "Isaac is the son through whom your descendants will be counted." Abraham assumed that if Isaac died, God was able to bring him back to life again. ▪ Don't you remember that our ancestor Abraham was declared right with God because of what he did when he offered his son Isaac on the altar? So you see, we are made right with God by what we do, not by faith alone.

The way to identify a tree or a person is by the kind of fruit that is produced. Not all people who sound religious are really godly. They may refer to me as "Lord," but they still won't enter the Kingdom of Heaven. The decisive issue is whether they obey my Father in heaven. ▪ You know these things—now do them! That is the path of blessing.

When someone claims to have faith, what he or she may have is intellectual assent—agreement with a set of Christian teachings—and as such it would be incomplete faith. True faith transforms our conduct as well as our thoughts. If our life remains unchanged, we don't truly believe the truths we claim to hold. *LAB note for James 2:14*

(JOHN 16:31) (JAMES 2:14, 17) (HEBREWS 11:17-19) (JAMES 2:21, 24) (MATTHEW 7:20-21) (JOHN 13:17)

November 17

May the Lord of peace himself always give you his peace no matter what happens. The Lord be with you all.

Grace and peace from the one who is, who always was, and who is still to come. ▪ You will experience God's peace, which is far more wonderful than the human mind can understand. His peace will guard your hearts and minds as you live in Christ Jesus.

Jesus himself was suddenly standing there among them. He said, "Peace be with you." ▪ I am leaving you with a gift—peace of mind and heart. And the peace I give isn't like the peace the world gives. So don't be troubled or afraid.

The Counselor—the Spirit of truth. ▪ When the Holy Spirit controls our lives, he will produce this kind of fruit in us: love, joy, peace. ▪ His Holy Spirit speaks to us deep in our hearts and tells us that we are God's children.

"I will personally go with you, Moses. I will give you rest—everything will be fine for you." Then Moses said, "If you don't go with us personally, don't let us move a step from this place. If you don't go with us, how will anyone ever know that your people and I have found favor with you?"

God's peace is different from the world's peace. True peace is not found in positive thinking, in absence of conflict, or in good feelings. It comes from knowing that God is in control. Our citizenship in Christ's Kingdom is sure, our destiny is set, and we can have victory over anxiety.

LAB note for Philippians 4:7

(2 THESSALONIANS 3:16) (REVELATION 1:4) (PHILIPPIANS 4:7) (LUKE 24:36) (JOHN 14:27) (JOHN 15:26) (GALATIANS 5:22) (ROMANS 8:16) (EXODUS 33:14-16)

November 18

We can rejoice, too, when we run into problems and trials, for we know that they are good for us.

If we have hope in Christ only for this life, we are the most miserable people in the world.

Dear friends, don't be surprised at the fiery trials you are going through, as if something strange were happening to you. Instead, be very glad—because these trials will make you partners with Christ in his suffering, and afterward you will have the wonderful joy of sharing his glory when it is displayed to all the world. ▪ Our hearts ache, but we always have joy.

Always be full of joy in the Lord. I say it again—rejoice! ▪ The apostles left the high council rejoicing that God had counted them worthy to suffer dishonor for the name of Jesus.

I pray that God, who gives you hope, will keep you happy and full of peace as you believe in him.

Even though the fig trees have no blossoms, and there are no grapes on the vine; even though the olive crop fails, and the fields lie empty and barren; even though the flocks die in the fields, and the cattle barns are empty, yet I will rejoice in the LORD! I will be joyful in the God of my salvation.

What a difference it makes to know Jesus! He cares for us in spite of what the world thinks. Don't let circumstances or people's expectations control you. Be firm as you stand true to God, and refuse to compromise his standards for living. *LAB note for 2 Corinthians 6:8–10*

(ROMANS 5:3) (1 CORINTHIANS 15:19) (1 PETER 4:12–13) (2 CORINTHIANS 6:10) (PHILIPPIANS 4:4) (ACTS 5:41) (ROMANS 15:13) (HABAKKUK 3:17–18)

November 19

My eyes are always looking to the LORD for help.

Is anything too hard for the LORD? ▪ Commit everything you do to the LORD. Trust him, and he will help you. ▪ Don't worry about anything; instead, pray about everything. Tell God what you need, and thank him for all he has done. ▪ Give all your worries and cares to God, for he cares about what happens to you. ▪ Take delight in the LORD, and he will give you your heart's desires.

Moses and Aaron were among his priests; Samuel also called on his name. They cried to the LORD for help, and he answered them. He spoke to them from the pillar of cloud, and they followed the decrees and principles he gave them.

I will answer them before they even call to me. While they are still talking to me about their needs, I will go ahead and answer their prayers! ▪ The earnest prayer of a righteous person has great power and wonderful results.

I love the LORD because he hears and answers my prayers. Because he bends down and listens, I will pray as long as I have breath!

"Is anything too hard for the LORD?" The obvious answer is, "Of course not!" Make it a habit to insert your specific needs into the question. "Is the communication problem I'm having too hard for him?" Asking the question this way reminds you that God is personally involved in your life.

LAB note for Genesis 18:14

(PSALM 25:15) (GENESIS 18:14) (PSALM 37:5) (PHILIPPIANS 4:6) (1 PETER 5:7) (PSALM 37:4) (PSALM 99:6-7) (ISAIAH 65:24) (JAMES 5:16) (PSALM 116:1-2)

November 20

Do people know where to find wisdom?

If you need wisdom—if you want to know what God wants you to do—ask him, and he will gladly tell you. He will not resent your asking. But when you ask him, be sure that you really expect him to answer, for a doubtful mind is as unsettled as a wave of the sea that is driven and tossed by the wind. ▩ Trust in the LORD with all your heart; do not depend on your own understanding. Seek his will in all you do, and he will direct your paths. ▩ He is the eternal King, the unseen one who never dies; he alone is God. ▩ Don't be impressed with your own wisdom.

"O Sovereign LORD," I said, "I can't speak for you! I'm too young!" "Don't say that," the LORD replied, "for you must go wherever I send you and say whatever I tell you. And don't be afraid of the people, for I will be with you and take care of you. I, the LORD, have spoken!"

Go directly to the Father and ask him, and he will grant your request because you use my name. You haven't done this before. Ask, using my name, and you will receive, and you will have abundant joy. ▩ If you believe, you will receive whatever you ask for in prayer.

Wisdom is not only knowledge, but the ability to make wise decisions in difficult circumstances. Whenever we need wisdom, we can pray to God, and he will generously supply what we need to guide our choices. *LAB note for James 1:5*

(JOB 28:12) (JAMES 1:5-6) (PROVERBS 3:5-6) (1 TIMOTHY 1:17) (PROVERBS 3:7) (JEREMIAH 1:6-8) (JOHN 16:23-24) (MATTHEW 21:22)

November 21

The suffering you sent was good for me, for it taught me to pay attention to your principles.

Even though Jesus was God's Son, he learned obedience from the things he suffered. ■ If we are to share his glory, we must also share his suffering. Yet what we suffer now is nothing compared to the glory he will give us later. ■ Whenever trouble comes your way, let it be an opportunity for joy. For when your faith is tested, your endurance has a chance to grow. So let it grow, for when your endurance is fully developed, you will be strong in character and ready for anything.

He knows where I am going. And when he has tested me like gold in a fire, he will pronounce me innocent. For I have stayed in God's paths; I have followed his ways and not turned aside.

Remember how the LORD your God led you through the wilderness for forty years, humbling you and testing you to prove your character, and to find out whether or not you would really obey his commands. So you should realize that just as a parent disciplines a child, the LORD your God disciplines you to help you. So obey the commands of the LORD your God by walking in his ways and fearing him.

Jesus' human life was not a script that he passively followed. It was a life that he chose freely—and a continuous process of making the will of God the Father his own. Because Jesus obeyed perfectly, even under great trial, he can help us obey, no matter how difficult obedience seems to be.

LAB note for Hebrews 5:8

(PSALM 119:71) (HEBREWS 5:8) (ROMANS 8:17-18) (JAMES 1:2-4) (JOB 23:10-11) (DEUTERONOMY 8:2, 5-6)

November 22

No one will succeed by strength alone.

David shouted in reply, "You come to me with sword, spear, and javelin, but I come to you in the name of the LORD Almighty—the God of the armies of Israel, whom you have defied." Reaching into his shepherd's bag and taking out a stone, he hurled it from his sling and hit the Philistine in the forehead. The stone sank in, and Goliath stumbled and fell face downward to the ground. So David triumphed over the Philistine giant with only a stone and sling.

The best-equipped army cannot save a king, nor is great strength enough to save a warrior. But the LORD watches over those who fear him, those who rely on his unfailing love. ▩ Riches and honor come from you alone, for you rule over everything. Power and might are in your hand, and it is at your discretion that people are made great and given strength.

I am glad to boast about my weaknesses, so that the power of Christ may work through me. Since I know it is all for Christ's good, I am quite content with my weaknesses and with insults, hardships, persecutions, and calamities. For when I am weak, then I am strong.

We should be confident of God's ultimate control over the events in our lives, and we should be thankful for the ways God has blessed us. By praising God for all good gifts, we acknowledge his ultimate control over all the affairs of life. *LAB note for 1 Samuel 2:1–10*

(1 SAMUEL 2:9) (1 SAMUEL 17:45, 49–50) (PSALM 33:16, 18)
(1 CHRONICLES 29:12) (2 CORINTHIANS 12:9–10)

November 23

Though the spirit is willing enough, the body is weak!

LORD, we love to obey your laws; our heart's desire is to glorify your name. All night long I search for you; earnestly I seek for God.

I know I am rotten through and through so far as my old sinful nature is concerned. No matter which way I turn, I can't make myself do right. I want to, but I can't. I love God's law with all my heart. But there is another law at work within me that is at war with my mind. This law wins the fight and makes me a slave to the sin that is still within me. ▩ The old sinful nature loves to do evil, which is just opposite from what the Holy Spirit wants. And the Spirit gives us desires that are opposite from what the sinful nature desires. These two forces are constantly fighting each other, and your choices are never free from the conflict.

I can do everything with the help of Christ who gives me the strength I need. ▩ Our only power and success come from God. ▩ My gracious favor is all you need.

We must never use the power of sin or Satan as an excuse, because they are defeated enemies. But without Christ's help, sin is stronger than we are. That is why we should never stand up to it all alone. Jesus Christ, who has conquered sin once and for all, promises to fight by our side.

LAB note for Romans 7:17-20

(MATTHEW 26:41) (ISAIAH 26:8-9) (ROMANS 7:18, 22-23) (GALATIANS 5:17) (PHILIPPIANS 4:13) (2 CORINTHIANS 3:5) (2 CORINTHIANS 12:9)

November 24

God made Christ, who never sinned, to be the offering for our sin, so that we could be made right with God through Christ.

The LORD laid on him the guilt and sins of us all. ▪ He personally carried away our sins in his own body on the cross so we can be dead to sin and live for what is right. You have been healed by his wounds! ▪ Because one person disobeyed God, many people became sinners. But because one other person obeyed God, many people will be made right in God's sight.

God our Savior showed us his kindness and love. He saved us, not because of the good things we did, but because of his mercy. He washed away our sins and gave us a new life through the Holy Spirit. He generously poured out the Spirit upon us because of what Jesus Christ our Savior did. He declared us not guilty because of his great kindness. And now we know that we will inherit eternal life. ▪ So now there is no condemnation for those who belong to Christ Jesus.

The LORD Is Our Righteousness.

When we trust in Christ, we make an exchange: He takes our sin and makes us right with God. In the world, bartering works only when two people exchange goods of relatively equal value. But God offers to trade his righteousness for our sin—something of immeasurable worth for something completely worthless. *LAB note for 2 Corinthians 5:21*

(2 CORINTHIANS 5:21) (ISAIAH 53:6) (1 PETER 2:24) (ROMANS 5:19) (TITUS 3:4-7) (ROMANS 8:1) (JEREMIAH 23:6)

November 25

The dust will return to the earth.

Our earthly bodies, which die and decay . . . now disappoint us. . . . They are weak . . . natural human bodies. ▪ Adam, the first man, was made from the dust of the earth.

You were made from dust, and to the dust you will return. ▪ One person dies in prosperity and security, the very picture of good health. Another person dies in bitter poverty, never having tasted the good life. Both alike are buried in the same dust, both eaten by the same worms.

No wonder my heart is filled with joy, and my mouth shouts his praises! My body rests in safety. ▪ After my body has decayed, yet in my body I will see God! ▪ The Lord Jesus Christ . . . will take these weak mortal bodies of ours and change them into glorious bodies like his own, using the same mighty power that he will use to conquer everything, everywhere.

LORD, remind me how brief my time on earth will be. Remind me that my days are numbered, and that my life is fleeing away. ▪ Teach us to make the most of our time, so that we may grow in wisdom.

Stripped of the life-giving spirit breathed into us by God, our bodies return to dust. Stripped of God's purpose, our work is in vain. Stripped of God's love, our service is futile. We must put God first over all we do and in all we do because without him we have nothing.

LAB note for Ecclesiastes 12:7-8

(ECCLESIASTES 12:7) (1 CORINTHIANS 15:42-44) (1 CORINTHIANS 15:47) (GENESIS 3:19) (JOB 21:23-26) (PSALM 16:9) (JOB 19:26) (PHILIPPIANS 3:20-21) (PSALM 39:4) (PSALM 90:12)

November 26

The LORD is more pleased when we do what is just and right than when we give him sacrifices.

The LORD has told you what is good, and this is what he requires: to do what is right, to love mercy, and to walk humbly with your God. ▪ What is more pleasing to the LORD; your burnt offerings and sacrifices or your obedience to his voice? Obedience is far better than sacrifice. Listening to him is much better than offering the fat of rams. ▪ I know it is important to love him with all my heart and all my understanding and all my strength, and to love my neighbor as myself. This is more important than to offer all of the burnt offerings and sacrifices required in the law.

Come back to your God! Act on the principles of love and justice, and always live in confident dependence on your God. ▪ Mary . . . sat at the Lord's feet, listening to what he taught. "There is really only one thing worth being concerned about. Mary has discovered it—and I won't take it away from her."

God is working in you, giving you the desire to obey him and the power to do what pleases him. ▪ May he produce in you, through the power of Jesus Christ, all that is pleasing to him. . . . To him be glory forever and ever. Amen.

Sacrifices are not bribes to make God overlook our character faults. If our personal and business dealings are not characterized by justice, no amount of generosity when the offering plate is passed will make up for it. *LAB note for Proverbs 21:3*

(PROVERBS 21:3) (MICAH 6:8) (1 SAMUEL 15:22) (MARK 12:33) (HOSEA 12:6) (LUKE 10:39, 42) (PHILIPPIANS 2:13) (HEBREWS 13:21)

November 27

The spirit will return to God who gave it.

The LORD God formed a man's body from the dust of the ground and breathed into it the breath of life. And the man became a living person. ▪ It is God's Spirit within people, the breath of the Almighty within them, that makes them intelligent. But sometimes the elders are not wise. Sometimes the aged do not understand justice.

We are always confident, even though we know that as long as we live in these bodies we are not at home with the Lord. ▪ I long to go and be with Christ. That would be far better for me. ▪ And now, brothers and sisters, I want you to know what will happen to the Christians who have died so you will not be full of sorrow like people who have no hope. For since we believe that Jesus died and was raised to life again, we also believe that when Jesus comes, God will bring back with Jesus all the Christians who have died.

There are many rooms in my Father's home, and I am going to prepare a place for you. If this were not so, I would tell you plainly. When everything is ready, I will come and get you, so that you will always be with me where I am.

It is not enough to recognize a great truth; it must be lived out each day. Elihu [Job's "friend"] recognized the truth that God was the only source of real wisdom, but he did not use God's wisdom to help Job. Becoming wise is an ongoing, lifelong pursuit. Don't be content just to know about wisdom; make it part of your life. *LAB note for Job 32:7-9*

(ECCLESIASTES 12:7) (GENESIS 2:7) (JOB 32:8-9) (2 CORINTHIANS 5:6) (PHILIPPIANS 1:23) (1 THESSALONIANS 4:13-14) (JOHN 14:2-3)

November 28

No one can take them from me.

I know the one in whom I trust, and I am sure that he is able to guard what I have entrusted to him until the day of his return. ▩ The Lord will deliver me from every evil attack and will bring me safely to his heavenly Kingdom. ▩ Overwhelming victory is ours through Christ, who loved us. And I am convinced that nothing can ever separate us from his love. Death can't, and life can't. The angels can't, and the demons can't. Our fears for today, our worries about tomorrow, and even the powers of hell can't keep God's love away. Whether we are high above the sky or in the deepest ocean, nothing in all creation will ever be able to separate us from the love of God that is revealed in Christ Jesus our Lord. ▩ Your real life is hidden with Christ in God.

Hasn't God chosen the poor in this world to be rich in faith? Aren't they the ones who will inherit the kingdom God promised to those who love him?

May our Lord Jesus Christ and God our Father, who loved us and in his special favor gave us everlasting comfort and hope, comfort your hearts and give you strength in every good thing you do and say.

Paul was in prison, but that did not stop his ministry. He trusted God to use him regardless of his circumstances. If your situation looks bleak, give your concerns to Christ. He will guard your faith and safely keep all you have entrusted to him until the day of his return.

LAB note for 2 Timothy 1:12

(JOHN 10:29) (2 TIMOTHY 1:12) (2 TIMOTHY 4:18) (ROMANS 8:37-39) (COLOSSIANS 3:3) (JAMES 2:5) (2 THESSALONIANS 2:16-17)

November 29

You will not be condemned for doing something you know is all right.

Keep away from every kind of evil. ▪ We are careful to be honorable before the Lord, but we also want everyone else to know we are honorable. ▪ It is God's will that your good lives should silence those who make foolish accusations against you.

If you suffer, however, it must not be for murder, stealing, making trouble, or prying into other people's affairs. But it is no shame to suffer for being a Christian. Praise God for the privilege of being called by his wonderful name!

For you have been called to live in freedom—not freedom to satisfy your sinful nature, but freedom to serve one another in love. ▪ The Kingdom of God is not a matter of what we eat or drink, but of living a life of goodness and peace and joy in the Holy Spirit. ▪ You must be careful with this freedom of yours. Do not cause a brother or sister with a weaker conscience to stumble. ▪ If anyone causes one of these little ones who trusts in me to lose faith, it would be better for that person to be thrown into the sea with a large millstone tied around the neck. ▪ When you refused to help the least of these my brothers and sisters, you were refusing to help me.

As Christians, we cannot avoid every kind of evil because we live in a sinful world. We can, however, make sure that we don't give evil a foothold by avoiding tempting situations and concentrating on obeying God.

LAB note for 1 Thessalonians 5:22-24

(ROMANS 14:16) (1 THESSALONIANS 5:22) (2 CORINTHIANS 8:21) (1 PETER 2:15) (1 PETER 4:15-16) (GALATIANS 5:13) (ROMANS 14:17) (1 CORINTHIANS 8:9) (MATTHEW 18:6) (MATTHEW 25:45)

November 30

Awake, O sleeper, rise up from the dead, and Christ will give you light.

Wake up, for the coming of our salvation is nearer now than when we first believed. ▪ So be on your guard, not asleep like the others. Stay alert and be sober. Night is the time for sleep and the time when people get drunk. But let us who live in the light think clearly, protected by the body armor of faith and love, and wearing as our helmet the confidence of our salvation.

Let your light shine for all the nations to see! For the glory of the LORD is shining upon you. Darkness as black as night will cover all the nations of the earth, but the glory of the LORD will shine over you.

Think clearly and exercise self-control. Look forward to the special blessings that will come to you at the return of Jesus Christ. ▪ Be dressed for service and well prepared, as though you were waiting for your master to return from the wedding feast. Then you will be ready to open the door and let him in the moment he arrives and knocks. ▪ If you do these things, your salvation will come like the dawn. Yes, your healing will come quickly. Your godliness will lead you forward, and the glory of the LORD will protect you from behind.

The imminent return of Christ should motivate us to live for him. This means being mentally alert ("think clearly"), disciplined ("exercise self-control"), and focused ("look forward"). Are you ready to meet Christ? *LAB note for 1 Peter 1:13*

(EPHESIANS 5:14) (ROMANS 13:11) (1 THESSALONIANS 5:6-8) (ISAIAH 60:1-2) (1 PETER 1:13) (LUKE 12:35-36) (ISAIAH 58:8)

December

The Giver of Life

Creator and Provider

Comforter and Friend

Eternal, infinite, awesome God

In this special season of giving, take a minute to reflect on God's generosity to you. He truly is the giver of all good things. How is your life changed by God's greatest gift on that first Christmas?

December 1

His royal titles: Wonderful Counselor, Mighty God.

The Word became human and lived here on earth among us. He was full of unfailing love and faithfulness. And we have seen his glory, the glory of the only Son of the Father. ▪ Your promises are backed by all the honor of your name.

He will be called Immanuel (meaning, God is with us). ▪ Jesus, for he will save his people from their sins.

Everyone will honor the Son, just as they honor the Father. ▪ God raised him up to the heights of heaven and gave him a name that is above every other name. ▪ He is far above any ruler or authority or power or leader or anything else in this world or in the world to come. And God has put all things under the authority of Christ. ▪ A name was written on him, and only he knew what it meant . . . King of kings and Lord of lords.

We cannot imagine the power of the Almighty. ▪ What is his name—and his son's name? Tell me if you know!

In a time of great darkness, God promised to send a light who would shine on everyone living in the shadow of death. He is both "Wonderful Counselor" and "Mighty God." This message of hope was fulfilled in the birth of Christ and the establishment of his eternal Kingdom.

LAB note for Isaiah 9:2-6

(ISAIAH 9:6) (JOHN 1:14) (PSALM 138:2) (MATTHEW 1:23) (MATTHEW 1:21) (JOHN 5:23) (PHILIPPIANS 2:9) (EPHESIANS 1:21-22) (REVELATION 19:12, 16) (JOB 37:23) (PROVERBS 30:4)

December 2

You judge all people according to what they have done.

No one can lay any other foundation than the one we already have—Jesus Christ. If the work survives the fire, that builder will receive a reward. But if the work is burned up, the builder will suffer great loss. The builders themselves will be saved, but like someone escaping through a wall of flames. ▪ For we must all stand before Christ to be judged. We will each receive whatever we deserve for the good or evil we have done in our bodies.

When you give to someone, don't tell your left hand what your right hand is doing. Give your gifts in secret, and your Father, who knows all secrets, will reward you. ▪ There will be glory and honor and peace from God for all who do good.

It is not that we think we can do anything of lasting value by ourselves. Our only power and success come from God. ▪ LORD, you will grant us peace, for all we have accomplished is really from you.

It is tempting to use honor, power, wealth, or prestige to measure people. We may even think that such people are really getting ahead in life. But God weighs us by different scales. Only the faithful work we do for him has eternal value. *LAB note for Psalm 62:9-12*

(PSALM 62:12) (1 CORINTHIANS 3:11, 14-15) (2 CORINTHIANS 5:10) (MATTHEW 6:3-4) (ROMANS 2:10) (2 CORINTHIANS 3:5) (ISAIAH 26:12)

December 3

Make every effort to live a pure and blameless life. And be at peace with God.

Now you are no longer a slave but God's own child. And since you are his child, everything he has belongs to you.

You should consider yourselves dead to sin and able to live for the glory of God through Christ Jesus. Do not let sin control the way you live; do not give in to its lustful desires. Do not let any part of your body become a tool of wickedness, to be used for sinning. Instead, give yourselves completely to God since you have been given new life. And use your whole body as a tool to do what is right for the glory of God. ▪ Obey God because you are his children. Don't slip back into your old ways of doing evil; you didn't know any better then. But now you must be holy in everything you do, just as God—who chose you to be his children—is holy. ▪ If you keep yourself pure, you will be a utensil God can use for his purpose. Your life will be clean, and you will be ready for the Master to use you for every good work.

So, my dear brothers and sisters, be strong and steady, always enthusiastic about the Lord's work, for you know that nothing you do for the Lord is ever useless.

We should not become lazy and complacent because Christ has not yet returned. Instead, we should live in eager expectation of his coming. What would you like to be doing when Christ returns? That is how you should be living each day. *LAB note for 2 Peter 3:14*

(2 PETER 3:14) (GALATIANS 4:7) (ROMANS 6:11-13) (1 PETER 1:14-15) (2 TIMOTHY 2:21) (1 CORINTHIANS 15:58)

December 4

God's deep secrets.

I no longer call you servants, because a master doesn't confide in his servants. Now you are my friends, since I have told you everything the Father told me.

And God has actually given us his Spirit (not the world's spirit) so we can know the wonderful things God has freely given us.

When I think of the wisdom and scope of God's plan, I fall to my knees and pray to the Father, the Creator of everything in heaven and on earth. I pray that from his glorious, unlimited resources he will give you mighty inner strength through his Holy Spirit. And I pray that Christ will be more and more at home in your hearts as you trust in him. May your roots go down deep into the soil of God's marvelous love. And may you have the power to understand, as all God's people should, how wide, how long, how high, and how deep his love really is. May you experience the love of Christ, though it is so great you will never fully understand it. Then you will be filled with the fullness of life and power that comes from God.

"God's deep secrets" refers to God's unfathomable nature and his wonderful plan—Jesus' death and resurrection—and to the promise of salvation, revealed only to those who believe that what God says is true. Those who believe in Christ's death and resurrection and put their faith in him will know all they need to know to be saved. *LAB note for 1 Corinthians 2:10*

(1 CORINTHIANS 2:10) (JOHN 15:15) (1 CORINTHIANS 2:12) (EPHESIANS 3:14-19)

December 5

Revive us so we can call on your name once more.

It is the Spirit who gives eternal life. ▩ And the Holy Spirit helps us in our distress. For we don't even know what we should pray for, nor how we should pray. But the Holy Spirit prays for us with groanings that cannot be expressed in words. And the Father who knows all hearts knows what the Spirit is saying, for the Spirit pleads for us believers in harmony with God's own will. ▩ Pray at all times and on every occasion in the power of the Holy Spirit. Stay alert and be persistent in your prayers for all Christians everywhere.

I will never forget your commandments, for you have used them to restore my joy and health. ▩ The old way ends in death; in the new way, the Holy Spirit gives life. ▩ If you stay joined to me and my words remain in you, you may ask any request you like, and it will be granted! ▩ We can be confident that he will listen to us whenever we ask him for anything in line with his will.

How can anyone pray at all times? One way is to make quick, brief prayers your habitual response to every situation you meet throughout the day. Another way is to order your life around God's desires and teachings so that your very life becomes a prayer. *LAB note for Ephesians 6:18*

(PSALM 80:18) (JOHN 6:63) (ROMANS 8:26–27) (EPHESIANS 6:18)
(PSALM 119:93) (2 CORINTHIANS 3:6) (JOHN 15:7) (1 JOHN 5:14)

December 6

Let us come boldly to the throne of our gracious God. There we will receive his mercy, and we will find grace to help us when we need it.

Don't worry about anything; instead, pray about everything. Tell God what you need, and thank him for all he has done. If you do this, you will experience God's peace, which is far more wonderful than the human mind can understand. His peace will guard your hearts and minds as you live in Christ Jesus. ▪ So you should not be like cowering, fearful slaves. You should behave instead like God's very own children, adopted into his family—calling him "Father, dear Father."

Yes, ask anything in my name, and I will do it! ▪ So, dear brothers and sisters, we can boldly enter heaven's Most Holy Place because of the blood of Jesus. Let us go right into the presence of God, with true hearts fully trusting him. For our evil consciences have been sprinkled with Christ's blood to make us clean, and our bodies have been washed with pure water. ▪ "The Lord is my helper, so I will not be afraid. What can mere mortals do to me?"

Prayer is our approach to God, and we are to come "boldly." Some Christians approach God meekly with heads hung low, afraid to ask him to meet their needs. Others pray flippantly, giving little thought to what they say. Come with reverence because he is your King. But also come with bold assurance because he is your Friend and Counselor.

LAB note for Hebrews 4:16

(HEBREWS 4:16) (PHILIPPIANS 4:6-7) (ROMANS 8:15) (JOHN 14:14) (HEBREWS 10:19, 22) (HEBREWS 13:6)

December 7

When darkness overtakes the godly, light will come bursting in.

Who among you fears the LORD and obeys his servant? If you are walking in darkness, without a ray of light, trust in the LORD and rely on your God. ▪ Though they stumble, they will not fall, for the LORD holds them by the hand. ▪ These commands and this teaching are a lamp to light the way ahead of you. The correction of discipline is the way to life.

Do not gloat over me, my enemies! For though I fall, I will rise again. Though I sit in darkness, the LORD himself will be my light. I will be patient as the LORD punishes me, for I have sinned against him. But after that, he will take up my case and punish my enemies for all the evil they have done to me. The LORD will bring me out of my darkness into the light, and I will see his righteousness.

A pure eye lets sunshine into your soul. But an evil eye shuts out the light and plunges you into darkness. If the light you think you have is really darkness, how deep that darkness will be!

If we walk by our own light and reject God's, we become self-sufficient, and the result of self-sufficiency is torment. When we place confidence in our own intelligence, appearance, or accomplishments instead of in God, we risk torment later when these strengths fade.

LAB note for Isaiah 50:10–11

(PSALM 112:4) (ISAIAH 50:10) (PSALM 37:24) (PROVERBS 6:23)
(MICAH 7:8–9) (MATTHEW 6:22–23)

December 8

That couldn't happen even if the LORD opened the windows of heaven!

Have faith in God. ▩ It is impossible to please God without faith. ▩ With God everything is possible.

Was I too weak to save you? Is that why the house is silent and empty when I come home? Is it because I have no power to rescue?

"My thoughts are completely different from yours," says the LORD. "And my ways are far beyond anything you could imagine. For just as the heavens are higher than the earth, so are my ways higher than your ways and my thoughts higher than your thoughts." ▩ I will open the windows of heaven for you. I will pour out a blessing so great you won't have enough room to take it in!

The LORD is not too weak to save you, and he is not becoming deaf. He can hear you when you call. ▩ O LORD, no one but you can help the powerless against the mighty! Help us, O LORD our God, for we trust in you alone. It is in your name that we have come against this vast horde. O LORD, you are our God; do not let mere men prevail against you.

We expected to die. But as a result, we learned not to rely on ourselves, but on God who can raise the dead.

Sometimes we become preoccupied with problems when we should be looking for opportunities. Instead of focusing on the negatives, develop an attitude of expectancy. To say that God cannot rescue someone or that a situation is impossible demonstrates a lack of faith.

LAB note for 2 Kings 7:2

(2 KINGS 7:2) (MARK 11:22) (HEBREWS 11:6) (MATTHEW 19:26) (ISAIAH 50:2) (ISAIAH 55:8-9) (MALACHI 3:10) (ISAIAH 59:1) (2 CHRONICLES 14:11) (2 CORINTHIANS 1:9)

December 9

Your days of mourning will come to an end.

Here on earth you will have many trials and sorrows. ▪ For we know that all creation has been groaning as in the pains of childbirth right up to the present time. And even we Christians, although we have the Holy Spirit within us as a foretaste of future glory, also groan to be released from pain and suffering. We, too, wait anxiously for that day when God will give us our full rights as his children, including the new bodies he has promised us. ▪ Our dying bodies make us groan and sigh.

These are the ones coming out of the great tribulation. They washed their robes in the blood of the Lamb and made them white. That is why they are standing in front of the throne of God, serving him day and night in his Temple. And he who sits on the throne will live among them and shelter them. They will never again be hungry or thirsty, and they will be fully protected from the scorching noontime heat. For the Lamb who stands in front of the throne will be their Shepherd. He will lead them to the springs of life-giving water. And God will wipe away all their tears.

As Christians we should expect continuing tension with an unbelieving world that is "out of sync" with Christ, his Good News, and his people. At the same time we can expect our relationship with Christ to produce peace and comfort because we are "in sync" with him.

LAB note for John 16:31-33

(Isaiah 60:20) (John 16:33) (Romans 8:22-23) (2 Corinthians 5:4) (Revelation 7:14-17)

December 10

Teacher, don't you even care that we are going to drown?

The LORD is good to everyone. He showers compassion on all his creation.

All the wild animals, large and small, and all the birds and fish will be afraid of you. I have placed them in your power. I have given them to you for food, just as I have given you grain and vegetables. ▪ As long as the earth remains, there will be springtime and harvest, cold and heat, winter and summer, day and night.

The LORD is good. When trouble comes, he is a strong refuge. And he knows everyone who trusts in him. ▪ Then God heard the boy's cries, and the angel of God called to Hagar from the sky, "Hagar, what's wrong? Do not be afraid! God has heard the boy's cries from the place where you laid him." Then God opened Hagar's eyes, and she saw a well. She immediately filled her water container and gave the boy a drink.

Don't worry about having enough food or drink or clothing. Why be like the pagans who are so deeply concerned about these things? Your heavenly Father already knows all your needs. ▪ Trust . . . in the living God, who richly gives us all we need for our enjoyment.

Think about the storms in your life—the situations that cause you great anxiety. Whatever your difficulty, you have two options: You can worry and assume that Jesus no longer cares, or you can resist fear, putting your trust in him. When you feel like panicking, confess your need for God and then trust him to care for you. *LAB note for Mark 4:38-40*

(MARK 4:38) (PSALM 145:9) (GENESIS 9:2-3) (GENESIS 8:22) (NAHUM 1:7) (GENESIS 21:17, 19) (MATTHEW 6:31-32) (1 TIMOTHY 6:17)

December 11

Your faithful work.

This is what God wants you to do: Believe in the one he has sent.

Faith that doesn't show itself by good deeds is no faith at all—it is dead and useless. ▩What is important is faith expressing itself in love. ▩ Those who live only to satisfy their own sinful desires will harvest the consequences of decay and death. But those who live to please the Spirit will harvest everlasting life from the Spirit. ▩ We are God's masterpiece. He has created us anew in Christ Jesus, so that we can do the good things he planned for us long ago. ▩ He gave his life to free us from every kind of sin, to cleanse us, and to make us his very own people, totally committed to doing what is right.

We keep on praying for you, that our God will make you worthy of the life to which he called you. And we pray that God, by his power, will fulfill all your good intentions and faithful deeds. ▩ God is working in you, giving you the desire to obey him and the power to do what pleases him.

The Thessalonians had stood firm when they were persecuted. Paul commended these young Christians for their faithful work, loving deeds, and anticipation of the Lord's return. These characteristics are the marks of effective Christians in any age. *LAB note for 1 Thessalonians 1:3*

(1 Thessalonians 1:3) (John 6:29) (James 2:17) (Galatians 5:6)
(Galatians 6:8) (Ephesians 2:10) (Titus 2:14)
(2 Thessalonians 1:11) (Philippians 2:13)

December 12

This is what God has testified: He has given us eternal life, and this life is in his Son.

The Father has life in himself, and he has granted his Son to have life in himself. He will even raise from the dead anyone he wants to, just as the Father does.

I am the resurrection and the life. Those who believe in me, even though they die like everyone else, will live again. They are given eternal life for believing in me and will never perish. ▪ I am the good shepherd. The good shepherd lays down his life for the sheep. The Father loves me because I lay down my life that I may have it back again. No one can take my life from me. I lay down my life voluntarily. For I have the right to lay it down when I want to and also the power to take it again. For the Father has given me this command. ▪ I am the way, the truth, and the life. No one can come to the Father except through me. ▪ So whoever has God's Son has life; whoever does not have his Son does not have life. ▪ For you died when Christ died, and your real life is hidden with Christ in God. And when Christ, who is your real life, is revealed to the whole world, you will share in all his glory.

Jesus has power over life and death as well as power to forgive sins. This is because he is the Creator of life. He who is life can surely restore life. When we realize his power and how wonderful his offer to us really is, how can we not commit our lives to him? *LAB note for John 11:25-26*

(1 John 5:11) (John 5:26, 21) (John 11:25-26) (John 10:11, 17-18) (John 14:6) (1 John 5:12) (Colossians 3:3-4)

December 13

Then the LORD did exactly what he had promised. Sarah became pregnant, and she gave a son to Abraham in his old age.

Trust in him at all times. Pour out your heart to him, for God is our refuge. ▪ David found strength in the LORD his God. ▪ God will surely come for you, to lead you out of this land of Egypt. He will bring you back to the land he vowed to give to the descendants of Abraham, Isaac, and Jacob. ▪ I have seen the misery of my people in Egypt. I have heard their cries. So I have come to rescue them. Now go, for I will send you to Egypt. And by means of many miraculous signs and wonders, he led them out of Egypt, through the Red Sea, and back and forth through the wilderness for forty years. ▪ All of the good promises that the LORD had given Israel came true.

God can be trusted to keep his promise. ▪ God is not a man, that he should lie. He is not a human, that he should change his mind. Has he ever spoken and failed to act? Has he ever promised and not carried it through? ▪ God also bound himself with an oath, so that those who received the promise could be perfectly sure that he would never change his mind. ▪ Heaven and earth will disappear, but my words will remain forever. ▪ The grass withers, and the flowers fade, but the word of our God stands forever.

Who could believe that Abraham would have a son at one hundred years of age—and live to raise him to adulthood? But doing the impossible is everyday business for God. Our big problems won't seem so impossible if we let God handle them. *LAB note for Genesis 21:1-7*

(GENESIS 21:1-2) (PSALM 62:8) (1 SAMUEL 30:6) (GENESIS 50:24) (ACTS 7:34, 36) (JOSHUA 21:45) (HEBREWS 10:23) (NUMBERS 23:19) (HEBREWS 6:17) (MATTHEW 24:35) (ISAIAH 40:8)

December 14

He will save his people from their sins.

You know that Jesus came to take away our sins, for there is no sin in him. ▪ He personally carried away our sins in his own body on the cross so we can be dead to sin and live for what is right. ▪ He is able, once and forever, to save everyone who comes to God through him.

He was wounded and crushed for our sins. He was beaten that we might have peace. He was whipped, and we were healed! All of us have strayed away like sheep. We have left God's paths to follow our own. Yet the LORD laid on him the guilt and sins of us all. He was oppressed and treated harshly, yet he never said a word. He was led as a lamb to the slaughter. And as a sheep is silent before the shearers, he did not open his mouth. From prison and trial they led him away to his death. ▪ It was written long ago that the Messiah must suffer and die and rise again from the dead on the third day. . . . Take this message of repentance to all the nations, beginning in Jerusalem: "There is forgiveness of sins for all who turn to me." ▪ He came . . . to remove the power of sin forever by his sacrificial death for us.

Then God put him in the place of honor at his right hand as Prince and Savior. ▪ In this man Jesus there is forgiveness of your sins. Everyone who believes in him is freed from all guilt and declared right with God—something the Jewish law could never do. ▪ Your sins have been forgiven because of Jesus.

Jesus came to earth to save us because we can't save ourselves from sin and its consequences. No matter how good we are, we can't eliminate the sinful nature present in all of us. Only Jesus can do that. Thank Christ for his death on the cross for your sin, and then ask him to take control of your life. *LAB note for Matthew 1:21*

(MATTHEW 1:21) (1 JOHN 3:5) (1 PETER 2:24) (HEBREWS 7:25) (ISAIAH 53:5-8) (LUKE 24:46-47) (HEBREWS 9:26) (ACTS 5:31) (ACTS 13:38-39) (1 JOHN 2:12)

December 15

The Philistine commanders demanded, "What are these Hebrews doing here?"

Be happy if you are insulted for being a Christian, for then the glorious Spirit of God will come upon you.

You will not be condemned for doing something you know is all right. ■ Be careful how you live among your unbelieving neighbors. Even if they accuse you of doing wrong, they will see your honorable behavior, and they will believe and give honor to God when he comes to judge the world.

Don't team up with those who are unbelievers. How can goodness be a partner with wickedness? How can light live with darkness? And what union can there be between God's temple and idols? For we are the temple of the living God. As God said: "I will live in them and walk among them. I will be their God, and they will be my people."

You are a chosen people . . . so you can show others the goodness of God, for he called you out of the darkness into his wonderful light.

Christ will send his Spirit to strengthen those who are persecuted for their faith, but not all suffering is the result of good Christian conduct. It may take careful thought or wise counsel to determine the real cause of our suffering. We can be assured, however, that whenever we suffer because of our loyalty to Christ, he will be with us all the way.

LAB note for 1 Peter 4:16

(1 SAMUEL 29:3) (1 PETER 4:14) (ROMANS 14:16) (1 PETER 2:12) (2 CORINTHIANS 6:14, 16) (1 PETER 2:9)

December 16

He calls his own sheep by name and leads them out.

God's truth stands firm like a foundation stone with this inscription: "The Lord knows those who are his." ▩ On judgment day many will tell me, "Lord, Lord, we prophesied in your name and cast out demons in your name and performed many miracles in your name." But I will reply, "I never knew you. Go away; the things you did were unauthorized." ▩ For the LORD watches over the path of the godly, but the path of the wicked leads to destruction.

I have written your name on my hand. ▩ Place me like a seal over your heart, or like a seal on your arm. For love is as strong as death, and its jealousy is as enduring as the grave. ▩ The LORD is good. When trouble comes, he is a strong refuge. And he knows everyone who trusts in him.

There are many rooms in my Father's home, and I am going to prepare a place for you. If this were not so, I would tell you plainly. When everything is ready, I will come and get you, so that you will always be with me where I am.

Jesus exposed those who sounded religious but had no personal relationship with him. Many people think that if they are "good" people and say religious things they will be rewarded with eternal life. In reality, faith in Christ is what will count at the judgment.

LAB note for Matthew 7:21-23

(JOHN 10:3) (2 TIMOTHY 2:19) (MATTHEW 7:22-23) (PSALM 1:6) (ISAIAH 49:16) (SONG OF SONGS 8:6) (NAHUM 1:7) (JOHN 14:2-3)

December 17

He will keep you free from all blame on the great day when our Lord Jesus Christ returns.

You who were once so far away from God . . . were his enemies, separated from him by your evil thoughts and actions, yet now he has brought you back as his friends. He has done this through his death on the cross in his own human body. As a result, he has brought you into the very presence of God, and you are holy and blameless as you stand in it firmly. Don't drift away from the assurance you received when you heard the Good News. ▩ Live clean, innocent lives as children of God in a dark world full of crooked and perverse people. Let your lives shine brightly before them.

And now, all glory to God, who is able to keep you from stumbling, and who will bring you into his glorious presence innocent of sin and with great joy. All glory to him, who alone is God our Savior, through Jesus Christ our Lord. Yes, glory, majesty, power, and authority belong to him, in the beginning, now, and forevermore. Amen.

The guarantee to be "free from all blame" is not because of our great gifts or our shining performance but because of what Jesus Christ accomplished for us through his death and resurrection. All who have received the Lord Jesus as their Savior will be considered blameless when he returns.

LAB note for 1 Corinthians 1:7-9

(1 Corinthians 1:8) (Colossians 1:21-23) (Philippians 2:15) (Jude 1:24-25)

December 18

He will protect his godly ones.

We are lying if we say we have fellowship with God but go on living in spiritual darkness. We are not living in the truth. But if we are living in the light of God's presence, just as Christ is, then we have fellowship with each other, and the blood of Jesus, his Son, cleanses us from every sin. ▩ Let us strip off every weight that slows us down, especially the sin that so easily hinders our progress.

I will teach you wisdom's ways and lead you in straight paths. If you live a life guided by wisdom, you won't limp or stumble as you run. Do not do as the wicked do, or follow the path of evildoers. Avoid their haunts. Turn away and go somewhere else. Look straight ahead, and fix your eyes on what lies before you. Mark out a straight path for your feet; then stick to the path and stay safe. Don't get sidetracked; keep your feet from following evil.

The Lord will deliver me from every evil attack and will bring me safely to his heavenly Kingdom. To God be the glory forever and ever. Amen.

How does Jesus' blood cleanse us from every sin? Jesus died for the sins of the world. When we commit our life to Christ and thus identify ourselves with him, his death becomes ours. He has paid the penalty for our sins, and his blood has purified us. *LAB note for 1 John 1:7*

(1 SAMUEL 2:9) (1 JOHN 1:6-7) (HEBREWS 12:1)
(PROVERBS 4:11-12, 14-15, 25-27) (2 TIMOTHY 4:18)

December 19

Try to understand what the Lord wants you to do.

God wants you to be holy. ▩ Stop quarreling with God! If you agree with him, you will have peace at last, and things will go well with you. ▩ This is the way to have eternal life—to know you, the only true God, and Jesus Christ, the one you sent to earth. ▩ We know that the Son of God has come, and he has given us understanding so that we can know the true God. And now we are in God because we are in his Son, Jesus Christ. He is the only true God, and he is eternal life.

We have continued praying for you ever since we first heard about you. We ask God to give you a complete understanding of what he wants to do in your lives, and we ask him to make you wise with spiritual wisdom. ▩ God, the glorious Father of our Lord Jesus Christ, . . . give you spiritual wisdom and understanding, so that you might grow in your knowledge of God. I pray that your hearts will be flooded with light so that you can understand the wonderful future he has promised to those he called. I want you to realize what a rich and glorious inheritance he has given to his people. I pray that you will begin to understand the incredible greatness of his power for us who believe him.

Being made holy is the process of living the Christian life. The Holy Spirit works in us, conforming us to the image of Christ. Do you seek for holiness in your daily life, with the Holy Spirit's help?

LAB note for 1 Thessalonians 4:3

(Ephesians 5:17) (1 Thessalonians 4:3) (Job 22:21) (John 17:3) (1 John 5:20) (Colossians 1:9) (Ephesians 1:17-19)

December 20

Be strong with the special favor God gives you in Christ Jesus.

You will be strengthened by his glorious power so that you will have all the patience and endurance you need. May you be filled with joy. ▩ Just as you accepted Christ as your Lord, you must continue to live in obedience to him. Let your roots grow down into him and draw up nourishment from him, so you will grow in faith, strong and vigorous in the truth you were taught. Let your lives overflow with thanksgiving for all he has done. ▩ The LORD has planted them like strong and graceful oaks for his own glory. ▩ We are his house, built on the foundation of the apostles and the prophets. And the cornerstone is Christ Jesus himself.

And now I entrust you to God and the word of his grace—his message that is able to build you up and give you an inheritance with all those he has set apart for himself. ▩ May you always be filled with the fruit of your salvation—those good things that are produced in your life by Jesus Christ—for this will bring much glory and praise to God.

Fight the good fight for what we believe. ▩ Don't be intimidated by your enemies.

Just as we are saved by God's special, undeserved favor, we should live by it. This means trusting completely in Christ and his power and not trying to live for Christ in our strength alone. Receive and utilize Christ's power. He will give you the strength to do his work. *LAB note for 2 Timothy 2:1*

(2 Timothy 2:1) (Colossians 1:11) (Colossians 2:6-7) (Isaiah 61:3) (Ephesians 2:20) (Acts 20:32) (Philippians 1:11) (1 Timothy 6:12) (Philippians 1:28)

December 21

Wonderful Counselor.

And the Spirit of the LORD will rest on him—the Spirit of wisdom and understanding, the Spirit of counsel and might, the Spirit of knowledge and the fear of the LORD. He will delight in obeying the LORD.

Listen as wisdom calls out! Hear as understanding raises her voice! She stands on the hilltop and at the crossroads. At the entrance to the city, at the city gates, she cries aloud, "I call to you, to all of you! I am raising my voice to all people. How naive you are! Let me give you common sense. O foolish ones, let me give you understanding. Listen to me! For I have excellent things to tell you. Everything I say is right, for I speak the truth and hate every kind of deception. Good advice and success belong to me. Insight and strength are mine."

The LORD Almighty is a wonderful teacher, and he gives the farmer great wisdom. ▩ If you need wisdom—if you want to know what God wants you to do—ask him, and he will gladly tell you. He will not resent your asking. ▩ Trust in the LORD with all your heart; do not depend on your own understanding. Seek his will in all you do, and he will direct your paths.

God takes all our individual circumstances and weaknesses into account, much as the farmer uses special tools to plant and harvest the fragile plants. God deals with each of us sensitively. We should follow his example when we deal with others. Different people require different treatment. *LAB note for Isaiah 28:23-29*

(ISAIAH 9:6) (ISAIAH 11:2-3) (PROVERBS 8:1-7, 14) (ISAIAH 28:29) (JAMES 1:5) (PROVERBS 3:5-6)

December 22

Mighty God.

You are the most handsome of all. Gracious words stream from your lips. God himself has blessed you forever. Put on your sword, O mighty warrior! You are so glorious, so majestic! In your majesty, ride out to victory, defending truth, humility, and justice. Go forth to perform awe-inspiring deeds! Your throne, O God, endures forever and ever. Your royal power is expressed in justice. ▩ Who is this . . . with his clothing stained red? Who is this in royal robes, marching in the greatness of his strength? "It is I, the LORD, announcing your salvation! It is I, the LORD, who is mighty to save!"

See, God has come to save me. I will trust in him and not be afraid. The LORD God is my strength and my song; he has become my salvation. ▩ But thanks be to God, who made us his captives and leads us along in Christ's triumphal procession.

The Son reflects God's own glory, and everything about him represents God exactly. He sustains the universe by the mighty power of his command. After he died to cleanse us from the stain of sin, he sat down in the place of honor at the right hand of the majestic God of heaven. ▩ Glory to God, who is able to keep you from stumbling, and who will bring you into his glorious presence innocent of sin and with great joy. . . . Amen.

What a glorious day it will be when Jesus Christ comes to reign over the earth! Even now we need to express our gratitude to God, thanking him, praising him, and telling others about him. From the depths of our gratitude, we must praise him. And we should share the Good News with others. *LAb note for Isaiah 12:1ff.*

(ISAIAH 9:6) (PSALM 45:2-4, 6) (ISAIAH 63:1) (ISAIAH 12:2) (2 CORINTHIANS 2:14) (HEBREWS 1:3) (JUDE 1:24-25)

December 23

Everlasting Father.

Hear, O Israel! The LORD is our God, the LORD alone.

The Father and I are one. The Father is in me, and I am in the Father. ▩ Since you don't know who I am, you don't know who my Father is. If you knew me, then you would know my Father, too. ▩ Philip said, "Lord, show us the Father and we will be satisfied." Jesus replied, "Philip, don't you even yet know who I am, even after all the time I have been with you? Anyone who has seen me has seen the Father! So why are you asking to see him?" ▩ Here I am—together with the children God has given me. ▩ When he sees all that is accomplished by his anguish, he will be satisfied. ▩ "I am the Alpha and the Omega—the beginning and the end," says the Lord God. "I am the one who is, who always was, and who is still to come, the Almighty One." ▩ I existed before Abraham was ever born! ▩ I AM THE ONE WHO ALWAYS IS. . . . I AM has sent me.

To his Son he says, "Your throne, O God, endures forever and ever." ▩ He existed before everything else began, and he holds all creation together. ▩ In Christ the fullness of God lives in a human body.

Monotheism—belief in only one God—was a distinctive feature of Hebrew religion. Many ancient religions believed in many gods. Then and today there are people who prefer to place their trust in many different "gods." But the day is coming when God will be recognized as the only one. He will be the king over the whole earth. *LAB note for Deuteronomy 6:4*

(ISAIAH 9:6) (DEUTERONOMY 6:4) (JOHN 10:30, 38) (JOHN 8:19) (JOHN 14:8-9) (HEBREWS 2:13) (ISAIAH 53:11) (REVELATION 1:8) (JOHN 8:58) (EXODUS 3:14) (HEBREWS 1:8) (COLOSSIANS 1:17) (COLOSSIANS 2:9)

December 24

Prince of Peace.

Help him judge your people in the right way; let the poor always be treated fairly. May the mountains yield prosperity for all, and may the hills be fruitful, because the king does what is right. Help him to defend the poor, to rescue the children of the needy, and to crush their oppressors. May he live as long as the sun shines, as long as the moon continues in the skies. Yes, forever! ▪ Glory to God . . . and peace on earth to all whom God favors.

Because of God's tender mercy, the light from heaven is about to break upon us, to give light to those who sit in darkness and in the shadow of death, and to guide us to the path of peace. ▪ There is peace with God through Jesus Christ, who is Lord of all.

I have told you all this so that you may have peace in me. Here on earth you will have many trials and sorrows. But take heart, because I have overcome the world. ▪ I am leaving you with a gift—peace of mind and heart. And the peace I give isn't like the peace the world gives. So don't be troubled or afraid. ▪ God's peace . . . is far more wonderful than the human mind can understand. His peace will guard your hearts and minds as you live in Christ Jesus.

What qualities do we want most in our leaders? God desires all who rule under him to be just and righteous. Think how the world would change if world leaders would commit themselves to these two qualities. Let us pray that they will! *LAB note for Psalm 72:1-2*

(ISAIAH 9:6) (PSALM 72:2-5) (LUKE 2:14) (LUKE 1:78-79) (ACTS 10:36) (JOHN 16:33) (JOHN 14:27) (PHILIPPIANS 4:7)

December 25

Thank God for his Son—a gift too wonderful for words!

Shout with joy to the LORD, O earth! Worship the LORD with gladness. Come before him, singing with joy. Enter his gates with thanksgiving; go into his courts with praise. Give thanks to him and bless his name. ▪ For a child is born to us, a son is given to us. And the government will rest on his shoulders. These will be his royal titles: Wonderful Counselor, Mighty God, Everlasting Father, Prince of Peace.

For God so loved the world that he gave his only Son. ▪ Since God did not spare even his own Son but gave him up for us all, won't God, who gave us Christ, also give us everything else? ▪ There was only one left—his son whom he loved dearly. The owner finally sent him. ▪ Everyone who believes in him will not perish but have eternal life. ▪ The whole world and life and death; the present and the future. Everything belongs to you, and you belong to Christ, and Christ belongs to God.

Let them praise the LORD for his great love and for all his wonderful deeds to them. ▪ Praise the LORD, I tell myself; with my whole heart, I will praise his holy name.

Oh, how I praise the Lord. How I rejoice in God my Savior!

God's love is not static or self-centered; it reaches out and draws others in. Here God sets the pattern of true love, the basis for all love relationships—when you love someone dearly, you are willing to give freely to the point of self-sacrifice. *LAB note for John 3:16*

(2 CORINTHIANS 9:15) (PSALM 100:1-2, 4) (ISAIAH 9:6) (JOHN 3:16) (ROMANS 8:32) (MARK 12:6) (JOHN 3:16) (1 CORINTHIANS 3:22-23) (PSALM 107:21) (PSALM 103:1) (LUKE 1:46-47)

December 26

Be strong and steady, always enthusiastic about the Lord's work.

You know that nothing you do for the Lord is ever useless. ❖ Just as you accepted Christ Jesus as your Lord, you must continue to live in obedience to him. Let your roots grow down into him and draw up nourishment from him, so you will grow in faith, strong and vigorous in the truth you were taught. Let your lives overflow with thanksgiving for all he has done. ❖ Those who endure to the end will be saved.

Stand firm in your faith.

All of us must quickly carry out the tasks assigned us by the one who sent me, because there is little time left before the night falls and all work comes to an end.

Those who live only to satisfy their own sinful desires will harvest the consequences of decay and death. But those who live to please the Spirit will harvest everlasting life from the Spirit. So don't get tired of doing what is good. Don't get discouraged and give up, for we will reap a harvest of blessing at the appropriate time.

Because of the Resurrection, nothing we do is useless. Knowing that Christ has won the ultimate victory should affect the way we live right now. Don't let discouragement over an apparent lack of results keep you from doing the work of the Lord enthusiastically as you have opportunity.

LAB note for 1 Corinthians 15:58

(1 CORINTHIANS 15:58) (1 CORINTHIANS 15:58) (COLOSSIANS 2:6-7) (MATTHEW 24:13) (2 CORINTHIANS 1:24) (JOHN 9:4) (GALATIANS 6:8-9)

December 27

He is able, once and forever, to save everyone who comes to God through him.

I am the way, the truth, and the life. No one can come to the Father except through me. ▪ There is salvation in no one else! There is no other name in all of heaven for people to call on to save them.

My sheep recognize my voice; I know them, and they follow me. I give them eternal life, and they will never perish. No one will snatch them away from me ▪ God, who began the good work within you, will continue his work until it is finally finished on that day when Christ Jesus comes back again. ▪ Is anything too hard for the LORD?

And now—all glory to God, who is able to keep you from stumbling, and who will bring you into his glorious presence innocent of sin and with great joy. All glory to him, who alone is God our Savior, through Jesus Christ our Lord. Yes, glory, majesty, power, and authority belong to him, in the beginning, now, and forevermore. Amen.

No one can add to what Jesus did to save us; our past, present, and future sins are all forgiven, and Jesus is with the Father as a sign that our sins are forgiven. If you are a Christian, remember that Christ has paid the price for your sins once and for all. *LAB note for Hebrews 7:25*

(HEBREWS 7:25) (JOHN 14:6) (ACTS 4:12) (JOHN 10:27-28) (PHILIPPIANS 1:6) (GENESIS 18:14) (JUDE 1:24-25)

December 28

For Christ himself has made peace between us.

For God was in Christ, reconciling the world to himself, no longer counting people's sins against them. This is the wonderful message he has given us to tell others. For God made Christ, who never sinned, to be the offering for our sin, so that we could be made right with God through Christ. ▪ By him God reconciled everything to himself. He made peace with everything in heaven and on earth by means of his blood on the cross. As a result, he has brought you into the very presence of God, and you are holy and blameless as you stand before him without a single fault. ▪ He forgave all our sins. He canceled the record that contained the charges against us. He took it and destroyed it by nailing it to Christ's cross.

I am leaving you with a gift—peace of mind and heart. And the peace I give isn't like the peace the world gives. So don't be troubled or afraid.

There are many barriers that can divide us from other Christians: age, appearance, intelligence, political persuasion, economic status, race, theological perspective. Fortunately, Christ has knocked down the barriers and unified all believers into one family. His cross should be the focus of our unity. *LAB note for Ephesians 2:14–22*

(EPHESIANS 2:14) (2 CORINTHIANS 5:19, 21) (COLOSSIANS 1:20, 22) (COLOSSIANS 2:13–14) (JOHN 14:27)

December 29

Your sins are forgiven.

I will forgive their wickedness and will never again remember their sins. ▩ Who but God can forgive sins!

I—yes, I alone—am the one who blots out your sins for my own sake and will never think of them again. ▩ Oh, what joy for those whose rebellion is forgiven, whose sin is put out of sight! Yes, what joy for those whose record the LORD has cleared of sin, whose lives are lived in complete honesty! ▩ Where is another God like you, who pardons the sins of the survivors among his people?

God through Christ has forgiven you. ▩ The blood of Jesus, his Son, cleanses us from every sin. If we say we have no sin, we are only fooling ourselves and refusing to accept the truth. But if we confess our sins to him, he is faithful and just to forgive us and to cleanse us from every wrong.

He has removed our rebellious acts as far away from us as the east is from the west. ▩ Sin is no longer your master, for you are no longer subject to the law, which enslaves you to sin. Instead, you are free by God's grace.

God wants to forgive sinners. Forgiveness has always been part of his loving nature. He announced it to Moses; he revealed it to David; and he dramatically showed it to the world through Jesus Christ. He forgives rebellion, puts sin out of sight, and clears our record of sin.

LAB note for Psalm 32:1-2

(MARK 2:5) (JEREMIAH 31:34) (MARK 2:7) (ISAIAH 43:25) (PSALM 32:1-2) (MICAH 7:18) (EPHESIANS 4:32) (1 JOHN 1:7-9) (PSALM 103:12) (ROMANS 6:14)

December 30

You saw how the LORD your God cared for you again and again here in the wilderness, just as a father cares for his child.

I brought you to myself and carried you on eagle's wings. ▩ In his love and mercy he redeemed them. He lifted them up and carried them through all the years. ▩ Like an eagle that rouses her chicks and hovers over her young, so he spread his wings to take them in and carried them aloft on his pinions. The LORD alone guided them.

I will be your God throughout your lifetime—until your hair is white with age. I made you, and I will care for you. I will carry you along and save you. ▩ For that is what God is like. He is our God forever and ever, and he will be our guide until we die. ▩ The steps of the godly are directed by the LORD. He delights in every detail of their lives. Though they stumble, they will not fall, for the LORD holds them by the hand.

Give your burdens to the LORD, and he will take care of you. He will not permit the godly to slip and fall. ▩ Don't worry about everyday life—whether you have enough food, drink, and clothes. Your heavenly Father already knows all your needs.

God wants us to give our burdens to him, but often we continue to bear them ourselves even when we say we are trusting in him. Trust the same strength that sustains you to carry your cares also.

LAB note for Psalm 55:22

(DEUTERONOMY 1:31) (EXODUS 19:4) (ISAIAH 63:9) (DEUTERONOMY 32:11-12) (ISAIAH 46:4) (PSALM 48:14) (PSALM 37:23-24) (PSALM 55:22) (MATTHEW 6:25, 32)

December 31

Much land remains to be conquered.

I don't mean to say that I have already achieved these things or that I have already reached perfection! But I keep working toward that day when I will finally be all that Christ Jesus saved me for and wants me to be.

You are to be perfect, even as your Father in heaven is perfect. ▪ Make every effort to apply the benefits of these promises to your life. Then your faith will produce a life of moral excellence. A life of moral excellence leads to knowing God better. Knowing God leads to self-control. Self-control leads to patient endurance, and patient endurance leads to godliness. Godliness leads to love for other Christians and finally you will grow to have genuine love for everyone.

I pray that your love for each other will overflow more and more, and that you will keep on growing in your knowledge and understanding.

No eye has seen, no ear has heard, and no mind has imagined what God has prepared for those who love him.

There is a special rest still waiting for the people of God. ▪ Your eyes will see the king in all his splendor, and you will see a land that stretches into the distance.

Our culture often glorifies the young and strong and sets aside those who are older. Yet older people are filled with the wisdom that comes from experience. They are very capable of serving if given the chance and should be encouraged to do so. Believers are never allowed to retire from God's service. *LAB note for Joshua 13:1*

(JOSHUA 13:1) (PHILIPPIANS 3:12) (MATTHEW 5:48) (2 PETER 1:5-7) (PHILIPPIANS 1:9) (1 CORINTHIANS 2:9) (HEBREWS 4:9) (ISAIAH 33:17)